The Well-Fed Writer
— *A Well-Praised Book!*

"Bowerman shows ... how almost anyone can forge ahead as an independent writer. His advice is good, couched in brassy prose ... He anticipates every conceivable question ... great common-sense tips ..."

Booklist

"... with a snappy conversational tone ... Bowerman spells out everything. ... For anyone interested in writing and willing to make a go of self-employment, this book should provide excellent guidelines and inspiration."

ForeWord, The Magazine of Independent Publishing

"... truly rewarding reading for aspiring freelance writers, copywriters, scriptwriters, columnists, journalists, and anyone else wanting to earn from what they write."

The Midwest Book Review

"This book is the best information on how to make more money with corporate clients I have ever read. It answers everything you want to know. Highly recommended."

Bob Bly, Author (20+ titles)
Secrets of a Freelance Writer, The Copywriter's Handbook
Regular Contributing Editor to *Writer's Digest* magazine

"A detailed roadmap to freelancing success, *The Well-Fed Writer* is brimming with nuggets of practical advice delivered in an enthusiastic, casual style. If you're serious about writing for fun and profit, you MUST buy this book!"

Bev Walton-Porter, Editor, BookStop
www.Inkspot.com
The Writer's Resource

"If you would rather be writing, get this book. Peter Bowerman, a successful freelance writer, has been there. In this book he shows you the way... I highly recommend this book."

Dan Poynter, Author (100+ books)
The Self-Publishing Manual, Successful Non-Fiction
www.ParaPublishing.com

"Engaging, motivating, and comprehensive—but above all, powerfully useful. An encyclopedic collection of freelancing fundamentals suffused throughout with the spirit of freedom and possibility all would-be freelancers crave."

Michael Perry, Author, Speaker
Handbook for Freelance Writing
www.sneezingcow.com

"Sharing practical information with great humor, *The Well-Fed Writer* pulls together in one easy-to-read package everything you need to know to be a freelance commercial writer—a topic most how-to-freelance books skip entirely."

Teresa Mears, Editor/Publisher
Freelance Success newsletter for writers
www.FreelanceSuccess.com

"An excellent book worth every penny of the cover price, and written in a conversational style that makes you feel like you're talking over coffee. There's so much information here you could read it three times and come away with something different each time."

Jerri L. Ledford
www.momwriters.com
Writer's Digest Top 101 Web Sites
Momwriters Mailing List
(momwriters@egroups.com)

"Writers regularly ask me how and where to find lucrative freelance work. From now on, I'll tell them to read *The Well-Fed Writer*. Unlike countless other writing books that promise the moon but deliver the doldrums, Peter Bowerman's advice is practical, insightful, and relevant."

Debra Koontz Traverso, Co-President
www.WriteDirections.com
Author (four books)
Adjunct Faculty, Harvard University

"Writing the Great-American-Novel isn't the only way for a writer to earn a living. If you love to write and want the flexibility of a work-at-home career, let *The Well-Fed Writer* and author Peter Bowerman guide you every step of the way with practical tips, straightforward advice, wit, and honesty. I highly recommend this book."

Cheryl Demas
Editor, *www.WAHM.com* – The Online Magazine For Work-At-Home Moms
Author, *The Work-at-Home Mom's Guide to Home Business*

"We have a school that teaches people to make a career out of writing—a fun well-paid career. *The Well-Fed Writer* is now on our recommended reading list. And even though I've been teaching people how to make a living as advertising copywriters for over 20 years, I'm amazed at how much this book has taught me in a couple of hours."

Norm Grey
President, The Creative Circus, Inc.
(School for Copywriting, Art Direction, Photography, Design/Illustration)
Former Sr.VP/Group Creative Director, *J. Walter Thompson*

"*The Well-Fed Writer* is one of the best books I have read about making a living as a professional writer. Practical tips in a fun-to-read style."

Priscilla Y. Huff, Author
101 Best Home-Business Success Secrets for Women

"Peter Bowerman knows his stuff. In simple, step-by-step fashion, and with a lucid style rare for how-to books, he shows how to turn the seeming madness of freelance writing into the magic of financial freedom. When it comes to writers' guides, this is the best. Toss the rest."

Jeff Gates, Author
The Ownership Solution, Democracy at Risk

"*The Well-Fed Writer* is a comprehensive guide, written in a clear, concise, first-person style. I highly recommend it to anyone who's seriously considering entering the writing field or to any working writer interested in substantially increasing their income."

Bill Watson, Author
9 Creativity-Required Businesses You Can Start From Home
www.BillWatson.net

"No starving in a garret for this author. If you've ever dreamed of becoming a freelance writer, you'll be hooked on *The Well-Fed Writer*. Peter Bowerman recommends his guidelines to career-changers, journalists, corporate staff writers, at-home moms, even recent college graduates. We do, too."

Linda Mitchell, Editor
Kennedy's Career Strategist

"*The Well-Fed Writer* is a comprehensive feast for writers of all skill levels. It's a "must read" for anyone interested in ... the lucrative field of freelance commercial writing."

Kim Lisi, Managing Editor
HOMEBusiness Journal
www.homebizjour.com

"Bowerman adopts the language and style of contemporary self-help books ... includes useful samples of promotional materials and ... commercial pieces. Public libraries should consider purchasing *[The Well-Fed Writer]* for their career sections."

Library Journal

"Over the years, those writers in our ***writers-editors.com*** network who have generated the most money with the least frustration have pursued commercial writing to some extent. I like *The Well-Fed Writer* because it leads the writer step-by-step through the 'how, when, if, and where' of being successful as a commercial writer."

Dana K. Cassell, Executive Director
www.writers-editors.com
(where editors/clients find writers; where writers find markets)
Editor, *Freelance Writer's Report*

And From Inside the Industry...

Listen to Corporate Writing Buyers and
Freelance Commercial Writers!

"As a former communications manager and employer of freelance writers, I believe *The Well-Fed Writer* does a great job describing the depth of opportunity in this lucrative field. The information and direction are right on the money."

Marsha Hawkins
(Former) Employee Communications Manager
BellSouth Corporation

"A friendly, well-organized, and thorough primer for the business. I'm still trying to figure out how he's amassed a career-ful of insight in less than a decade!"

Paul Glickstein
Commercial Staff Writer from 1972
Freelance Commercial Writer since 1986

"After freelancing for nearly six years, I can vouch for the fact that Peter Bowerman tells it like it is. Even at this stage in my career, his book has inspired me to push beyond the status quo."

Lisa Rubilar
Rubilar Communications
Freelance Commercial Writer since 1994

"Wow! A veritable feast of practical information on the ins and outs of freelance copywriting. Armed with *The Well-Fed Writer* when I started out more than a dozen years ago, no doubt I'd have avoided some mistakes—and made more money!"

Steve Knapp
Intelligent Copy for High-Tech Products
Freelance Commercial Writer since 1988

The Well-Fed Writer

*Financial Self-Sufficiency
As a Freelance Writer
In Six Months or Less*

By Peter Bowerman

Fanove Publishing - Atlanta, Georgia
2000

This book includes information from many sources and gathered from many personal experiences. It is published for general reference and is not intended to be a substitute for independent verification by readers when necessary and appropriate. The book is sold with the understanding that the neither the author nor publisher is engaged in rendering any legal, psychological, or accounting advice. The publisher and author disclaims any personal liability, directly or indirectly, for advice or information presented within. Although the author and publisher have prepared this manuscript with utmost care and diligence and have made every effort to ensure the accuracy and completeness of the information contained within, we assume no responsibility for error, inaccuracies, omissions, or inconsistencies.

ISBN: 0-9670598-4-4

Publisher's Cataloging-in-Publication
(Provided by Quality Books, Inc.)

Bowerman, Peter
    The well-fed writer: financial self-sufficiency as a freelance writer in six months or less / Peter Bowerman
  – 1st ed.
      p.   cm.
    Includes index.
    LCCN: 99-97023
    ISBN: 0-9670598-4-4

    1. Authorship–Marketing. 2. Authorship. I. Title

PN161.B69 2000   808.02
                                          QBI00-500042

Second printing: 2001
Third printing: 2001

Dedication

To Bob Bly, who gave me the idea in the first place. You're my hero.

Table of Contents

- Ability to Market Oneself
- Discipline—I'm Lazy, Believe It Or Not
- Technical Expertise—If I Can Do It…
- Flexibility, Curiosity, A Non-Conformist Nature
- Being Easy to Get Along With—Your Secret Weapon
- Assertiveness—Take a Stand for Quality
- Ability to Ask Lots of Dumb Questions
- Humility, A Quick Study, Discretion

- Remember: The Client Is The Boss
- Use Every Advantage You Have
- Pick A Specialty ... Maybe
- Sow The Seeds, Get Referrals
- Remember: Nothing Is Forever
- Luck (and the Lazy Client) Favors the Visible
- Go Out and Meet Your Market
- Don't Go "Direct"
- Follow Up After Meetings and Phone Calls
- Listen More, Work Less
- Send Note Cards
- Save Your Junk E-mail
- Keep Your Word, Earn Your Money
- "Give Back" Through Pro Bono
- Partner with a Designer and Other Writers

Chapter Fourteen
What Will You Be Writing? 181

Chapter Fifteen
The Home Stretch 211

Acknowledgments

My sincere thanks to:

David and Richard, my loyal and always available technical gurus. Countless times, they came to the aid of this committed techno-phobe in his moments of digital despair. I would never have gotten this far without you both.

Fellow writer Kathy Couch, who so graciously volunteered to edit my initial manuscript. Your voluminous and invaluable feedback absolutely made this a much better, stronger, and more focused book.

Paul Glickstein, for being there in the confused and stumbling early days, with the right advice and the right answers as I slowly broke the code on this business. May all my readers be so fortunate.

Chris DiNatale, my brilliant graphic designer. Thanks for a cover design that has turned heads around the globe—literally.

Michael Höhne and Angela Werner, my wonderfully patient, soothing, easy-going, and talented typesetters. Thanks for caring as much about this as I did.

Mom, for her eternal faith in me, and her constant loving "nudges" to get this thing done.

All my clients, who've provided me with the golden opportunity to learn, hone my craft and make a healthy living in this great field. You've all made this book possible.

All who buy this book. I'm honored to play a part in the realization of your dreams.

Peter Bowerman
June 2000

Introduction

WHEN WAS THE LAST TIME you did something for a living that *really* and truly lit you up? Where work felt like play, you looked forward to getting out of bed in the morning, you were consistently stimulated, as busy as you wanted to be, along with lots of freedom, creative fulfillment, and comfortable working conditions? *And* all the while earning a handsome income with the time to enjoy it? Have you ever had such an experience? Can you even imagine it? If you have been there but aren't now, don't you think a lot about how to find it again?

LET YOURSELF DREAM   Have you dreamed of becoming a writer but never took it too seriously because after all, the words "starving" and "writer" are pretty much joined at the hip? Or are you already a writer but either working for someone else or struggling financially?

What would you say if I told you that there's an arena of writing, that if pursued with reasonable diligence by an even moderately talented and minimally creative individual, could generate self-sufficiency inside of six months and all the above-described goodies in only about a year or two?

That's what *The Well-Fed Writer* is all about. Becoming a well-respected, well-compensated, fulfilled writer. A person who, when asked what you do, can proudly respond "I'm a writer." Talk about a conversation piece. You watch.

When you're around someone who's doing what he or she really enjoys, it shows, doesn't it? Well, speaking of it "showing," I'm going to share my 1994 Christmas letter with you. Lucky you.

For years, I swore I'd never do one of those form letters at Christmas time. You know, those incredibly dull travelogues of the past year, outlining every inconsequential thing that happened to every major and minor family member (and usually not even *your* family) over the past 12 months.

Feel The Excitement   Then, in late 1992, after finding myself in my eighth straight hour of doing Christmas cards, I decided that the next year, I would actually do that which I loathed—my own Xmas letter. Anyway, let these excerpts from my Seasons Greetings 1994 give you a snapshot of the excitement and enthusiasm I felt for my new career.

I ask again: When was the last time you were really excited about what you did for a living? That's possible when you find the right direction, and for some of you, this kind of writing may be it.

Dear Friends,   Christmas 1994

Guess what I did this year? Climb Mt. Everest? Wrestle an alligator? Get elected to public office? Hey, that was a low blow ....

I became a writer. Not in some ethereal sense of the word, like, "I declare myself merged with the essence of" 'writer-ness.' I'm talking a "paying-the-bills-by-writing" writer.

I was spurred on by the advice given Sarah Caldwell (famous opera producer) by her mother: "Find something you love to do, and someone who will pay you to do it." Amen to that.

After spending January buying a second-hand computer, talking myself in and out of the idea about 50 times, and alternately experiencing anxiety attacks and delusions of grandeur, I finally took the plunge as a freelance commercial writer on Monday, January 24th at approximately 9:36 a.m. Company name: *WriteInc.*

On the 26th of February, at approximately 1:45 p.m., my mailman delivered an envelope with a $50 check enclosed. My first official paycheck as a writer of anything came for a column entitled, "Petiquette in the Park"—the lighter side of people and their pets. The quintessential humble beginning.

However, operating on the pragmatic assumption that most writers who insist on writing only books, articles, and columns tend to eat a lot of baloney and ramen noodles, I decided to pursue commercial writing—writing for business: marketing brochures, ad copy, video scripts, corporate image pieces, speeches, and so on.

Within three and a half months, I literally had more business than I could handle. There's no more frustratingly satisfying feeling than having to turn down work. My current tally (are you growing weary of this self-enshrinement?) since early February is 19 brochures, four video scripts, two radio spots, two 40-page technical manuals, a half dozen ad campaigns and sales promotion projects, a 44-part educational CD-ROM, ... oh, and a book.

In mid-May, I landed a job ghost-writing a motivational book for a very successful mortgage broker/speaker, entitled: *Life Mastery: The Ultimate*

Power of Relationships. It was a beautiful thing. Three months and almost 230 pages.

I had over 45 columns published in five local papers. Everything from humor/satire and political /social commentary to business advice. Doesn't pay much, but provides food for the soul. Sorry for talking shop so much, but frankly, it's how I spent most of my year.

Built From Nothing Think I was excited? You bet I was. I'd created this life direction out of nothing other than a dream and it had taken flight. Is it fun all the time? Of course not. Did I work a lot that first year? Absolutely, but it didn't feel like work. Would I trade it for the life I had before? Not for a second. Does that mean I'll be doing it forever? Probably not. But that's just me.

In all likelihood, I'll be changing careers another, oh, six or seven times or so in my life. You might find that this direction is it for you. I've got a number of professional colleagues who've been doing this for anywhere from 10-25 years—for someone else originally and eventually for themselves—and wouldn't want to do anything else. And as you'll soon discover, it's not hard to see why.

$2000/Month Part-Time The freelance commercial writing direction can be tremendously lucrative on either a full- or part-time basis. If you choose to pursue it full-time, I challenge you to find an easier way to make a very hand-some living as a writer (the very few Stephen Kings and John Grishams of the world notwithstanding). By the same token, you may decide that part-time is the way to go, as a way to supplement your more creative writing pursuits—your "passion" writing. If so, great! In that case, making $2000 a month part-time is extremely feasible. Heck—that's just 2–3 medium-size marketing brochures.

HOW DID I GET STARTED? I'd love to tell you some wonderfully heart-warming story about how I knew I wanted to be a freelance commercial writer from the time I was crawling. How I rewrote the endings to Dr. Seuss at age five, walked around the house at age eight coming up with new jingles for Mrs. Paul's Fishsticks and Durkee canned onion rings. Or that I revamped the Boy Scout manual at 12 and at 17, submitted suggested revisions of my high school his-tory book to Prentice-Hall.

Alas, not so. I did take one journalism course in both high school and col-lege and at 15, did write a column covering little league baseball for three local newspapers in my little tri-town community on the North Shore of Massachusetts. That's it. Impressive, huh?

Zero Experience I'd never been a writer before I started this business. I had no industry background and no advertising agency experience. I was a Russian Studies major in college. I had no contacts in the industry, no client list. Nada. Zippo. Zilch.

Given all that, while my success certainly says something about me, it says just as much about the accessibility of the opportunity.

I found that in any job I'd held over the years, I gravitated to the few writing tasks that did crop up—an occasional letter or little brochure—and typically got good feedback from those around me. Do we have anything in common there?

All in all, there was very little in my past to refer to. Just that I'd decided that this was the next step in my life journey that I wanted to take, and I had a sense that I was a good enough writer and a good enough marketer to be successful.

So, if you're thinking about this field and have no formal experience or writing background, rest assured, it's no hindrance to success. You might have to work a little harder to get established than say, a staff writer for a corporation, but it's totally do-able. And as you'll also undoubtedly be delighted to discover along the way here, I'm not a super disciplined, aggressive, or technically-savvy guy and yet, I've done quite well.

IT'S CLOSER THAN YOU THINK   I've written this book as a realistic guide to approaching this business. And here's what I mean by "realistic": Given that we're all human beings, and as such, have a rather substantial lazy, slug-like streak in us, I didn't want to write a book that would make becoming a freelance commercial writer seem akin to climbing Mt. Everest.

If I did, you'd finish the book—maybe—and it would become just another one of those things you checked out but never did anything about. And let me say this about my profession. As businesses go, this business *is* a lot easier than most to get off the ground. And compared to other areas of freelance writing, it's not only much easier to get into—it's much more lucrative once you do.

SIMPLE, REPEATABLE SYSTEMS   With an emphasis on simple, repeatable systems, I believe I've created a strategy for operating this business that achieves the best of both worlds: potential for healthy financial success without killing yourself to get there.

In fact, in many ways, it epitomizes the concept, "Work smarter, not harder." Bottom line, you can work this business hard, like a *Type A* personality would, and I'll show you how to do that, if that's what you want. If however, you're like me and prefer to have a life *and* make a solid living, I can show you how to do that, too.

WHY SO SOON? Some readers might ask, "Why start writing this book after a little more than two years at it? Wouldn't most people put a decade or two in before writing a how-to book?" Even though I've been at it for over six years at press time, I wanted to start this book early, for one simple reason: to show people that it just doesn't take very long to achieve healthy financial success in this business—two years or less. And only six months to financial self-sufficiency.

Have you ever gone to a how-to seminar, where the speaker has been practicing his or her craft for 15–20 years? How intimidating is that? If you're brand new to something, and you're confronted with a double-decade expert, you might just feel like it's going to take you forever to reach even a fraction of the success that he's had. No wonder he's successful, you say, he's been at it for most of his life! I want you to feel like this is an accessible and "within-reach" opportunity, because it is.

LEVERAGE WHAT YOU KNOW   In that regard, you may be that much ahead of the game. If you're coming from a specific field—such as healthcare, financial services, real estate, retail, hi-tech—and don't mind writing about that field, that's a huge plus. That's how many people get their start. They may eventually transition into writing for other fields, but at the outset, they establish a solid business base writing about what they already know, using years of established contacts.

Maybe you're in the industry and already writing, but working for someone else. You want to jump out on your own, and would appreciate some kind of a trail to follow. Whatever your reason, this book can help get you headed in the right direction.

WHAT'S AHEAD?   What are we going to cover along the way? While we'll spend one chapter near the end delving into the stylistic side of writing—how to actually write certain kinds of projects—the main focus of this book is on how to build a freelance commercial writing business from nothing other than your vision.

I'm assuming that you wouldn't be reading this book unless you felt that you were a pretty decent writer already (but rest assured, you do *not* have to be great), but that you just need some guidance in parlaying that ability into a lucrative profession.

Since there are plenty of books and courses around on improving your writing skills, I'll let them pick up the slack in that arena.

I'll be sharing with you my experiences in building a successful business. Not the *right* answers or *only* answers, just some things that have worked for me. Take on what works for you and don't use what doesn't. But know that this is one very solid path to follow if you want to build a business of your own.

Do I do everything I suggest in this book religiously? No. If I did, would I make a lot more money than I currently do? Absolutely. If you followed these guidelines to the letter, would you earn an even healthier living than I do? I'd bet on it.

Subscribing to the idea that learning not only *can* but *must* be fun, I've tried to make it light and readable. If you actually use this book to launch a new career for yourself, well, that would be just about the coolest thing I could possibly imagine. Let's get started....

Chapter One

An Enviable Lifestyle

PICTURE THIS   On a Friday morning client phone call, you pick up a job writing a marketing brochure. Several hours later, a couriered package of background material shows up at your door. In a follow-up call, the client answers some questions and you spend a few hours on Sunday night reviewing the material. Monday morning, you meet them at their offices just ten minutes away.

You work on the project at home, on your deck, under that great shady tree, phone by your side, tall glass of lemonade nearby. By Wednesday morning, between the client call, background reading, the Monday meeting, and crafting a first draft, you have 16 hours in the project (16 x $75 = $1200). You fax them your draft Wednesday morning, and you won't get it back until Friday.

The Phone Keeps Ringing…   In the meantime, you put in six hours on some edits for an event presentation script that's been on-going for two weeks now. (6 x $65 [long-term client gets a break] = $390). After turning the edits around late Wednesday, you get a call from some new clients who've been hiring you recently to edit their hi-tech brochures. They e-mail you the file, you take the night off, and start working on it Thursday morning. It takes you four hours @ $75/hr. = $300. You e-mail it back, and bill them immediately.

And Ringing… In the early afternoon, you get a call from a relatively new regular client asking about your availability for a brochure project the next week—probably 12–15 hours worth of work. You set up a meeting for Monday afternoon. Later that same afternoon, one of your regular clients calls, needing a few headlines for a store display. She says, "My brain is fried. Just come up with a few lines. Don't spend a lot of time on it."

You've done 30+ projects like this, so it's a breeze. You charge her your two-hour minimum, $150, grab your microcassette recorder, head to the gym, knocking out half of it on the way over. That night, sitting outside at your favorite neighborhood eatery with a clipboard, you get the rest done, having put in a total of maybe an hour of time. You get home, take 10 minutes to type them up and fax them on.

It's Not Unusual That's just a hair over $2000 by Thursday night, for under 30 hours of work, minimal running around, comfortable work, almost completely by phone, fax, and e-mail, and with plenty of time left over to have a life. And you've got about $1000 worth of work lined up for next week to boot.

OK, it's not always this easy or rosy and you'll have your share of $500 weeks, too. This is no get-rich-quick thing. In the beginning, you'll be working a lot harder for a lot less, and in any given week, there's a lot of other work to do—prospecting, marketing, and paperwork (though less than you'd imagine). But, develop the right work habits early and you'll be surprised at how soon and often you'll be having weeks like the above.

THE LIFE OF A FREELANCE COMMERCIAL WRITER Good money, flexible hours, stimulating work. Go to bed when you want, get up when you want (most of the time), wear what you want, take vacations when you want, shower and shave when you want. Do you have a lot of outside interests? *Would you* if you had more time of your own? Well, you can.

Your income is up to you. Want a raise? Work harder, make more phone calls, put in more hours. It's that simple. Sure, you'll be working hard to get established, but it's not nearly as difficult as you'd think, and as we discussed earlier, depending on your present situation, you could be halfway there right now.

Do You Have "Quality of Life"? Have you taken a "quality audit" of your life lately? Does this sound like you? Get up early, put on the suit, drive 30–45 minutes (on a good day) through glacial rush hour traffic, work in some climate-controlled windowless cubicle in a high-rise all day, deal with office politics, eat unhealthy food on the run, sit in endless boring meetings using words like "re-purpose," "actionable" and "value-added," get stressed out, be nice to people you think are morons, leave the office late, maybe get in a rushed work-out, get home by 8:30–9:00, wolf down some dinner, fall asleep in front of the TV, have weird dreams because you went to bed on a full stomach, collapse on Friday night, run errands and do wash on Saturday, look forward to your one to two weeks of vacation every year, and 40 more years of that.

The Good Life Granted, not everyone lives a life like that, but more than just a few do. My life is very different, and at some point early in my fourth year, I started realizing how good I actually had it. I'd be out and about and people would ask me how things were. I'd reply, "Everything is wonderful actually."

Of course they'd do a double take since they couldn't remember the last time they heard that. Most people don't even want to hear about it. But, you know what? If I can do it, you can do it. Get used to hearing that mantra throughout this book.

WHAT'S THE FIRST STEP?   Well, it's the thing that most people have the hardest time doing: imagining it. That's right. They can't picture themselves there. Oh sure, they'd really *like* to have a lifestyle like this, and if they're blow-ing the candles out on their birthday cakes and the thought crossed their minds, they'd certainly *wish* for it, but they see it as some out-of-reach thing other peo-ple get to do, but not them. After all, a job is a job. It's not supposed to be ful-filling. That would be almost un-American, right?

Can You Imagine It? Robert Allen, the *Nothing Down* real estate guru, said the same thing in explaining why most people won't ever be wealthy. It wasn't that they weren't smart enough or capable of making it happen. Many mil-lionaires never even finished high school. Just about everyone is capable, he observed, but they just can't imagine themselves successful.

For those of you who've owned other businesses, imagining it may not be that much of a stretch. For others who've only worked for someone else and are very used to that steady paycheck and the routine, it might take a bit more effort.

Yet, the fact that you're reading this tells me that you're motivated to make a change. Here's the good news. If you can get the mental side of this equation handled, you're halfway there. You won't be subconsciously sabotaging your-self because you can't quite picture yourself in the role.

QUESTION THE NORM   In our ultra high-performance, waste-no-time, always-be-producing world, there's this not-so-subtle mindset that frowns on you if you're not crankin' 16 hours a day. While few of the people doing the crankin' seem very happy, they nonetheless want you to be just as slammed.

Shift Your Thinking I came across a wonderful Spanish proverb in a book called *Traveler's Tales: Spain.* Each story dropped you into a strange and wonderful world, where you could truly see, hear, smell, taste, and feel a different reality. A place where people lived—and more importantly, *thought*—very differently than we do.

I walked away from the book, and from any foreign travel I've done as well, realizing that the way we do things here isn't the *only* way, the *right* way, or the best way. Just a way. The line went: *Que bonito es no hacer nada, y luego descansar.* Translation: "How beautiful it is to do nothing, and then rest afterwards." I love it.

Share that with most Americans, however, and their eyes will glaze over. They won't get it. It's a sentiment that's totally, completely, absolutely incompatible with our work ethic in this country.

Busy for Busy's Sake? Being busy has become a badge of honor in our culture. And not just busy, but moving at Mach 4 with your hair on fire from sunup to way past sundown. Not having enough time to do basic life stuff, not to mention personal time for fun, has in some twisted way become a welcome point of commiseration for many.

The popular culture—TV, advertising, MTV, movies—constantly bombards us with images designed to show us exactly what we need to be happy, successful, sexy, in love, or any other state that is obviously eluding us at present. And it all takes money. Lots of it.

Compared to the rest of the world, Americans take achievement and accomplishment to a ludicrous level. We measure our worth and that of all our citizens based on how much we 'produce.' As young children, it is constantly driven into our heads that the overall goal of our lives should be to grow up and become "productive, contributing members of society."

Don't hear this as an indictment of our system and philosophy. We do feel better about ourselves as human beings, when, through our own labor, we're able to carve out a good life for ourselves and our loved ones. And America is a can-do culture, with a solid reputation for getting things done. But it's gotten a little nuts in the past few decades.

Skewed Priorities Across the world, we're known as people who work way too much, put work above time with our families—despite our protests to the contrary—are overly stressed out, unhealthy, overweight, unhappy professionally, and in general, have a skewed sense of priorities. Pretty accurate and well-deserved, no?

Take vacation time. While here, most corporations start with one week of vacation and slowly work up to four after 20+ years of service, in Europe and most other western industrialized nations, you *begin* your career with four weeks of vacation and work up from there. 50–70 hour weeks? Try about 35–40 or less. Last October, I took a month off and went to Asia. It's possible.

THE ALTERNATIVE It all underscores a fascinating phenomenon: that an inherently illogical *modus operandi*, if accepted widely enough and practiced long enough, will become the "way things are done." Of course, if you don't feel compelled to follow this path, whole new possibilities open up. Like working fewer hours, having less stress, and owning more of your life while making the same money.

With a career as a Freelance Commercial Writer (henceforth abbreviated to FLCW), you can craft a healthy income *and* a lifestyle that when held up to our conventional work model, may at times look somewhat "slack" or "lazy."

Type A **Not Required** Can you tell I'm not a *Type A* personality? Never have been and you know what? Don't let anyone tell you that success will only come to those who are. Of course, my definition of success—i.e., a well-rounded life—may be different from the norm. If you're a *Type A,* no problem. You can be just as much of a workaholic in this business as any. The only difference is that because you're paid in direct proportion to your efforts, you'll probably make more money and have fewer hassles than you would in corporate America.

Remember the scenario I described at the beginning of the chapter? $2000+ for a relatively light workweek (30 hrs.) by society's standards? I'll have even lighter weeks like writing one medium brochure and a few headlining projects, which might net me $1200. Fifty of those means about 60K a year, and with enough time to do everything you might want to do—take up a hobby, volunteer, spend more time with your family, etc.

But of course, this is a business and there's work to be done. And feast/famine is very much a part of our lives, as we'll soon discuss. But once you've established the business, the freedom and flexibility are most enviable.

What Do You Need to Be Happy? OK, so 60K isn't all the money in the world, but would you be happy with it, especially with the time to really enjoy life? You want to work harder and make more, say 100K? You can absolutely do it in this business, and probably working a lot less than you would in other businesses. It's your choice, and that's the key. No one is limiting your income…but you. I happen to like that arrangement and if you try it for a few years, I'm guessing you'd never go back.

And no, you probably won't have a lifestyle like this right out of the gate. But hey, bust your rear just as hard for someone else for three years, and where will you be? More money and less time to enjoy it? More importantly, are you doing what really turns you on? Might writing be the thing? If so, you can't put a price tag on that.

It only took me about four months to become self-sufficient and awfully close to the point I'm at now by the end of year two. By self-sufficiency, I mean paying my bills and doing it full-time (i.e., no moonlighting), and accepting no large cash infusions from anyone.

When you go beyond that and create the lifestyle as well, you're likely to catch some grief from your friends about being lazy. They're just jealous. Their idea of paradise is having a day to catch up on laundry. Meanwhile, yours might be a weekend cruise.

LET'S GET TO IT! OK, time to get into the nitty-gritty: What exactly does a FLCW do? And what—besides the great lifestyle—are the reasons why this is a solid career direction? And yes, what are the downsides of this business? With these questions rolling around in our minds, let's move on to our next chapter….

Chapter Two

Why Be A
Freelance Commercial Writer (FLCW)?

WHAT IS A FLCW?   So, what exactly does a Freelance Commercial Writer (FLCW) or "copywriter" do? (I prefer FLCW—sounds a little more like a profession, which it most definitely is. Nonetheless, you'll still be referred to as a "copywriter" by many in the business, especially in the ad copy realm.) And why start a freelance commercial writing business? There are tons of reasons.

YOU LIKE TO WRITE AND ARE GOOD AT IT   Just making sure…

HIGH DEMAND FOR TALENT   Don't take my word for it. I contacted a number of commercial writing buyers in Atlanta and asked them to share their thoughts on finding good writing talent in this field. As you'll see from their comments, there's plenty of room for you if you're a good writer.

"Although I manage a staff of three professional writers and do a lot of writing myself, we occasionally get covered up and need freelance help.
Unfortunately, it seems I always have to scramble to find someone. That's

because I rarely receive a call or letter from a writer asking for work. Apparently, the freelancers in Atlanta either have all the work they can handle or aren't actively marketing themselves."

Michael J. Baker
Sr. Writer/Editor and Copy Team Manager
MCI WorldCom Marketing Communications

"Finding good copywriters is probably one of the toughest challenges we have. We're a small agency, but I bet we try 3–4 new writers a year. Most experiences are very disappointing—for many different reasons. So we usually end up rewriting most copy in-house."

Doug Warner, CEO
Fountainhead Advertising
Atlanta, Georgia

"As a broker for both technical and marketing writers, I have found that good talented creative writers are in short supply. A combination of talent and good disposition is rare and especially attractive to any employer. I most enjoy working with a writer who doesn't realize how good he/she really is."

Diane Eissler
Vice President
Writers of Atlanta Associates, Inc.
(Writers Broker)

"Without question, it is hard to find a good freelance writer. We're not lacking for choices, but really good ones are rare. It's taken us several years to build up a stable of writers spread out over the country who are talented and reliable. There are probably currently 7 or 8 freelancers on our 'A list' and we keep them very busy."

Ken Sternad
Vice-President, Public Relations
UPS

"We produce multiple publications, collateral and direct marketing materials. It's critical that we maintain a pool of talented writers who understand our business and can adhere to our deadlines. Once I find a writer who 'gets it,' they can rely on a steady customer."

Nancy Knauf
Associate Director of Public Relations
Shepherd Center

"Finding a talented writer can be a nightmare and trying to find one you 'connect' with is even worse. I have been fortunate enough to work with a team that is well networked and knows the right people. Once I located such a writer, I found myself giving him more and more assignments. It not only made the projects come to fruition faster, but presented a similar message and image."

Adriana Cadavid
VP International Marketing
FOCAS, Inc.
(Fiber Optics Cable and Systems)

"As a former award-winning journalist and current owner of a multi-media communications firm, I am struck by the scarcity of good writing in the business arena. Regardless of your background, there is huge corporate demand for good, solid, coherent writing."

Bob Hamilton
Multiple Associated Press Award-winner
President, In-Focus Communications

"Once you find a copywriter who is talented, strategic, creative and reliable—hold on to them for dear life! The demand for these individuals is extremely high in the fast-paced world of corporate marketing and advertising. A writer who takes the time and initiative to really get to know your business becomes a valuable asset that you just can't afford to live without."

Kristi Sumner
Marketing Director - Creative Development
Mercedes-Benz Credit Corporation

"In my business I need a wide variety of writers on call all the time. My writing needs vary from editorial, to technical, to business consulting, to promotional to more ad-like. Rarely can one writer do all of these well. Good writers are hard to find. I'm willing to pay top dollar if I get top quality writing the first time and every time. That means getting the big idea fast, understanding the audience and nailing the style on the first pass."

Karlenne Hager Trimble
Deeley Trimble & Company
Partner - Creative Director
(Internal Marketing and Communications Company)

"When it comes to writers, my motto is 'Good, Fast, Affordable—pick any two.' It's a challenge to find writers with strong grammatical skills, let alone those who can write well and adapt their style. And there's an incredible shortage of people who can write good technical copy."

Lisa Amdur Frazier
Marketing Communications Manager
Tensar Earth Technologies, Inc.

"While I put myself through college writing video scripts, I decided that I really wanted to be a film and video producer and began to leave my writing credits and writing awards off my résumé. When the offers weren't exactly pouring in, I called a client, the manager of a large corporate video production department, to get his advice. He said, 'You're a great writer and you need to lever-age that talent. I can pick up the phone and in ten minutes I can find ten video producers. But, I'll sometimes spend two weeks looking for a good writer. Good writers are rare, but when I find one, I use them over and over again.'

"The next day I began marketing myself as a writer/producer/director. The work began coming in and never stopped. While I've since phased out of the writing end of film and video projects, it was undoubtedly my writing skills that opened doors and gave me the greatest credibility. When I find good writ-ers, I tell all of my colleagues about them. Word of mouth is priceless.

"So many people these days are graduating with degrees in communica-tions and journalism, but simply do not have strong writing skills. In my col-lege lectures to communication graduates, one of the first things I tell them is to hone their writing skills, no matter what their career choice is. Freelance writing, scripts or copywriting, is one of the few flexible jobs that can keep food on the table while you pursue other career interests."

Carmie McCook
Video Production Manager &
Olympic Communications Manager
UPS

Starting to get the picture? Your writing skills are needed by a whole host of top companies willing to pay handsomely for them.

UNLIMITED WORK   Marketing brochures, corporate image pieces, adver-tisements, newsletters, direct mail campaigns, industrial video scripts, trade articles, educational/industrial CD-ROM scripts, press releases, radio spots, TV commercials, event scripting, business letters, sales promotion material, mar-keting manuals, technical manuals, corporate profiles, annual reports, product documentation, product spec sheets, proposals—shall I go on? Every single one of these—and a lot more that I didn't mention—have one thing in common: they all have to be written by someone.

The sheer volume of work in any good-sized metropolis is staggering. Take Atlanta. Put me with a bunch of my professional colleagues and we'd whole-heartedly agree on one thing: there's more work in this town than all of us can handle. If I'm not busy, it's my own lack of motivation in running down the work.

Plus "Unfinished Business"   I just had dinner with my writers group (the creation of which I discuss in Chapter Thirteen: "Dos, Don'ts and Don't

Forgets"). We were lightheartedly commiserating about the surprisingly sizable number of "start-stop-die" projects that are a standard fixture in the commercial writing arena. That is, projects that begin, get to a certain point, and then, for any number of reasons (new management, new product, new marketing direction, new crystal ball), the project gets suspended—usually temporarily at first, but often evolving into permanent demise.

It's pretty common in big corporations, especially ones going through transition. Of course, you still get paid for all the hours you've put into it up till that point. It just never turns into a sample. So, remember: the sphere of possible paid writing projects include not only the ones that must get done, but those that *never* get done as well.

THE TIME IS RIGHT FOR FREELANCERS OK, why don't these companies do the work themselves? Well, many corporations do have marketing or communications departments in-house. In the last decade, however, two huge trends have sculpted the corporate American landscape: downsizing and outsourcing.

It's a lean, mean business world out there, and corporations across the country and around the world are doing more with less. Fewer people, less resources, smaller budgets. The creative, marketing and communications departments are being scaled back or eliminated altogether.

When an organization downsizes, these areas are often the first to go. Consequently, many organizations rely on freelancers heavily to get their work done—and not just because they have to. There are many solid benefits of dealing with freelancers: no salaries, no vacation time or sick days, and no health insurance or benefits. Not to mention that a variety of talent can ensure a consistently fresh writing perspective, often a challenge with full-time staff writers.

A manager of a telecommunications firm in Atlanta noted, "Most people would assume that a company of our size would do the bulk of our writing in-house, and they'd be wrong. It's amazing how much writing we outsource. When I started here, I was talking to a marketing manager about the huge writing workload. I asked, 'Why don't we do some of it ourselves?' He replied, 'I don't know, but we just don't.' And it's the same in many other places, including my last company, which was also huge and a prolific outsourcer. My writing needs these days are pretty steady, and I pay anywhere from $65–85/hour, depending on a writer's experience."

Even when companies do the work in-house, and especially with small creative departments, crunch times are inevitable. A competent freelancer can pick up plenty of work when things get hairy. We'll get into the specifics of approaching these departments in Chapter Five—"Where's The Business?"

The Other Side of the Story To editorially digress for just a moment, having been a freelancer for more than six years has given me a completely different perspective on corporate downsizing. Typically the media paint this trend in the worst possible light, filling the rag sheets and air waves with one-sided screeds about the big bad greedy 'pigwigs' in Corporate America, more concerned about their own selfish profit-mongering than their own employees. And certainly, I'm not here to suggest that profits aren't the overriding motivation of corporate America.

What gets forgotten, however, in these emotional, shrieky discussions of the real horrors of job loss and displacement are the inevitable opportunities created for the independent and entrepreneurial-minded out there. There's a whole segment of the population out there, sizable and growing, that's richly benefiting from these seemingly universally-reviled trends.

Its members look just like those in corporate America. single, married, starting out, well-established, raising families, raisin' hell, you name it, our ranks include the whole gamut. Bottom line: no trend is universally negative. The economy taketh away, the economy giveth.

In Competence There Is Security You may be one of those displaced souls looking to carve out your own share of the pie. Well, the time couldn't be better for it. Work hard for a few years, get your name out there, build something solid and you'll understand the true meaning of the phrase "job security."

In competence there is security. That security will be in your hands, not someone else's. You decide how hard you want to work, and ergo, what you want your income to look like. Then, the whole downsizing thing becomes this only mildly interesting news item that has virtually no negative ramifications for your life, and plenty of positive ones.

BE YOUR OWN BOSS As a huge control freak, I don't take too well to having to be somewhere every day working for someone else. I like to be the boss, and I'm actually a whole lot tougher on myself than anyone else could ever be.

Then there's the schedule thing. In the 9–5 working world, your hours of productivity have essentially been dictated to you, regardless of the wants and needs of your internal clock.

If we're playing the corporate game, we've got to pretty much march in lockstep with the rest of the troops. For some of you, given your rhythms, that arrangement works fine, but not so for others. If you're a morning person by edict, trapped in a night owl's body, your time (so to speak…) has come.

If you want to go to bed at 2 a.m. and sleep till 9 a.m.—my preferred schedule—go for it. Contrary to popular belief, you don't need to align your schedule with the rest of the working world to be successful. Sure, as a night owl, there are times when I feel I really should get up early and blend in with the rest of the world, but I usually get over it.

Perhaps some of you fellow kindred spirits who are now forced to operate under someone else's insane idea of a sensible workday schedule will relate to this column I wrote a few months back.

NIGHT OWLS UNITE!

10:06 a.m. The phone rings. It's one of my clients getting back to me on some ad copy I faxed them late the night before. My spoon is poised over my just-poured-the-milk-in bowl of cereal as she asks if I can go over a few revisions. Getting up from dining room table and heading north to my upstairs office, I hedge briefly, even letting a tiny whine escape my white-mustachioed lips.

Should I come out of the closet finally? Living this lie has become unbearable. After all, they like my work and aren't too likely to replace me just because I'm living an "alternative" lifestyle. Taking a deep breath, I begin. "Um, I'm sort of a night person; I stay up late and get up late and (I'm picking up steam now) I'm actually right in the middle of breakfast."

There. It's out. Let the chips fall where they may. Gotta train em' sometime. "Oh," she replies, caught off guard. Pause. I can see her checking her watch. This is a new one, she's thinking. "Wanna call me back?"

Fifteen minutes later, we're chatting again, and happily, she understands completely, especially when I tell her that cold cereal was on the menu this morning. Heavy on the corn flakes. "And with cereal," she commiserates, "every second counts."

You got that right. In fact, in the time it took me to walk halfway upstairs, turn around, and dig back in, I experienced an estimated 25–30% breakdown factor in my cereal bowl. Welcome to Sog City. I hate that.

I am not a morning person. Never have been and though I've tried diligently over the years to adjust my clock to get into step with most of my fellow earthlings, I still end up sawing my Z's between the hours of 2–9 a.m. In fact, I come from a long line of night owls. Sorry, it's genetic. That's my story and I'm sleepin' with it.

Just my luck. The present work day was obviously conceived by a morning person. Think about it. No one in his right mind would have everyone getting up and hitting the highways all at the same time. Hello? No wonder so many people are grumpy in the mornings and have pathological caffeine addictions. HELLO?

Me, I never touch the stuff. Don't have to. I get to wake up (most days anyway) when my inner clock nudges me awake. Yeah my alarm works, though I rarely make it punch in. No bags under these eyes. Don't hate me because I'm beautiful.

Of course, our culture tries to brainwash us into thinking that only the early risers will make it to the top. The clichés are everywhere: "Early to bed, early to rise… The early bird catches the worm… Early is as early does… Blessed are the early, for they shall inherit the earth… Early waters run deep… A night owl and his money are soon parted…" I mean, geez, the list goes on and on.

I recall a conversation with a former colleague—and fellow night owl—who was recounting the unpleasant and short-lived experience of a 7 a.m. college French class. After several weeks of somnambulistic agony, he finally went to the professor and dropped the course, explaining that at 7 a.m., English was as much a foreign language to him as French would ever be.

So, fellow nocturns (new word), stand firm and be proud. And remember: To rise with the sun is human, but to dance with the moon is divine.

Bottom line, in this business, an 8:30 a.m. meeting is rarely truly necessary. People may suggest it, but I'm not at all above putting on my best regretful voice, and lying though my teeth:

"Gee, I'd love to get an early start *(Actually, I hate getting an early start, and I can't believe you'd even suggest it)*, but I've already got another appointment scheduled *(…with my pillow and blankets)*. Can we make it at 10:30? I should be done by then *(though I'll have to cut my normal leisurely breakfast short, and frankly, I'm not very happy about that.)*

Do What You've Got to Do By this point in my career, most of my clients know not to call me much before 10. And frankly, they're welcome to. That's what voicemail and Caller ID are for. Of course, if that's the only time the client can meet (or so they *say*…I guess two can play this game), then do what you've got to do.

And just to clarify this: in your first year, when you're building your business, you'd better be meeting clients when and where they want. Build it up and once they realize that they can't live without your awesome talents, *then* you can start making a few of your own scheduling preferences known.

MINIMAL INVESTMENT/LOW OVERHEAD Here's all you need to get start-ed and be successful:

- *A room—or some dedicated space*
- *A phone—with answering machine/voice mail capability*
- *A late-model computer—with e-mail capability*
- *A fax machine (or a fax program on your computer)*
- *A printer*
- *Printer paper and floppy diskettes*
- *A nice business card*
- *A dictionary and a thesaurus*

That's about it. OK, nice letterhead and envelopes once you get a few bucks rolling in, but certainly not necessary in order to hang out your shingle. If you're working out of your home, you save rent on an office. Put it all together, and its one of the most minimal start-up investments out there.

Sure, if you don't have a computer, you'll have to bite the bullet on that, but they're getting so reasonable, it just doesn't take much to get set up right.

If you're willing to look at a used machine, bargains abound, although some awesomely powerful machines are out there for a relative pittance. Rule of thumb, according to all the experts: Buy as much computer as you can afford. See Chapter Seven for a significantly more in-depth discussion of technology.

SHEER VARIETY OF WORK One of the things I love most about this busi-ness is that every day is different, new and interesting, full of opportunities to learn something. I'm happiest when I've got 3–4 jobs going on simultaneous-ly and I can switch back and forth between them.

Over the years, I've learned and written about UPS's Canadian shipping operations, BellSouth's product line and small business division happenings, Coca-Cola's alliance with The Boys & Girls Clubs of America, fiber optic cable companies that bring utilities and telecommunications companies together, seminars to teach chiropractors how to become Olympic doctors, the charita-ble activities of a prestigious Chattanooga hospital, how one event production company would design an entertainment pavilion for the Olympics, and on and on.

OK, so you might not seek these subjects out on your own, but when some-one's paying you pretty well to learn about something, encapsulate it, and put it on paper, you'll get into it and enjoy it.

Variety not only implies a broad spectrum of work but new clients/bosses all the time as well. Working for a wide range of people and businesses always makes things interesting.

Another plus is you never have to deal with any situation—such as a particularly egregious case of office politics—for very long. You get in, get the project done and get out.

NOT ENOUGH GOOD WRITERS   It doesn't matter which major metropolitan area you call home. The situation is pretty much the same everywhere, and it's very good news for you if you're considering this business: There just isn't a ton of good copywriters out there. There are a lot of people who are calling themselves copywriters, but they certainly aren't making a positive impression on anyone. If you're half-way decent and somewhat aggressive about getting the word out, you'll have plenty of work.

Make Sure You're Suited for This   Now, as we assumed earlier, you like to write and you feel you're pretty good at it. If you're not sure of your skills and have little formal experience, you'd be well-advised to get some input from someone—a successful businessperson, English professor, another writer or someone else who *does* know what he or she is talking about in this department.

Because frankly, the last thing this field needs is more mediocre or just plain bad writers. We've got plenty. And the sad part is that their clients often don't know any better, and some pretty scary stuff ends up circulating on a fairly wide scale.

VERY HEALTHY INCOME   Maybe you're a purist and being a writer to you means writing books and articles. Perhaps, you're thinking that there's something terribly mercenary about writing for Corporate America, right? Well, it's about tradeoffs. Living the "starving artist" lifestyle does have its advantages. The main one of course, is that you get to live this romantic, tortured, angst-ridden existence. You get to feel vastly superior to the typical working stiffs who've obviously sold out and furthermore, wouldn't know good writing if it came up and mugged them.

Finance Your Dreams   If you are trying to go the "purist" route— writing only articles and books—and you end up moonlighting to make ends meet, you might as well do something closer to your field that actually pays well. Then, with the bills paid, you've got the time and space to pursue that arena of writing which really lights you up—that future Oscar, Pulitzer, Emmy, or Tony-award-winning screenplay, novel, TV series, or Broadway play.

We should all have those dreams that drive us forward. Never give them up. I certainly don't aspire to just do commercial writing for the duration. I have my own pet projects—such as this one—that turn me on, and that I can happily work on, thanks to my bread and butter income from this business.

For Those of Us Who Like Nice Stuff… Now, it *is* hard to imagine any downside to the "starving artist" scenario except, perhaps, the "starving" part. Some of us out there like a little comfort in our lives. I know. It's so hopelessly conventional, but I like nice, relatively new clothes, good healthy food, nice digs, an occasional night out in a restaurant, and a couple of nice vacations a year. I'm funny that way.

Do It the Hard Way Or… But seriously, you could make a go of it writing articles and books, but it can be a long, tough road. Don't get me wrong. Writing articles for publication can get into fascinating arenas. But, unless you're really, really good and can climb into the high-paying, ultra-competitive circles of the big-time, big circulation national weeklies and monthlies, where the money is good, the financial side of periodical writing is typically pretty sad and sorry.

Of course, if busting your hump for three weeks and making, say, $1200 is your idea of a successful writing career, you'll be happy. In the business I'm talking about in this book, you could very realistically make that much in one week or less, on a reasonably consistent basis to boot and not wear yourself out in the process.

Will you make that much right away? Probably not. Do you need to? Again, probably not. While this business doesn't pay off overnight, it is a solid career opportunity that takes virtually no special training, pays pretty handsomely and affords you a level of freedom and flexibility most of the world would kill for.

How Much Can You Make? Without revealing my tax returns, let me put it this way: if you have even an inkling of intelligence along with *minimal* ability and drive, you can sleepwalk your way to $30,000 a year. If you're halfway decent and reasonably aggressive about getting the word out, you should easily top $50,000. And once you get a good reputation, and the referrals start coming in, who knows? There are a pretty healthy number of writers in this business grossing $100,000 a year or more.

Can you make more than $100,000? Of course. I would never discourage anyone from any aspiration, regardless of how ambitious, because I have no idea what you may have inside you that could drive you to that level and beyond. Suffice it to say, 50–100K in this field is very common. Does that work for you, especially with the freedom/lifestyle worked into the equation? It does for me.

How about expenses? Well, once you're set up with a computer, printer, software, etc., the overhead for a FLCW is one of the lowest around. We're talking paper, diskettes, toner, pens, pads.

TAX ADVANTAGES I won't be spending a lot of time in this book discussing all the ins and outs of legally setting up your own business. That's why there are accountants and attorneys. If you don't at least have an accountant, get one. It'll be one of the best things you could ever do for yourself. Suffice it to say, I'm set up as an "S" corporation, and each year, come tax time, I get to deduct a portion of my house note, utilities, phone, all business-related expenses, any equipment, and much more. Here's my standard disclaimer: I am not qualified to offer professional legal or accounting advice. Please consult your own professional attorney or accountant to learn the full range of options, responsibilities, and benefits available to you as a home-based (most likely) small business owner.

IMPRESS PEOPLE AT COCKTAIL PARTIES I'm only half-joking here. I mean, it seems like such a superficial reason, and essentially it is, but, there's something to be said for ego gratification and being a freelance commercial writer can give you that. When people ask that inevitable "make-conversation" question, "So, whattaya do?" when you answer, "Oh, I'm a writer," I promise you you'll get more than "That's nice. I need to get a refill."

A writer is very interesting to people. I've joked about this with a lady friend of mine whose profession seems to have the opposite effect on people. When she tells people she sells ear plugs for a living … well … where do you go from there?

WHAT'S YOUR STORY? OK, so why are you considering this direction? Perhaps, you're simply looking to change careers, take a completely new direction with your life. You've always felt you're a good writer and now you want to put that skill to work. Great. That's my story.

No Experience, No Problem I knew nothing about this business when I first started out. Had no contacts, hadn't been traveling in the creative circles at all, so I had to build it from nothing. Now a whole lot of people in this town know me.

An In-house Writer? Perhaps you're currently collecting a steady paycheck as a staff writer for a large company but looking to make the transition to self-employment. While you may have an advantage over the "never-written-for-money" masses in terms of grasping the rhythm, pace, and discipline of the craft, you're still looking for a roadmap to self-sufficiency. This can get you there.

Journalist? Might you be a journalist or news reporter who loves the business of writing but longs to make more money and have more freedom than you currently enjoy? A former journalist turned business owner shared these thoughts with me:

> *"Professional journalists get a lot of practice at making ideas easy to understand. However, because of low pay and often terrible working conditions, most want to make a career change within a few years of graduating. With their experience at expressing ideas in a clear, concise, logical manner, they are very well positioned to escape the shackles of poverty and earn $50–$85+ an hour in the freelance commercial writing market… [where] there is a huge demand for good, solid, coherent writing skills."*

Restless Mom? Maybe you're an at-home mom who would love to have a flexible, lucrative business on the side that meshes nicely with motherhood. If you were in advertising, marketing, or PR in your last life, this can be a perfect fit. Or perhaps, as previously discussed, you can leverage your past career experience—healthcare, financial services, real estate, hi-tech, telecommunications, retail—and seek writing projects in your former field. Given your familiarity with the field and your established contact network, you can make your life dramatically easier out of the gate. (See Appendix C: For Women Only – Interviews with "At-Home-Moms" /Writers.)

New College Grad? Or perhaps you're a recent college graduate, looking for a solid career opportunity. Having little professional experience will make it a little tougher, but if you're smart, hardworking, and you follow this game plan, there's nothing to say you couldn't pull it off.

"AM I GOOD ENOUGH?"   How do you decide that you're good enough to do something like this? By all means, get input from those whose opinions you respect, but don't let people intimidate you into thinking that you need to start small and work up to freelancing.

How many times did I hear from people, "Oh, you really need to go to work for an agency for a couple of years. It's going to be really hard for you to get work." Yeah, whatever. Thanks for sharing. If I believed them, then it would have been true. If you think you can do it, and you've got a reasonable grip on reality about your own talents and ability, that's all you need to listen to.

At one of my accounts recently, I was introduced to a woman who I realized was one of those who, five years ago, told me how hard it was going to be to get established. When she saw how well I was doing, she was amazed and said something very interesting.

The year I started my business (when I'd called her) and the following one, the local creative industry was going through a very rough time. So rough, in fact, that she had to close her business and go to work for a big corporation. And while businesses were apparently closing left and right, I knew nothing about it, so it never became an issue for me.

Had I heard all that talk then and took it to heart, I might never have tried. What I didn't know didn't hurt me. If you want anything badly enough, the "facts" don't matter.

Trust Yourself   If you just know that you're a good writer, you don't need anyone to tell you so. Listen to yourself, not someone who doesn't know what's inside you. Trust your instincts, listen to your heart, and never, ever, let anyone tell you you can't. OK, so is it all wine and roses? Are there some minuses here?

THE DOWNSIDES:

THE CLIENT IS THE BOSS; DON'T FORGET IT   How big is your ego? You don't want to be a *prima donna* in this business and get a reputation as someone who gets very attached to his or her writing and doesn't take too kindly to people changing it.

Get attached to your "after-hours" writing—your poetry, columns, short stories, books, etc. A word to the wise, however. You think corporate clients are brutal editors? Just wait till a newspaper, magazine, or book editor gets ahold of your sacred scribblings. You ain't seen nothin' yet.

But if you take this field seriously and pursue it diligently, it can be your bread and butter. And that's the trade-off. If I write a column and a newspaper publishes it, I'll be lucky to get $75–$100.

On the other hand, if I do a simple marketing brochure, I might make $600–$1000 or more. If you have a problem giving the client what he wants, whether or not you think it's the best way to say it, you'll probably have a short lifespan in this business.

Do the Right Thing Now, I'm not talking about unethical practices. I've never been asked to do something that offended my sense of morality, but if I did encounter such a situation, I'd walk. It's not worth selling your soul for a few bucks.

What I'm referring to here is simply a difference of opinion as to how something should be written. There will be plenty of times, when you *know* that keeping it the way you've written it would be more effective communication, but the client wants to change it. That's life. She's the client. She wins. Now, don't get me wrong. I'm not talking about being a wimp here. Let me explain.

Be a Valuable Consultant I was in sales and marketing for about 15 years before I started writing—a background I used as a strong selling point. "I may not have lots of direct writing experience, Mr. Prospect, but my sales and marketing background allows me to bring a persuasive selling tone to my writing, if that's appropriate."

Given my decent grasp of sales and marketing issues, I'm not shy about pressing a point if I feel the client is making a mistake. Make your case eloquently, and the client will appreciate it. This is classic "value-added": delivering more than just copywriting. You're providing valuable consultation, and as such, you're simply going to be worth more to your clients. Give them more than they bargained for, and they won't even think of going somewhere else.

Most smart clients expect your input. If you've got some good creative suggestions—even non-writing related ones that'll improve the delivery of their message—speak up. Recommend a certain direction very different from their original vision, which they end up using effectively, and you'll evolve, in their eyes, from copywriter to marketing/creative consultant. Your value rises, along with the likelihood of being hired again, and perhaps for a higher fee as well. Next chapter, we'll discuss *assertiveness* in more depth, a very important quality for any aspiring FLCW.

All that said, while you have an obligation to do your best to create the most effective piece you can, ultimately, your job is to give your clients what they want. If they choose to ignore your suggestions, that's their prerogative. Suck it up, smile, do it their way, and collect your check. Then go home, stick pins in a voodoo doll likeness of one of them, and you'll feel much better.

Trade-Offs With this arena of writing, given the financial potential, you might have to give up that romantic notion of a tortured and angst-filled writer-ly existence.

I know, it is harder to conjure up suffering and anguish when your bills are all paid and you've got money in the bank, but you'll adapt. Seriously though, the trade off is this: 1) you don't get to dictate what you write, and, 2) the client gets to change whatever you've written (again, substitute "editor" for "client" and you're talking about *any* writer).

THE LIMITS OF COMPENSATION As a freelancer, you're basically paid for your time. In the course of doing a promotion for a company, maybe you come up with a tagline, for instance, that becomes their new signature slogan and ends up on all their materials and in their advertising. Well, generally speaking, all you're going to receive is pay for the hours you've been contracted for.

Don't bother to dwell on the unfairness of it all. This is simply the nature of the beast. That's not to say that if you do come up with something that you know is a winner, you shouldn't try and maximize the compensation for your efforts.

I say "generally speaking" because if, in fact, you did come up with a particularly high-profile slogan for a company like Coca-Cola that perhaps became the next company tagline with huge national and international recognition and exposure, this would warrant what is known as "value billing": a higher fee than just the hours expended because of the promotional value the slogan earns them. This is a very familiar concept in creative circles, so don't be shy about pressing the point if it's appropriate.

Don't Give It Away I'm working on a direct mail campaign right now, where we (my designer and I, the two-man team concept I'll talk about later) have been asked to come up with a theme and three ideas off that theme to take them through three months.

It so happens I came up with a great idea for a year-long campaign that will probably be a lot more effective than four three-monthers. While I could show them all 12 ideas on the theme, why should I? I'll give them three and let them pay for the other nine if they like the first ones.

You're entitled to be fairly compensated for your creativity, so don't let clients milk you for more than they've contracted for under the guise of "seeing where you're going with this thing." If they want the tour, they need to pay the toll.

DON'T HAVE F.I.T.S. (FREELANCER ISOLATION—THE SYNDROME) As I hinted at earlier, this business, if done from your home, can significantly reduce your contact with other human beings. So, what can you do to counteract the inevitable loneliness, isolation, and slow creep of social atrophy inherent with a solitary field such as this?

Let me say at the outset that being single, my comments, though in some ways applicable to anyone, are geared primarily towards singles. If you're married and/or have kids, you'll have a whole different set of challenges.

Now, you'd better be meeting people in the job or you won't build a business very fast. However, in these amazingly high-tech times, once you've secured new clients, you'll probably be able to do a lot of work electronically—by phone, fax, and e-mail.

Meetings will get fewer and farther between and that's a positive thing for everyone. In fact, therein lies the double-edged sword inherent in this craft. You want to get to a point where you're not running all over town to get your business done. Picture this:

Technology Has Its Benefits, But... You get a call from a client about a new project. He sends the info to you by courier or fax and then you get on the phone with him and nail down the parameters and expectations.

You work on the project, check in by phone if you have any questions, conduct any necessary interviews by phone, fax him drafts until you get final approval, e-mail him the final copy in file form, and send a bill. Thirty days later, you get a check in the mail.

You've never set foot in his office and never met with anyone face-to-face. You're truly working from your home with all the wonderful pluses of that scenario. Even if he does want a meeting, that's at the front end and it's over in a few hours.

Of course, while it probably sounds absolutely fabulous to anyone currently forced to get up at 6:30–7:00 every morning and fight rush-hour traffic to be somewhere by 9:00, believe it or not, you can get used to it very quickly. Not that you ever completely take it for granted. Daily, I remind myself of how good I have it. It's just that you start seeing the other side of the equation.

Working for yourself and alone does require some adjustments and takes a subtle, imperceptible toll on you. Kind of like the frog in the boiling water thing. Put a frog in boiling water, he'll jump right out. But put him in cool water and turn the heat up slowly, and he'll just end up boiling because the change was so gradual. Stay a cool frog, not a boiled one.

Get Out & About! When you work for corporate America and you're around people all day long, you might just want to come home and be by yourself. Do that when you're working at home and the walls begin closing in on you. So, what's the answer?

Make sure you get out at least three nights a week doing something, whether it's to take a class, join a choral group, take karate, volunteer your time, go to the health club, have dinner with a friend or friends and so on. But the important thing is just to be around people. Get creative.

Scoping Other Freelancers When you're out and about, in whatever setting, keep an eye out for other freelancers like yourself. Make some new friends, swap cards, get together for lunch. I'd wager that unless they're in a very contact-intensive arena like video production, or photography, they'd welcome the opportunity to expand their social circle.

Decide that you're going to become a "contact commando," aggressively pursuing opportunities to rub elbows with your fellow homo sapiens in fun, interesting, stimulating settings.

Check your city's alternative newspaper every week or the Saturday edition of your daily paper, which is where they usually have the "What's Going On Around Town" section. Pick at least one activity to do each week. Join a book club, go to a lecture or concert, teach someone to read, try that new Ethiopian restaurant, go to a poetry reading. Make yourself do it. You'll be glad you did.

And don't say, "Well, all that stuff costs money. If I'm just starting out, I may really have to watch my spending." Right you are, but that's why I suggested the alternative magazines. They're generally stuffed full of all kinds of cheap or free activities going on around town.

Get yourself one of those 2-for-1 discount books—you know, the one you said you'd never buy because they make you look like a cheapskate? Right. *That* one. In addition to two-fers for scillions of restaurants around town, they've got similar deals on the symphony, theater companies, museums, the botanical gardens, the zoo, movies, etc..

You save money and discover a lot of interesting, little-known (which is why they're in such a book) activities.

An Outside Office? I still work from home, but recently, I've been pondering that. In addition to the isolation, there are distractions at home: refrigerator, bed, television, washer-dryer, swimming pool, etc.

I have friends who've bitten the bullet, gotten an office outside their home for $350–600 a month and are glad they did, because when they go to the office, they're "at work" which means they work. For about $500 a month, you can do an "officeshare," where you'll have your own office, along with shared receptionist, fax machine, copier, and conference room.

The crucial human contact also provides the opportunity to network amongst a wide variety of other businesses. This is key, simply because there are very few businesses in this world that won't, at one time or another, have a need for copywriting services. If you're across the hall, and just as good as the guy across town, why not use you? But this move is more down the line.

So, what are the qualities that make for a good FLCW? What attributes will boost your odds of success? That's the subject of our next chapter. Right this way….

Chapter Three

What Does it Take to Be Successful?

So, what qualities are good predictors of future success as a freelance commercial writer? Well, let's take a look….

WRITING ABILITY   As discussed, I'm assuming you think you're a pretty decent scribe and are interested in writing for a living. Also, as mentioned, you don't have to be a crackerjack writer to make a good living in this business. If you're not, it may only mean that you won't get as much work in certain fields like ad copywriting, which requires consistently tight, snappy, and creative copy.

Average Ability Is More Than Enough   There are plenty of fields, however, whether they be healthcare, banking, manufacturing, insurance, high technology, and many, many more that need oodles of clear, concise copywriting that just simply doesn't have to be a work of art. As a matter of fact, they don't *want* a work of art. They simply want to convey information, *simply*. If you can position yourself as *the* writer to call when someone needs solid, dependable, consistent copy in one or more fields, you'll do well.

I have a friend who writes copy for a very specific industry, and has been getting plenty of work for eight-plus years now. Yet, he's a very average copywriter and is the first to admit it. Doesn't mean you can't improve your skills, but know that there's more than enough work for the less-than-brilliantly-gifted.

ABILITY TO MARKET ONESELF This business is, first and foremost, a sales and marketing venture. Since I began in this business, I've heard a line used over and over again: Assuming a healthy, growing business, "You'll spend 60% of your time finding the business and 40% actually doing it." Of course, in the beginning, it's going to be a lot more like 100/0, and as you get much more established, it'll get to a more balanced ratio and eventually, very likely weighted the other way.

Of course, don't forget the other business-related activities that will grab time from you besides just marketing and writing—i.e., bookkeeping, equipment purchasing, software mastery, etc.

And just a word of comfort and advice for those of you who've "never sold anything in my life" or "hate sales" or "hate salesmen": Don't get too wigged out by the sales thing.

A Different Kind of Sales First of all, if you've ever held a job in your life, you've sold something—yourself, or your ideas.

Secondly, I would assert that the discomfort most people feel in the sales arena stems from having to sell a product with which they're not completely familiar or worse, not sold on themselves.

I promise you, should you embark on this particular journey, it'll be because you have confidence in your ability to write. That means you're not only familiar with the product but sold on it as well, because it's you. And when you're selling *you* and what you know you do well, it's a whole other ballgame.

That said, all the confidence in the world in yourself and your abilities won't pay the bills unless you get the word out on a pretty wide scale. Unless you've got a huge client base built up from a previous job, you're going to have to reach out by phone and mail to your business community. More on that in Chapter Six: "Let's Get Started!" Just know that they need you. Believe me, they do.

DISCIPLINE When I tell people I'm a freelance writer, many say, "Oh, you must be so disciplined. I could never do that!" Frankly, I'm not very disciplined, but when I have work on my desk, I'd better do it if I, 1) want to eat and pay my mortgage, 2) want to continue living this wonderful lifestyle that I do, and 3) ever want to be hired by that company again.

Certainly, if I don't have a project going, and I've got a little money in the bank, that new paperback starts calling to me, or the bed seems to be beckoning for a post-lunch siesta. And frankly, I can do that, which is one of the perks of this gig. It's my show.

TECHNICAL EXPERTISE   These days, the individuals who've managed to avoid learning the basics of computerese are about as rare as mall parking spaces at Christmas. It just doesn't take much to get up to speed on what you need to know to do this business. If you already know *Microsoft® Word,* your learning curve just got even shorter.

I'm one of those people on the Minimum Daily Requirement technical track: I learn the least I can possibly get away with to do my job. Hey, I'm curious in most other areas, but I'm just not eternally searching for the latest and greatest software program, and in this business, you don't have to (See Chapter Seven—"Technically Speaking…" for more details).

TENACITY   It really helps to have a thick skin and a healthy dose of "stick-tuit-iveness." The beginning can be very lonely and very unprofitable. Plan on having at least 3–4 months of living expenses set aside. Perhaps you're fortunate to have a financial support system while you're growing the business, which is why this business makes a lot of sense for married moms who used to be in the business world and want to get back into it gradually.

A potentially sensitive sidebar here. I don't know what it's like to be a minority or a woman in this business. I do know that women make up the majority of copywriters in the field, so being a woman will in no way hinder your progress.

If you're a minority, in addition to marketing across a wide spectrum, definitely approach as many minority-owned businesses as you can. Maximize what you have. Superior performance will convince just about anyone. Here's where you can work to control the "controllables" like integrity, reliability, and consistency and set yourself apart from the pack.

Having to make it on your own—while certainly providing moments of despair, panic, or outright terror—can be very motivating. A motivation, incidentally, that may be more difficult to muster if there are no particularly unpleasant financial consequences should you not make a go of it. Put simply, being "hungry" can be a major asset as you begin on a path like this.

FLEXIBILITY   If you're the type of person who needs a lot of structure in your life, this business can be very frustrating. Because when you hit the inevitable slow periods, it can be very rough on your attitude and your self-concept.

This seems to be easier for women to handle than men, because women tend to be more multi-dimensional in their personalities than men. As a man, I'm more likely to define myself largely by what I do for a living day in and day out. If I have no work, who am I?

And when I don't have jobs going on, I find that it's amazingly easy to quickly fill up my day with "stuff'—running errands, working out, going shopping, meeting friends for lunch, etc, etc. If you can roll smoothly between the feasts and the famines, and know that your workload will alternately balloon and shrink, you'll be fine.

CURIOSITY   Are you the kind of person who loves learning all about new and different people, places, and things? Do you like trying exotic, ethnic restaurants, traveling to places you've never been before, reading National Geographic, or dating three different people at a time? If this describes you, (not counting the last part…. OK, maybe counting the last part), you'll like this field.

Freelance commercial writers who have been at it for awhile know a lot of stuff about a lot of stuff. One day, I'll be steeped in a brochure for a trade show exhibit, another project might require me to become an expert on the Korean War for an educational CD-ROM, while another day has me studying the ins and outs of forms printing technology.

And incidentally, a nice by-product of always searching for and writing about the positive, unique, and wonderful aspects of any product, service, or company is that you naturally start doing the same for the rest of your life. And that's a good thing.

A 'NON-CONFORMIST' NATURE   If you don't think like the masses, then you're in good shape for this business. If you happen to subscribe to the notion that it's possible to love what you do, make good money, and have the time to enjoy it, then we're going to get along just fine.

Not that true conformists can't make it too. If you're of that ilk, and you want to work 60-70 hours a week, you can do that too, and probably make a lot more than your peers working similar schedules.

ORGANIZATIONAL SKILLS   The more organized you are, the easier this job will be. We'll get into the specifics of what that means in Chapters Seven ("Technically Speaking") and Eight ("The System Is the Solution"). An anal-retentive nature can be a very good friend in this business. But, while there can be a healthy amount of minutiae to keep track of, it's never too much to handle.

EASY TO GET ALONG WITH   The surest way to keep clients coming back is to make it an easy, enjoyable, professional experience for them. Don't have an attitude and think you're going to make it in this business. Don't think you're smarter than everyone and all they need is your wisdom to see the light of truth. You may be smarter than many. That's fine. Just think it.

I'm sure there are a number of mediocre writers out there making good livings in this town because they're easy-going, cooperative, and accommodating. Clients like to work with people like that. Wouldn't you? By the same token, there are undoubtedly some very talented writers here who have to struggle for work because they're such arrogant pains in the butt.

Remember, many prospective clients may realize that they're lousy writers which is why they're in the market for your services. If they're not very savvy about what caliber of writer is available out there, chances are, even an average writer will impress them and more importantly, might be all they need. If that writer is easy to work with on top of all that, then the client's won all around.

While this field can often be a wonderful outlet for creative expression, in the end, it's still a job, full of things you'll like *and* hate. On balance, however, you'll always come out ahead.

EXCITED ABOUT WHAT YOU'RE DOING   You have to really want to do this. If what you're doing doesn't turn you on, then find something that does. Now, I don't bound out of bed with an ear-to-ear grin every morning, but I look forward to getting to work. Too many people are walking around unhappy with their work, and making life miserable for everyone around them.

I believe we all have an obligation, not only to ourselves, but to the world around us, to find that which turns us on, because when we are lit up, we're just that much nicer to be around.

ASSERTIVENESS/CONVICTION   Be willing to take a stand for what you feel is best for the project in the face of a client's suggested revisions. Remember, you're the professional. Clients may not accept your recommendation, but presumably, they hired you because they believe you possess some skill that they don't. In the beginning, it will be a challenge to remind yourself of that fact.

I remember during that first year, and even now occasionally, a client will solicit my specific input on something, asking, "What do you think? After all, you're the professional." And my internal voice is screaming, "Me?!? The Professional? I'm Just Some Guy Who Was Selling Dating Service Memberships A Year Ago (the sad truth) Who Decided That He Could Write!! What Do I Know?!?!?"

Of course, I don't say that. I wisely nod my head, rub my chin, and begin, "Well, given the target audience and the objective of the piece, my recommendation is…" Live it and you'll become it.

"Docile" Copywriters Need Not Apply The good clients will appreciate your expertise and your commitment to a quality outcome. The morons won't, but provided you make your views known in diplomatic fashion, that's their problem, not yours.

I pride myself on not being a docile copywriter. I will be very outspoken when I feel the client's off-base and about to do something that will compromise the impact of the piece. And you better believe that my regular clients love that. In their minds, it's what separates me from the pack—the "value-added."

If you just obediently go along with every single copy change your client suggests, she may just start wondering how good you really are. Then again, when the Client From Hell is insisting on one idiotic change after another, your desire to get the stupid thing done far outweighs any nobler commitment to creative integrity. You're entitled from time to time. Just don't cave too early.

ABILITY TO ASK LOTS OF DUMB QUESTIONS Translation: Good Interrogation Skills. One of my trademarks is asking tons of questions at the beginning, many of which may seem dumb or painfully obvious. I also happen to nail my first drafts about 95% of the time. It's no coincidence.

My regular clients understand my approach and know that it leads to a high quality outcome. When I'm with new clients, I may explain what I'm doing so they don't think they've hired a dim bulb.

I remember one occasion when, in the midst of these multiple, possibly silly sounding questions with a regular client, I started apologizing, and my client interrupted and said, "That's why we like working with you. You take the time to find out exactly what we want and end up hitting the mark 'most every time." Wow. She'd noticed and definitely appreciated it.

Delve deeper, ask more questions: What sentiment, message, feeling would you like the reader to be left with after reading this? What's your purpose in creating this piece? What do you want it to accomplish? Get them talking. They'll usually end up telling you what to write, how to write it, and even serve up a golden concept.

By definition, you will be coming into every project "in the middle." Questions help you be a quick study. Ask plenty.

Don't Freak Out! I had a client meeting today, during which I experienced something that's happened many times before. Now, just assume that when you enter a project kickoff meeting (like this one was), the people with whom you're meeting will have been stewing in the subject matter for so long (especially if it's high-tech) that they'll have a hard time pulling back far enough to realize that you're essentially coming in blind. Sure, you may have some knowledge of the field, but their specific focus is new to you.

Consequently, they will often assume a knowledge level you don't have and throw unfamiliar terms and jargon at you at breakneck speed. In situations like these, it's not at all uncommon to feel overwhelmed at the beginning. All your "I'm-not-good-enough" stuff will rear its ugly head in such moments. Don't panic. Stay calm, ask a million questions and make sure you get printed material to take with you. After getting home, reading it all, reviewing your notes, and asking a few more questions, I promise that in about 95% of the cases, you'll feel 95% better.

Don't assume for a moment that your clients will present the information to you in a logical and coherent manner, and that if you're not getting it, it's your fault. I can't tell you how many times I've come to discover how disorganized the participants (often multiple contributors to one piece and coming in with their own objectives, goals, and agendas) in these meetings really are. Not to mention that often, it's later become clear that they overloaded me with an enormous amount of extraneous, unnecessary information (the "Let's Throw Everything He Might Ever Conceivably Need at Him at Once and Let Him Sort It Out" approach to content development). No wonder it didn't make sense at the time! The first time it happens, you'll probably be looking for the life preserver. Hang in there. It's like breaking a code. It'll come.

HUMILITY/GOOD LISTENING SKILLS   There's a wonderful saying in spiritual self-growth circles: "Before enlightenment, chopping wood, carrying water. After enlightenment, chopping wood, carrying water." It speaks to the importance of humility, never thinking you're better than, too good for, or above it all, no matter what level of accomplishment and success you've attained.

Don't Be So Sure   Humility, unfortunately, is rare among copywriters (and human beings in general). Many truly feel they're a whole lot smarter than most clients out there, which frankly, is true in many cases. The problems begin when these folks let this sentiment affect how they approach any job.

They'll walk into a new situation and in a few minutes, are just sure they've got it sized up. They *know* what the client wants (translation: they know how they'd like to write it) and then when they return a first draft that's off the mark, they'll get ticked at the client who obviously 1) doesn't know what he wants, and/or 2) can't appreciate good writing, when in fact, they just didn't listen long enough or closely enough to the client.

Approach this business with humility and in addition to being viewed as easy to work with (a priceless reputation), you'll have less anxiety, and get more jobs finished more quickly and competently, all of which will put more money in your pocket.

Small Can Lead to Big   Humility also means not being so "big for your britches" that you can't or don't take little jobs that come along. I have a friend in this business who smugly declares, "I don't pick up a pen for less than $500." Well, that seems to work for her, but I doubt she was always like that.

If you're not too busy, can get a small job knocked out in a few hours, and make $200 in the process, why not? Remember, small jobs done well can lead to big jobs later on—and not necessarily from that same client. On several occasions, I've been referred by clients for whom I'd done a few small jobs to friends of theirs who had much bigger projects on tap.

DISCRETION   In the course of your work, you will be exposed to some mighty sensitive information, i.e., details of a company's product launch, consumer demographic information, a company's multi-million-dollar proposal to a big client who's also getting proposals from three or four other vendors, and more.

Bottom line, you'll be privy to information that competitors would practically kill for. You can start feeling pretty darned important, like a major player in a spy novel. Fine. Feel whatever you want. Just keep it to yourself. Don't even discuss the info innocently with friends, while leaving out the names. It's not worth it. If the client or worse, your market, gets even a whiff that you betrayed a client confidence, you might as well find a new line of work.

PRIDE IN A JOB WELL DONE   Sometimes I think that my success in this endeavor is largely due to my unwillingness to turn in a product that is substandard. Which, judging from the quality of writing in the marketplace about which I have heard clients speak, is certainly not a sentiment universally shared by other writers out there. So, if you are the type who would be ashamed to turn in anything that isn't really good, it'll hold you in good stead.

Now that you know the optimum qualities of a successful FLCW, how do you start? What are the steps you can take—mentally, physically, financially—to get yourself prepared for this exciting career direction? Onward and upward....

Chapter Four

Ready for Self-Employment?

TAKE FULL RESPONSIBILITY   Starting your own business and making it work is a game for adults. Sure, you can cut corners, pretend you're working harder than you really are, blame circumstances when things don't go your way, and all those other things people often do when they work for someone else. You might be able to get away with it there. Here, you can't, because you're only cheating yourself.

Decide right now, right this very minute, that regardless of how this venture pans out, wonderfully or not at all, that you'll assume full responsibility for the outcome. Good advice for life in general. I heard a wonderful line several years back. Put it on your wall: "When we look back on our lives later on, we'll either have what we want out of life, or we'll have the reasons why we don't."

This may not be the right opportunity for you, but get out of the habit of assigning blame to externals in your life. Why the self-awareness lecture? Because I assert that it's important to understand how human nature fits into this equation and how to make it work for, not against us.

REALITY CHECK   Up till now, we've looked at the fun, promising, and profitable potential of the business. That's all there and valid. But if you're coming from the corporate world, starting your own venture can be daunting if you're not used to being completely self-motivated, which is exactly what it's going to take.

It Can Happen Fast   As all business owners know, the nitty-gritty of building a business is hard, repetitive, grueling, and generally unprofitable work at the beginning. How long that unprofitable period has to go on is largely a function of the time and effort you're willing to put into it. The good news? It can happen fast if you hit it hard, and even faster in this business because you're not having to dig yourself out of a huge hole of capital investment.

How long did it take me? Three and a half months into my fledgling career, I got a deal to ghost-write a book for a local businessman and was essentially self-sufficient from that point forward.

Develop Good Habits Early   If you establish good habits at the outset and stick to them, freelancing doesn't have to be difficult. The thought of having to go back and work for someone else is so painful and unpleasant that there are few things I wouldn't do to make sure that I can keep this gig going. So, I hunt up the work and when I do get a job, I do it, on time and well, so that I make a good impression and I get hired again.

Here's a strange statement, but oh-so-true. The reason I work hard to keep this going is because I'm a lazy person. It's the truth. I'll periodically bust my butt so I don't have to constantly bust my butt, or at least so I don't have to drive to a job every morning.

ATTITUDE IS EVERYTHING   You've probably heard enough lectures about having a positive mental attitude to last you ten lifetimes, but this one's a little different.

Life isn't always wonderful, and we've all seen those people who seem to have a smile plastered on their face all the time, and then find out they had a nervous breakdown. I'm just not Mr. Constantly Cheerful. Maybe someday, but I'm not holding my breath.

What Do You "Know"?   I'm talking about self-perception here—taking a good long look at just how you perceive yourself. What limitations have you put on yourself? What do you just "know" about yourself? What are you just "sure" you can—and more importantly, *cannot*—do? What inner dialogue yammers on in your head about your capabilities, limitations, and past defeats?

How many of you are reading this book because the idea is intriguing to you, but inside a little voice is saying, "You'll never do this. It'll just be another thing you checked out, spent a few bucks on and never did anything with. Who are you kidding?"

I say this part of the book is *the* most crucial. It's often the weakest link. You can memorize all the information in the world about how to build a business like this, but if you're not clear upstairs, nothing's going to happen. On the other hand, you can know nothing about this business whatsoever, but if you want it badly enough, I'd bet on you in a heartbeat.

For many, it's one of the toughest hurdles they'll have to get past to make a go of *any* self-employment. Like the classic conversation between a salaried employee and a self-employed person. The salaried guy asks, "How can you stand not knowing what you're going to make every month?" To which the self-employed guy, in typical entrepreneur fashion, replies, "How can you stand *knowing* what you're going to make?" Amen to that.

GET MENTAL, MAKE MONEY   You have to be mentally prepared to make good money. Sort of like what we discussed before about imagining yourself in the role. A very interesting thing happened in my fourth year in the business. A little background. When I first started this business, I didn't have huge financial aspirations for my first year. My goal was simple: to be able to make a living at this full time, and not have to moonlight.

That's quite an achievement just by itself. I didn't start out saying, "OK, I'm going to make 50K my first year." And I'm certainly not saying that you shouldn't set such a goal. If you're determined, you absolutely can make that—and more!

Reachable Goals   So my goal was to make ends meet solely by my pen, and I did it. In my second year, I didn't have a very firm target. I just threw something out like, "I want to have enough to pay the bills and then some." Again, I made it. Big deal, right?

Year three was a little different. I started out great guns, set an ambitious monthly goal and actually hit it for the first six months. I was doing really well. And all I did differently was to set a number.

Instead of just saying I wanted to pay the bills and a bit more, I set my sights on an amount that would cover significantly more than just "the bills and then some." And what do you know, I was rockin' 'n rollin' and right on target by June 30. So what happened?

Well, truth be known, my semiannual bout of Attention Deficit Disorder kicked in, as I got a little bored with what I was doing, and got a little side-tracked. I wasn't as focused in my goals, certainly not as aggressive about beating the bushes for new work.

Bottom line, my income dropped for several months. I ended up getting back on track and finished the year strongly, but there's a whole bunch of good news in this story.

You're in Control First of all, this points to a fundamental and perhaps obvious truth about working for yourself in general, and certainly this writing profession in particular: You control your income. Want a raise? Just work a little harder. Make a few more phone calls. Get out and meet a few more people. Network. Let more people know you're out there. Your income *will* rise.

Of course the flip side is just as true. Slip into typical lazy, instant-gratification-seeking human being mode, and the well starts going dry. But I love it. Even the downside is a constant wonderful reminder that I am the master of my own destiny.

Sure, I made less money for several months, but I also took time to have a life. I sang in a chorus in the summer. I started Tai Chi in September. I took a couple of nice trips. All because my time was my own. And I paid my bills and put money in the bank.

Little Change, Big Difference This year, one slight adjustment in my mental processes made all the difference in the world in my income. I was sitting in a lecture geared to freelancers and the whole subject of "Goal Setting" came up. Yawn. Geez, how many times do I have to listen to this in my life? Obviously, as many times as it takes for it to finally sink in.

If you're like me, when you see the words "Goal Setting," you get this feeling in the pit of your stomach. You know you really need to do it, but just haven't made the time. If you're already a committed goal-setter, then this business is going to be even easier.

Good news. My version of goal setting is not difficult and doesn't take some huge commitment of time and energy. Would you be willing to invest five minutes to put a system in place and about two minutes a day after that, if it meant dramatically increasing your income over the course of the year?

I decided that I wanted to make $100,000 this year. Now, just saying "I'm going to make 100K a year" is like trying to fit a whole pizza in your mouth at once. You need to break it down into more manageable bite-size pieces. So, I created a chart on my computer, which looked like this:

$100,000 a year
$8000 a month
$2000 a week
$400 a day
Where's the $400 coming from today?

I made a few copies of it, put one on my bathroom mirror and tacked another up on the wall next to my computer. I read the chart out loud to myself in the mirror for one minute in the morning and another minute at night before bed. Just having this sheet of paper to focus on made a huge difference.

My mind started working to make it a reality. When you've got to make $400 in the day, you get busy. The amazing thing about this is that once you get into the mindset, it isn't that difficult to do. The goal naturally propels you forward and suddenly presents you with opportunities. It's almost eerie, but it works.

What's interesting is that you start considering $2000 a week a baseline amount. Whereas before you might have thought of $1000–1200 as a decent week, now that sounds awfully low. It naturally drives up your own expectations of yourself. How did it go, you ask? Well, the year's not over yet, but I'm actually right on track.

How much is a lot of money to you? $30K? $50K? 100K? If the most you've ever made in one year is 30K, then it's going to be a big stretch, mentally and realistically, to make 100K. It certainly can be done, but you want to pick a figure that excites you but doesn't seem unreal and out of reach. It should be a stretch, but very do-able.

GET YOUR FINANCES IN ORDER   What's your present financial situation? You'll want to take good stock of your balance sheet and your lifestyle at this juncture. Do you have a lot of debt? Do you have healthy cash reserves? Lots of credit cards with high balances? Expensive car? High mortgage payment? Extravagant lifestyle? How hard is it going to be to scale back?

Go Low-Maintenance   Unless you're just an amazing marketer, with tons of contacts to start with, or a built-in client base from your last job, count on not making a lot of money right out of the gate. Consequently, it makes sense to structure your life and your monthly obligations to be as low-maintenance as possible.

In the beginning of any venture, *and I can't stress this enough,* the last thing you need is to be worrying about paying your bills. But it's a fine line. There is something to be said for being "hungry" as a source of inspiration but if you're too concerned about where the money's coming from to pay the light bill, it's going to make you crazy and have you wondering why in God's name you went in this direction, and wait'll I get my hands on that Peter Booberman guy.

Lower Your "Monthlies" Try and pay off, or at least pay down, your credit cards. If you start out without an extra $200-300 a month in debt service, you'll have a lot fewer tense moments while in business-building mode. Do you have a steep car payment—$350-500 a month? Think about trading down for something in the $200 range, or better yet, selling what you've got and outright buying something a lot cheaper that'll get you around town.

What's Really Important? I went from a Jeep Cherokee at about $400 a month to a Ford Escort at about half that. Suffice it to say, I discovered how attached I was to the image my car provided me. Sad, I know. As a single guy, I really was concerned about what sort of havoc such a vehicle would wreak on my social life.

But, you know what? It didn't make a damn bit of difference to anyone I went out with that year. As a matter of fact, I probably had more dates because all of a sudden I was doing something that really turned me on and it showed in my confidence and attitude. And that's a zillion times more important than your wheels to the people who are really worth your time.

As far as clients and your car are concerned, chances are remote that they'll ever see it and even if they do, so what? Don't expend valuable energy on things like this. If you're lucky enough to be driving a paid-off car that's still healthy, now is not the time to buy something new.

WHERE'S MY PORTFOLIO? So, how do you get work when you have nothing to show? Who's going to take you on faith? Well, there are some pretty easy ways to solve this problem. For starters, think of any type of writing project you've ever done in any job at any time that might be used to beef up a starter portfolio.

Have you written some particularly effective business sales letters? Some ads perhaps? A marketing manual? Press release? Marketing brochures? Internal newsletter? Rack your brain. If the pickins' are lean in that department, time for Plan B.

Pro Bono Is there a charity you already donate time to? If not, pick one. I chose the American Heart Association, probably because they were the first one to return my call, so they got lucky. It could be the Arthritis Foundation, a hospital, an environmental group like the Sierra Club, a political organization, a small theater group, whatever. What would turn you on?

What groups in your city might need to create printed materials and may not have high budgets to do it? Simple tri-fold or more complex brochures, newsletters, and ad campaigns are all possibilities.

Just make sure that what you do will result in a reasonably attractive sample and in an arena of work you're likely to be pursuing. Alternately, work on something which will entail a reasonably significant chunk of writing that will showcase to a prospective client your ability to "tell a story" for a business.

If the project is a sales brochure, corporate image piece, ad, or anything else that requires strong aesthetics, the client will most likely have a graphic designer to professionally produce the piece, which is good news for you. By pursuing more "copy-focused" projects such as simple tri-fold brochures, press releases, marketing/training manuals, video scripts, or the like—where the writing *is* the job—you eliminate the need for a designer.

Lay the Groundwork Now With careful planning, you can start constructing this pro bono portfolio while you're still working full-time. Offer to meet people before work for breakfast, after work for a bite, or even on weekends. Make it happen.

Over the course of a year or so before I officially launched my business, I put together close to a half dozen pieces for my book, all pro bono. There were three press releases for the American Heart Association, a marketing manual for a start-up hi-tech firm, a video script and fundraising proposal for a non-profit organization, and a marketing brochure for a small video production company.

As I was doing these projects, I didn't exactly know why. Just that it would probably lead to something, even if I didn't know what at that point. And boy did it.

The Power of the Team Another very effective strategy to ensure your work will look good is to team with a freelance graphic designer, in a pro bono version of the same teaming I'll discuss later in Chapter Thirteen—"Dos, Don'ts and Don't Forgets."

By finding a graphic designer who's also starting out and trying to get established, you could make a pretty attractive offer to a charity, non-profit, or a small company.

You'll create a promotional brochure, for instance, at no charge for the copywriting or design services. In return, you'll get plenty of samples when it's done *and* have a healthy amount of creative latitude to create a piece that'll wow 'em. Just make sure your client has the resources to produce the piece or at least that you have access to a good color printer.

The reason I mention "creative latitude" is that one of the most unpleasant scenarios in this business is a client who micro-manages a project: hires you to do a job, but then doesn't let you do it, edits the copy till it's embarrassingly bad, kills off any design creativity, and in the end, you have a piece you wouldn't want to show anyone.

The one saving grace of a situation like that is that at least you're making money, and you just chalk it up to the necessary evils of the business. Now, imagine that exact same scenario, except this time *you're not getting paid.* That's the stuff nightmares are made of.

By the way, another great source for a graphically-talented teammate is a local arts college or institute. Very often, students are looking for an opportunity to add to their portfolio by doing "real world" work. You might be able to swap out services and help them with copy for their own marketing/promotional piece.

If they don't need copywriting any time soon, they'll probably want to be paid, which is only fair. You want your talents valued even when you're starting out and so do they. However, chances are good you'll be able to get them at low "starving artist" rates and they'll get a piece for their books.

Go Through the Back Door Just try to get to these students directly, as opposed to going through the school administrators. Occasionally, the staff of these schools, in an attempt to protect their precious charges from those who would "exploit" them financially, will demand you pay full rates. Meanwhile, many students themselves, if given the choice, would gladly do it for less, in return for the experience and the sample for their books. But they never get the chance, thanks to those who would protect their honor. My libertarianism is showing....

Start-Ups Another whole group of pro bono prospects are start-up businesses. And you'd be wise to approach them like they're real paying prospects, because indirectly, they are. If they let you do some work for them, and you walk away with a good sample, then they've propelled you that much closer to the day when you can call on real live companies—the ones with money—and have something to show them. Perhaps even them, once they're really on their feet.

Of course, your start-up may never start up, in which case all you may have to show for it is a few pages of copy. Better than a sharp stick in the eye, as they say here in the South, but not ideal.

And remember: you're doing them a favor, but by giving you—an unproven entity—a chance, they're doing you a favor too. Keep your humility front and center. Treat them like a real prospect and you'll get some practice at prospecting, an absolutely essential, if not always joyous part of the job.

'Create' a Portfolio Another option to consider if you're teaming with a designer is to create a portfolio. Make 'em up. Why do you even need an actual assigned project from a company? If you've ever driven down the road, seen a really lame billboard that you just knew you could improve on, you're halfway there. If you do head in that direction, what's keeping you from approaching that company and selling them on your ideas?

The obvious drawback of the "make-up-a-portfolio" scenario is that you need to create things that look good coming from just a color printer or color copier (which a graphic designer, even a wannabe, will either have or have cheap access to), because you won't be professionally producing these pieces.

But you can do some pretty impressive mock-ups of a whole array of project types even with these constraints. Besides, it absolutely doesn't have to be perfect. If you can show a prospective client 4–5 pieces for even imaginary companies (which, incidentally, shows some added creativity), you've given them a good feel for what you might be able to do for them.

Local Publications Another great—and fun!—way to beef up a portfolio in your spare time is to get a few local publishing credits under your belt. There are undoubtedly any number of daily, weekly, and monthly publications in your area that are always on the lookout for material (especially the weeklies and monthlies, which often rely heavily on freelanced content). Got a subject you're interested in that you feel others would find stimulating? And is it a fit for a particular publication? Approach the editor and make your pitch. While not always the case, I think you'll be surprised at how accessible these folks generally are. Think about it—you're calling to make their lives easier! Granted, this isn't the type of work that pays a lot—usually enough for a few bags of groceries—but it can move you along the path toward much more lucrative freelancing!

So, where to next? Well, now that we've gotten a few personal things handled, and have a reasonable facsimile of a portfolio to show, who are we going to show it to? What sort of companies hire folks like you and me? Let's find out....

Chapter Five

Where's the Business?

WHO WILL HIRE YOU?   This part of the equation is pretty simple. You'll either be, A) doing a writing project for the people who will ultimately be using it or, B) for the people who are producing the project for the people who will ultimately be using it. It's A or B. Period. That means you'll be dealing with two types of clients, the end user (EU) or a middleman (MM) who's dealing with the end user. EUs means any company from small to Fortune 100, while MMs include, but aren't limited to: ad agencies, graphic design firms, marketing companies, PR firms, event production companies, writers agents/brokers, etc.

I like to think of MMs as "bird dogs" of sorts. Because they're hunting work for themselves and need to hire people like you to do it, in essence, they'll "find" work for you while you're off doing other stuff.

End Users: Pros and Cons The main disadvantage of dealing with the end users (EUs) is that there's often more educating necessary with them than with the MMs—though usually less so with big corporations than with smaller firms. Large corporations have obviously done a lot of this work already, so they usually know the score, unless the person running the project is new, inexperienced, or newly reassigned from a completely different area.

You'll run into the educating scenario more with smaller firms that are doing their first formal and professional brochure, ad, or marketing campaign.

The big advantage of dealing with EUs is just that—they're end users. That saves lots of time and frustration inherent in working with MMs, as I'll explain shortly.

If EUs are used to dealing with MMs, that'll work to your advantage when you're dealing directly with an EU. Why? Because they're used to paying inflated rates for copywriting—a normal rate plus the MM's premium, commonly added on as a vendor (that's the writer) management fee. So, your rates won't scare them.

Middlemen: Pros and Cons Typically, MMs need little educating. They know what they need, what it should cost, what's fair, that you need concepting time (those critical hours of thinking and contemplating that precede your actual creative explosions), and they won't ask for 27 rewrites at no extra charge.

The first downside to a MM is that by definition, your copy is going through one more layer of review and approval than if you were dealing with the EU directly, resulting in longer copy cycles and possibly more frustration.

You'll also have less control over the final product, and in fact, many MMs will restrict your contact to the EU, wanting you to deal with them exclusively (afraid you'll steal their clients). This often makes it difficult to get your questions answered and to make an eloquent case for your copy.

Too Many Cooks... An extra layer means more people, which means more potential for egos and an increased possibility that your brilliant copy will be butchered. And often not for any particularly good reason other than to allow team members to justify their existence. Gotta change something so they can demonstrate to the powers-that-be that they can "take ownership" of a project. As one of my professional colleagues so elegantly described this process: "Everyone's got to pee on it."

Now, by no means does this always, or even usually, happen. I've received excellent editing suggestions from clients. Just realize it's a possibility and if it arises, it won't come as a complete shock to you.

Don't Look Back... After a certain point in the process, when the copy has gotten to tweaking stage, the MM may just say, "Go ahead and bill me. We've only got minor edits left and we can handle it from here." Great. Now you can move on to the next project.

Just don't think too much about what they could still do to your copy—especially with ad agencies—or you'll get very sad. But remember. This is one of the few downsides to this business.

Another minus is that occasionally, MMs will want to beat you down on price. Because you didn't have to hunt for the specific job they're bringing you in on (even though you hunted for them), they'll occasionally want you to give them a break on price—maybe $10/hour off your normal rate.

If you cave quickly, you'll set a bad precedent and they'll always know you're easy. Stick to your guns and you'll probably get your rate. It shows that you have confidence in your abilities, which people like to see. If they make a "take-it-or-leave-it" offer, you need to decide. But it may never get to that point.

If your stellar reputation precedes you, I wouldn't give up a dime. If you're starting out, be open, but again, try to gauge whether they're playing hardball or just trying to get a few bucks out of you simply because they think they can.

END-USERS (EU)

Corporations Far and away, the biggest source of potential business in the EU arena is corporate America. There are opportunities in academia, such as communications departments of major universities or in government offices, but suffice it to say, you'll have your hands full with the corporate folks. The larger the company, the more different types of work are available.

Think about a company like Coca-Cola. They've got a zillion different departments, each with their own needs. Those include: ad copy, marketing brochures, POS (point-of-sale) display signage, promotional materials, training videos and manuals, product sheets, sales aids, CD training programs, proposals, internal publications, and the list goes on and on. As discussed earlier, while some corporations may have in-house staffs to handle writing needs, these days, thanks to the prolific downsizing bloodbaths (case in point: Coca-Cola) going on out there, many more outsource their work to freelancers.

Big companies like Coca-Cola, UPS, and BellSouth, for instance, hire a huge number of freelancers to handle their workload and they're not the exception.

First Stop – Corporate Communications Who do you contact in a large corporation? Typically, your first stop might be the corporate communications department. The CC department is entrusted with turning out a wide array of different literature, brochures, product information, videos, ad campaigns, promotional material, internal newsletters, and so on.

This can be a great clearinghouse for lots of work as well as connections to many other departments that you might deal with directly. In the absence of a CC department, per se, your best bet is to contact the marketing department, sales department, and when all else fails, human resources.

I say "when all else fails" because HR is so often the "conventional" route, meaning it's the best way to make absolutely sure that your name and promotional literature get held up for the longest amount of time.

It always makes more sense to ferret out the actual folks who have ultimate, specific, well-known needs—*and* the ability to hire you—as opposed to the department serving those people. That's an extra and usually unnecessary step.

In some cases, however, you've got little choice, since everything having to do with hiring outside help is automatically routed to HR. In these cases, polish up your skills in schmoozing and persistence.

MIDDLEMEN (MM)

Graphic Design Firms I've gotten a rather large chunk of my business over the years from graphic design firms, but don't think of them as these artsy creative companies. If they're successful, count on them to be consummate marketers as well, able to use their creative gifts to create high-impact pieces that effectively reach the target audience and get the job done. That "job" might be to boost sales with a marketing brochure or increase employee satisfaction and morale in the case of an internal communications program.

Not surprisingly, graphic designers are a very visual bunch. If you meet with them to show them your book, no matter how good your copy is, if it's ensconced in, shall we say, aesthetically-challenged layouts, you'll be fighting an uphill battle to get noticed.

I remember visiting a graphic designer when I was just starting out, with a growing but still graphically-undernourished portfolio. While the copy was good, he, predictably, was gazing at the design. Finally, he oh-so-diplomatically commented, "Your designers haven't been very kind to you." Meanwhile, I'm screaming (to myself), "Read the freakin' copy!" C'est la vie.

Good Reasons to Outsource Typically, few graphic design firms (unless they're huge, which is rare) have in-house copywriting talent, choosing to outsource instead. They do this not only to stay "lean 'n mean" but for a very sensible reason as well. Given that these companies work with a broad spectrum of industries with wide-ranging needs, it makes sense for them to cultivate a stable of writers, each with their own strengths and style, so they can form-fit the writer to the specific job.

While there are writers who can do professional, lofty, elegant, chatty, and humorous copy equally well, most have a specialty. And even if you can do it all well, your clients are more likely to cubby-hole you based on what you've done for them. So if you want to do different kinds of work, it's your job to educate them as to your creative range.

Don't Ignore the "Lone Rangers" In addition to making contact with the large and small graphic design firms, make a point to meet a bunch of the "lone rangers" out there, the one-man/woman freelancer shops that are doing what you're doing, except in graphic design. Establish a good rapport and friendship with four or five of these people, and you'll be their copywriter of choice when projects arise.

Think about it. Because they're just one-person shops, the relationships you develop with them are likely to be much more stable (and hence profitable) than ones you develop with a larger firm, where things can and do always change, ie., people leave, new people come in with their favorite copywriters, etc.

At the midway point of last year, I was looking at my invoicing journal for the year-to-date. I was having a very good year, and for a brief period, my #1 account was a freelance graphic designer—a one-woman shop—and when she wasn't #1, she was at least in the top three or four. So, don't let size fool you.

You cultivate a small but loyal group of freelancers and they can do a lot more than just help fill the slow times nicely, not to mention providing opportunities to team up on projects, as we'll discuss later.

And Staff Designers, Too... One more suggestion. Definitely get to know the most talented staff designers within a graphic design firm, marketing company or any other MM client. I can't overstate this. If someone's really good, it's only a matter of time until he or she goes solo. And when they do, they're going to need writing resources. On several occasions, I have been brought in on hugely lucrative, exciting, and creatively fulfilling long-term client relationships by former staff designers, putting many tens of thousands of dollars in my pocket over time.

Advertising Agencies These firms vary widely in size, scope, and specialty. The largest ones will concentrate on the most lucrative high-profile national campaigns, print ads, and TV spots.

Most of my colleagues agree that barring some disaster that takes out Biggie Ad Company's crack copywriting staff overnight, the average freelancer is unlikely to land the juicier, high-end, Fortune 100 concepting and headlining work—IBM, Delta, Ford, Kellogg's, American Express, etc, etc. They'll be keeping that work for themselves.

Your best bet with the big boys is what's known as "collateral"—brochures, internal campaigns, and other peripheral supporting projects that are, by definition, less prestigious and less lucrative to them. In the larger agencies, you've got bigger supporting casts—the account executive (the salesperson on the account), the creative director, art director, and production people. By contrast, in smaller agencies, fewer people handle more jobs.

According to some of my colleagues, whose accounts of working with ad agencies fairly drip with cynicism, an agency's real goal is to enter work in ad industry shows. And it's true that in the incestuous world of big-time advertising, it's often the cleverest stuff and not the most effective that win awards. We'll talk more about that subject in Chapter Fourteen: "What Will You Be Writing?"

While I have limited experience with larger agencies, I grilled several colleagues who've worked with them, and their experiences are generally more negative than positive. By the larger, more arrogant firms, you are often considered "the help," and simply a little cog in the wheel.

I just don't have this overwhelming need to play in the big boys' sandbox just to say I am, especially if the price is that I'm some bit supporting player, well out of the mainstream excitement. I'd rather be the big fish in the small pond. Heck, maybe it's just sour grapes on my part, since I've done little work for the big boys, so I've decided "it's not worth it anyway." Check it out for yourself.

Bigger Opportunities with Smaller Firms Smaller advertising agencies offer many more opportunities to get into the fun, creative concepting and headlining projects for, in all likelihood, small and local end users. But, it can be just as interesting and far more rewarding work, because with a smaller firm, you've got a much better chance of having your best efforts see the light of day. That translates to more job satisfaction and creative fulfillment.

Marketing Firms As we'll see, marketing firms, like PR firms, offer a variety of services. While typically they specialize in a particular industry (high-tech, healthcare, real estate, retail, etc.), occasionally they'll work with a broad spectrum of industries.

Marketing firms help growing companies market their products and services when those companies have generally hit a certain point in their evolution: they've achieved some success by sheer hard work, but in order to take that success to the next level, they could benefit from some professional expertise—and can afford it.

Smaller "Outsourcers" Perhaps a high-tech firm has made its mark in a local market but is looking to have a national impact. A good marketing firm might come in and design a comprehensive strategy and campaign to take the company to the next level. It might involve ad campaigns, public relations, direct mail, Internet solutions such as Web page creation, and the like.

While much of the work may get done in-house, many of these companies keep their permanent staff pretty lean (often fewer than 10 people), opting to bring in freelancers in a variety of specialties (graphic design, copywriting, photography, public relations, video production, etc.) on a contract basis. As discussed, this strategy allows them to be very nimble and responsive to their clients, finding just the right person for the job.

Companies like these are always on the lookout for good talent in many fields, and like to keep a healthy pool of human resources such as writers, photographers, and designers. One of the best sources for marketing companies is in the Yellow Pages under Marketing Companies or Marketing Firms.

Public Relations Firms While PR firms are ostensibly entrusted with fostering the best possible image of their clients in the eyes of the public, that responsibility takes many forms.

Because of the similarities and inevitable overlap between advertising agencies and PR firms, you'll find many larger ad agencies have PR divisions and vice versa. PR firms can be heavily weighted to newspaper articles, print advertising, collateral, speeches, or any combination.

While MMs like graphic design firms and marketing companies lean toward the smallish end in size, ad agencies and PR firms span the gamut, with a healthy number of huge ones in any large market. As is the case with ad agencies, chances are awfully good that as a FLCW, you won't see too much of the really high-profile work in a PR firm, but don't let that dissuade you from getting your name in front of them anyway.

Don't Idolize the Big Boys A year or so back, I decided to do a little marketing push to the PR firms. I called the top 50 firms in the city (using *The Book of Lists* I'll discuss in Chapter Six), sent info to about half of them and nothing happened. But a few months later, I got a call from one of the big companies (offices in 25–30 cities) who needed me to help rewrite a consumer presentation for a big local utility company. Another writer had cranked out something that just hadn't hit the mark.

I learned several important lessons. First, let things gestate. Just because you call 50 folks and nothing happens right away doesn't mean a thing. Plant the seeds and eventually some will bloom.

The other lesson was to not assume that just because these folks are with a BIG PR FIRM, they know what they're doing. Yes, they knew something was off with the project, but they couldn't figure out what it was, even though it was glaringly obvious to me. Be careful not to put the big boys on a pedestal while discounting your own talents and ability to effectively address a company's—even a big one's—challenges.

It never ceases to amaze me how much bad writing is floating around out there and a lot of it with big-name companies behind it—clunky, awkward, unfunny, obtuse, confusing, scattered, boring. You name it, it's everywhere. That's good news if you're good.

Event Production Companies (EPCs) EPCs will work with large corporations to produce their annual conferences, trade shows, conventions, meetings, product launches, and anything else that's big, involved and needs to be outstanding.

Many handle absolutely everything from soup to nuts: design and construction of all tradeshow exhibits, all printed literature before, during, and after the show, conference signage, speaker support, meeting rooms, catering, entertainment, the gargantuan job of shipping every single piece necessary to pull off the above to a location often across the country, and much, much more.

Work Across the Spectrum As you might guess from the above list, EPCs hire a lot of writers for a bunch of different types of work. Contact the producers, creative directors or account executives (if it's a good size firm, there will be multiples of all three) for inroads into proposals (the EPC's first step to getting awarded these huge contracts), creative treatments (mini-proposals outlining the EPC's ideas about how to execute certain parts of the program), conference literature, speaker support (writing, editing, or tweaking the comments of the various participants), event scripting (see a more detailed explanation in Chapter Fourteen), and lots more.

Show Up Regularly In contrast to most other entities, the key to getting work with EPCs is to show up in their hallways on a regular basis. Typically, they operate in more or less constant crisis mode, and rarely have much time to think about where to find a writer. Sure, they have a lot of names on their rolodex, but if you happen to be walking by their door when they need a writer (or just were in the past few days) and they're reasonably comfortable with you, you'll get the job. I'm totally serious.

I found this out the hard way when I went to a semi-annual networking function run by one of these firms. I'd done several projects for different groups within the company in the fall of 1995, and then I didn't hear from them again till January of 1997, at which point I got several more.

It should have occurred to me that in both cases, I got additional work after the initial jobs because I was around and visible. Both times, people stopped me in the hall and asked, "What's your availability in about a week or so?" And I was booked once again. Once out of sight, I was out of mind. One creative director even went as far as to say—only half-joking—"Heck, if you sit out in our lobby for an hour, you'll get work."

Agents/Brokers Another avenue is writers' agents or brokers, who contact large corporations that have large writing projects, usually in the technical arena.

A software or telecommunications firm needs to create a huge documentation manual, for instance. A project like that might keep one writer busy for six months and be a 30–60K+ job. My main broker keeps a sizable number of writers in her stable and matches the writer with the job, taking anywhere from 10–30% of the total project fee as her commission.

While many brokers deal with technical or large-scale internal policy manual-type work, you could just as easily find one that had marketing/creative work as their focus.

And though many have a technical slant, as mine does, that can actually work to your advantage if you're looking for creative work. Because she has plenty of technical writers to draw from, and very few marketing/creative writers, when the inevitable non-technical jobs come up, I'm the first one she thinks of.

This is the ultimate "bird-dog" situation and it definitely pays to ferret out companies like this. By no means should you count on them for a big chunk of your work but it's always nice when you get a job you did nothing to generate. In my first year of business, I actually got about 30% of my work from her. It's gone down since then, but the phone still rings from time to time.

I give up a percentage of my fee (10-15% typically), but since my agent typically prices me out higher than my normal rate to a potential client, I generally end up netting out close to my usual fee. Look in the Yellow Pages under "Writers" or ask around the network—other writers, your clients, etc.

HOW ARE YOU BEING REPRESENTED? When dealing with any of the above MMs (with the exception of agents/brokers) always ask how they're representing you. Some companies, in the interest of fostering an image of being a bigger firm with more in-house resources than is actually the case, will want to present you as an in-house writer with their firm (Scenario #1).

While I prefer to be introduced as freelance talent brought in for the project (Scenario #2, and the truth), and avoid any potentially embarrassing moments, I don't mind the first scenario.

Given the reality of the whole industry, however, Scenario #2 is much more likely these days as many firms turn what could be considered a negative into a positive: "We found the most appropriate writer for this particular project." It's true, and to most clients, that is a plus, when the alternative is an in-house writer who may or may not be well-versed in their business. But, in any case, you must get that little detail squared away at the outset, so your stories will jibe.

In Scenario #1 (you're the in-house writer—nudge, nudge, wink, wink), you'll obviously be billing the MM. In Scenario #2, as an outside freelancer, it could go either way. Just ask the MM how he'd prefer to do it. Most MMs will "mark up" your services, charging the client say, $100 an hour for copywriting, when you're charging the MM just $75, for instance. Clearly, you'll be billing the MM in this case, and not uttering Word One about any money issues to anyone but the MM.

Other MMs (usually small firms or "lone rangers") don't want to mess with it, so they'll let you go ahead and bill the client directly, which is usually preferable. See the *"Don't Go Direct"* section in Chapter Thirteen ("Dos, Don'ts & Don't Forgets") for further elaboration.

GETTING TO THEM   Go to the people. Or more specifically, go to the Yellow Pages or the *BusinessWise* directory or its equivalent in your area (see Chapter Six for more discussion of *BusinessWise*) to find the people. When searching any of those sources, look up these categories directly: advertising agencies, public relations firms, graphic designers, marketing companies, etc.

When you get some of these people on the phone, ask them for names of other companies in their category or different ones.

Use What You Have   If you have expertise specific to a particular industry, your best bet is to go after that industry directly. Contact the marketing or corporate communications department. Remember downsizing and outsourcing. Chances are good that the big companies in your former industry are running leaner than ever.

But, the show must go on and the work must get done. In some cases, former in-house copywriters go the freelance route, hunting for and often picking up work from their former employers.

More frequently, however, these displaced souls wander about aimlessly for a short time, before securing full-time work at another company, leaving a void in their last home. I promise you, the people now entrusted with getting the work done are happy to hear from anyone who can make their lives easier, especially if you "speak their language."

Change—The One Constant Besides death and taxes, the one thing you can always count on is change. The same goes for our business. While I'd love to tell you that the clients you get in your first year of business will be loyal and lucrative for years to come, I'd be telling stories. I'm actually doing business with very few, if any, of my first customers.

Everything Changes Clients move on to other jobs, their replacements have their favorite copywriters and you're out. Companies go out of business, your clients join other firms that have their own copywriters and you're out. Companies merge, and one of the firms has their own in-house copywriters and you're out.

And of course, the unthinkable happens too. Another copywriter contacts your clients, does better work, in the client's opinion, and you're out. Notice I said, "in the client's opinion." Frankly, that's all that really matters. Whether or not you think you're actually a better copywriter than the other person means little to anyone except you.

Sure, clients can make mistakes and I've gotten several calls over the years to "rescue" a project. That's always a great feeling, especially when you come through for them. Bottom line, if you're a serious player in your market, then just as often, you'll be that "other" copywriter to whom a competitor loses out.

Always Be Selling The bad news: marketing yourself is a continuous process. The good news: if you can do it regularly, you'll be ahead of about 95% of your competitors.

Most creative types—including copywriters—just aren't very good business people. In their idea of a perfect world, corporations would sincerely appreciate the nobility of their craft and line up to pay handsomely for their efforts. Of course, most writers (myself included) take it a step further and fantasize that we should be able to sit around and write poetry and be paid similarly well.

OK, so how do we make the contacts and get in front of these folks? It's called prospecting and I've come to realize that the hardest part of the prospecting process is just getting started. Boy, it's tough to pick up that phone for the first time and start telling your story, but once you get going and get into a groove, it gets easy and believe it or not, you'll actually end up having a lot of fun. So, let's go prospecting. We'll have fun. Trust me.

Chapter Six

Let's Get Started!

GOTTA GET NOTICED!   This business—and most of life, if you want to get philosophical about it—is all about getting noticed. Letting the world know you're out there. Figuratively (and sometimes literally) waving your arms wildly above your head and screaming, "Hey! Over here!"

The more effectively and regularly you can inform the world about who you are, what you do and why they should hire you, the more work you'll have and the more money you'll make. Period. I can show you how to do that very simply and cheaply.

Have I always been consistent in my own marketing efforts? Absolutely not. When things are going well, I've acted like most human beings: fat, happy, and complacent, and then when the phones got quiet later, I kicked myself.

NO TIME TO HUNT   Here's a fact about your future clients. While I mentioned that folks at event production companies are the ultimate version of this, to a certain extent, it's true for most prospects: they're overworked and when they need a copywriter, they don't want to spend a lot of time hunting for one.

If you show up in front of them in a direct mail piece, on their phone line, in their e-mail box, or in their face at just the moment when they're in the market for a writer, you've got an excellent chance of getting the nod. Even if you've never been hired by them, if your timing is good, you could get the job. It's happened to me several times. Moral: Keep showing up.

The Grapevine Delivers Once you get in the door, and do several pieces for a client, you'll learn a lot about them and their business, which makes you very valuable. There's minimal learning curve on new projects, and that makes your client's life easier, which is always their goal and should be yours as well.

This scenario is especially true in large corporations, where once you've done a good job, people talk. If the first guy likes you, you *will* get phone calls from their colleagues when they have projects. Just like a good mechanic, hair stylist, or financial planner, the word spreads. Of course, it works the other way too, and probably even quicker when you're lousy, so to save a lot of hassle and make a lot of money, just write well!

Now, we're going to assume that you followed my suggestions in previous chapters on creating a portfolio and you now have something to show, no matter how humble. It's time to go prospecting.

PROSPECTING MADE EASY...SORT OF In one sense, prospecting is a simple task. First, you get a frontal lobotomy (that *would* help...). Seriously, you get a list of names, you pick up the phone and you start calling. What's so difficult about that? Just a teensy issue called ego.

Dial up a few cretins on a power play who get their jollies telling hard-working folks like you that you're not smart enough, sophisticated enough, or savvy enough to play in their sandbox, and you're ready to pout your way through a couple of hot fudge sundaes and a matinee double-feature.

However, with a little planning and attention to detail, you can take this often challenging task, and have a lot of productive fun with it—no drugs required. The key is controlling those things you can, and managing the rest. Remember, if this was easy, everyone would be doing it and getting paid six bucks an hour, not $60-80. Let's take it step-by-step:

Dumb Down The first step to successful prospecting is to check your brain at the door—the analytical side anyway. Keep the rest; it might come in handy later. The analytical side is the one that alternately stares at the list and then out the window, asking a bunch of pointless questions, all beginning with, "Should I...", "Would they..." and "I wonder if..." Lose it.

A Reality Check Here's the real world of prospecting. Understand it and you'll stay emotionally level. Forget it and you'll freak. The Bad News: Most (as in 75+%) of the people you talk to won't be interested in your service (though you'll be pleasantly surprised at how many are).

Overwhelmingly, they'll be nice about it. A few won't. If you come across a few nasty ones, just realize that for them to get ugly with a polite, hard-working person that they don't even know means that their life must be pretty unpleasant. Feel sorry for them. Most importantly, don't take it personally.

The Good News The Law of Averages is etched in stone. I sold books door-to-door for two summers in college, and I'll never forget my sales manager's words: Tie an order book to a dog's tail, set him loose in the city and eventually someone will buy from him. Keep calling and you'll find the business.

Your List Know who your prospects are. The phone book, as discussed, is your first stop. If you're starting with MMs, just look up the specific categories such as graphic designers, advertising agencies, marketing companies, public relations firms, etc.

If you're starting with a specific field in which you have some expertise, go after the corporations directly, starting with corporate communications and branching out to marketing and sales.

Make photocopies of the pages from the phone book so you can mark them up. Given that phone book type is pretty small, you might even split a page into sections and enlarge them on the copier to give yourself more room to work.

Perhaps you've got a local publication dedicated to the creative industries—advertising, graphic design, photography, copywriting, video and multimedia production, etc. In Atlanta, ours is called *Oz*, and annually, they publish their *Creative Index,* a listing of all the companies in all the above categories and more. You get most of the same categories as the phone book but with more detail on names, specialties, etc. If you have no equivalent in your town, the phone book is the way to go.

If you need more help compiling a sufficiently detailed list, check with your friendly librarian. In Atlanta, we have a company called *BusinessWise* that puts out a directory that is perfect for generating a local prospect list. *BusinessWise* lists companies about eight different ways and includes industry classification, officers' names, number of employees, whether it's a solitary branch, regional, or headquarters office, address and phone, how long in business, etc.

According to the *BusinessWise* folks, check with your local Chamber of Commerce for a company that fits the above description. Most cities will have the equivalent. Your library should carry it.

"The Book of Lists" Be sure your list is long enough. You don't want any excuses to stop calling (except maybe that it's Saturday or something). Another great source is the annual directory put out by your city's local weekly business publication. In Atlanta, ours is the *Atlanta Business Chronicle,* which is part of a large 40+ strong nationwide family of business publications, most of which end in *Business Journal* (as in the *Los Angeles Business Journal,* the *Philadelphia Business Journal,* etc.) For the complete listing of these publications along with contact information, point your browser to *www.amcity.com.*

Each year, our *Chronicle* comes out with its annual *Book of Lists,* a highly impressive 200+ page compilation of just about every industry category and the top 10, 25, 50, or 100 players in that business locally—attorneys, ad agencies, PR firms, marketing companies, architectural firms, real estate companies, insurance companies, and I haven't even scratched the surface.

I'd wager that all the *Journals* produce their own respective *Book of Lists* as well. Check it out. It's about $30 for non-subscribers (still a great deal) and free if you subscribe yearly (around $50), which, by the way, is a pretty good idea. It'll keep you on top of your market—new companies, who's changed jobs, who's been promoted, which firms have closed their creative departments, etc.—all that juicy info that can spell new business.

Keep these same resources in mind when you're going to do direct mail campaigns to new prospects, a topic I discuss in more depth in Chapter Eight. Both *BusinessWise* and the *Book of Lists* (or their equivalents) are great places to put together lists as long as you need them to be.

Your Script In my opinion, this is a critical secret to staying focused during prospecting, while removing one potential source of anxiety from the process: Know exactly what you're going to say when your prospect answers the phone. Write it out word-for-word on a 3x5 card and keep it in front of you. Always say it, and never say anything but.

Keep it brief (15 seconds or less), simple and to the point. It's a very powerful psychological anchor. If you hang up from a rude prospect, or lunch is calling, it's invaluable to be able to physically zero in on something, get back on track and keep from getting bummed out or distracted.

My basic version goes like this: "Good morning, my name is Peter Bowerman, and I'm a freelance copywriter, making contact with local banks (for instance), to determine whether you have any on-going or occasional needs for a good freelance copywriter to help create marketing collateral material: brochures, newsletters, ads, etc. Who might be the best person to talk with?"

Ideally, you'll have a name, but if not, this'll do and it's always enough to get some reaction, which then drives the rest of the call. Hopefully, you know what to say if they respond, "Great! Your timing couldn't be better." It happens.

How To Talk Slowly, clearly, and evenly. When you get someone on the phone, don't just chat away like you normally would. Adjust to accommodate people who don't know you, aren't expecting your call, probably don't want to talk to you and were very likely busy doing something else when you called (I'm just full of good news). You're asking them to switch gears and turn on a dime. Make it easy for them to catch up.

Get Your Mind Right Before you begin, get yourself into the right frame of mind. Imagine that your goal is simply to talk to people, ask a few questions, and have some nice conversations. You want to come across to prospects as relaxed, easy-going, and confident and it's easier to do that when you feel there's less at stake. You both know why you're there: to drum up business. But you don't want to come across as desperate or trying too hard. Bottom line, people like to talk to people who make them feel comfortable, and will be more receptive to anyone (and their message) like that.

What Not to Say Refrain from cuteness like an ultra-cheerful, "How are you today!?" unless they ask you first. Coming from you, it fairly screams "Salesman Butter-Up Line!!" If they ask, it can be like a cool drink of water, especially if you've just crawled through the desert for the past 25 calls, getting only voice mail, rude receptionists, and arrogant *artistes*.

Simply reply politely, "Very well, thank you. And yourself?" Resist the urge to jump all over them with dirty paws like a golden retriever greeting its master after a two-week absence.

While not always the case, too often the people who are the nicest to you on the phone are the ones in no position to help you. When you're starved for civility and friendliness (an occupational hazard of cold-calling) it's very human to want to hang out with these people, but you'll just be wasting your time, unless they're your liaison to the top. Try to get to the Indian chiefs.

Keep a Log Keep track of your calling. I created a form (turned sideways: 11″ x 8½″), with columns for company name, contact person, address, phone, fax, e-mail, along with date and results of first, second, and third contacts, info sent out, etc.—with space for about 10 entries per page. Print out multiple copies, put 'em in a three-ring binder and go to work with a pen or pencil. At a glance, you'll always be able to see where you're at. If you're handy with *Microsoft Excel* or a good contact management program, you could do it that way too.

The Law of Averages Delivers When I started my writing business, I made close to 700 calls in one four-week period. I don't care what you're selling—you make that many calls, and something's going to happen. It's called critical mass. With that much momentum, progress is inevitable. I'm sure the thought of making that many calls is not a comforting one. But it works. Guaranteed.

How do you eat an elephant? One bite at a time. Make 50 calls a day, over the course of one month, and you've hit 1000. I can't think of a single better way of kickstarting this business, especially if you have few contacts and aren't planning on leveraging an existing knowledge base. And even if you are, count on the phone being your most valuable tool right from the beginning.

During the process, it's critical to alter your definition of accomplishment. For instance, if I make 50 calls before noon and find virtually no one interested in hearing my fine story, it would be easy to conclude that it was a wasted morning. Au contraire.

Actually, that's great work, because it means the real thing is right around the corner. Believe it. Out of 50, you might have only spoken to 10, and gotten voice mail and over-protective secretaries on the rest. Nature of the beast. Keep calling.

Dealing with Secretaries Speaking of that… Depending on your prospective clients, there's a good chance that some of them have a formidable layer of barbed wire around them. That's par for the course. While corporate communications folks are typically more accessible, creative directors for ad agencies, graphic design firms, and marketing companies or the president/owner of smaller firms are often hard to pin down.

They're extremely busy, stressed, overworked, and fight a never-ending battle to get their work done and stay focused. They don't have time to waste, and for that reason, only phone calls immediately germane to their lives will typically get through. I'm painting a particularly grim picture, and it absolutely isn't always the case, but it's important to be mentally prepared for a not-uncommon scenario.

Many will screen their calls through secretaries or other assistants. In response to your request to speak to Mr. Big Creative Cheese and Hirer of Unworthy Copywriters and Other Lower Forms of Life, when these administrative types coldly and pointedly inquire, "And what's this regarding?" you *will* want to reach through the phone and strangle them. How dare they question you, when you're here to make their life a breeze?

If you are actually able to deal with that response graciously and from an enlightened space, good for you. Now, see how well you do when—after you tell them who you are—they reply, "I don't think we'd be interested in that." Gnash, gnash.

Just remember, no matter how busy these people are, if they hire freelancers, they *will* need you *and* come looking for you at some point. So the more times and the more ways you've shown up in front of them, even if you've never spoken to them, the more likely it is they'll think of you.

Voice Mail Is Your Friend While human contact is certainly richer and more interesting, voice mail can be very expeditious. Write out a slightly expanded version of your basic greeting script for voice mail. It's over in 30 seconds, you've thrown a line out, and you can forget it for awhile. Keep track of the messages you've left, and if you hear nothing back, call once more. If you hear nothing again, let it go and move on.

But don't be surprised if those occasionally pan out. Just last week, I got a call from a prospect who'd received a cold call from me 3½ months ago. In our recent meeting, she showed me the note, where the secretary had jotted down, "Freelance writer." Though she had no needs then, she kept the note and called me when things changed.

Had I just left my name, minus my mission, it would have been in the landfill long ago. Instead, we're discussing upcoming projects. And that's the point. While you'll be planting seeds forever (if you're doing it right), in the beginning, it seems as though that's all you're doing. It may not look like progress, but progress takes many forms.

Maximizing Your Success While you can convince yourself that any particular period of the day or week is a good time or lousy time to prospect, here's a few tips to get the most from your efforts. Early morning (7:30–8:30) and late afternoon (5:00–6:00) are often the best times to reach the decision-makers.

They got to that position by starting early and staying late. They'll be calmer and more receptive then. Mondays and Fridays are not typically the best phone days. Mondays are busy "get-on-track" days and Fridays are… Fridays. Catch people when they're focused.

Tell the Truth Some books on "guerrilla prospecting" suggest all sorts of cute ploys to get through to the decision-makers. Like telling the receptionist you're returning your prospect's call, that you have some information they requested, or some other tall tale. Not my style. If they see what you're doing, you'll irritate them and that's a lousy first impression. Just be honest.

Get Out and Meet Your Market When you get some folks interested in seeing your work, *always* try to get a face-to-face appointment. Letting clients meet you in the flesh is absolutely critical to the growth of your business.

Early on in my career, a fellow writer shared a statistic: you'll get hired by one of ten prospects to whom you send information and one of three who meet you. Guess what I started doing really soon after that? I made a point to put a face with at least one or two voices each week and my business took off. It's also a lot more fun than cold-calling.

If someone agrees to meet you, you can safely assume that he's in the market for your services at some point. No guarantees, but it's a good sign. If he's not at all interested and just jerking you around with a request for a package, I promise he'll scare up some excuse not to meet, unless he's bored, lonely, and starved for human contact.

Of course, if he's not immediately receptive to your request for a meeting, it certainly doesn't mean he's not a prospect. Again, just listen to how he answers and his level of sincerity. If you're paying attention, people aren't that hard to decipher.

The "Info" Trap If you end up sending out info as opposed to getting in the door, do it wisely. Don't get caught in the trap of sending out info to anyone who sounds even remotely interested, because many will be just that—*remotely* interested.

There were days when I sent out a pile of packages, and in reviewing them, realized how few stood out as genuinely interested. One thing to always remember: People will always take your information, and often just to get you off the phone. In those cases, you'd do as well to shred it as to mail it.

I never ask prospects if I can send them information. I wait for them to ask me if I have any. Even then, I listen to how it's asked and what sort of dialogue preceded the request. Separate the buyers from the tire-kickers.

It's also a good idea to tier your mailings. For the hot-sounding ones ("Yes, we regularly use freelancers"), send out your good stuff. For the shaky ones ("Well, we occasionally use freelancers"), send your basic cover letter/résumé/business card mailing. Shortly, we'll be getting into exactly what the package of info you send out entails.

By sending *something* out, you ward off Murphy's Law: the one person you don't send to would've become your biggest client. Not very likely, but you'll feel better. When you follow up the next week, you get to revisit their interest level and proceed accordingly.

Follow-up on a package about a week after mailing it. Strongly suggest that "Copies of clips just aren't like the real thing, so let's get together for a meeting…." and then keep following up until you can make that happen.

Are You Too Nice? If you're very good on the phone, you can sometimes develop such a good rapport with someone that he hates to say, "Gee, we just don't have any writing needs", which believe me, is vastly preferable to "Well, we haven't used freelancers in the past, but that could change" coming from someone who's never hired a writer but hates to tell you that. Stay friendly but businesslike enough that people feel comfortable telling you the truth.

Better Bets Now, folks who say, "Well, we have a few writers we use right now whom we're pretty happy with" are obviously much better prospects, and as good as the "we-regularly-use-freelancers" set. After all, they definitely use writers, are specific about it and…nothing is forever. Stay on top of them with regular calls (assuming that's OK with them) mailings, and occasional samples of the work you know they do. Position yourself to be able to quickly step in should things change, which, in time, they usually will.

Make a point to get in and meet them as soon as you can, making it sound as casual and innocent as a walk in the park. "Listen, I understand that you're being taken care of pretty well right now by some other folks, and that's great, but I'm going to be out and about next week, and wondered if I might stop in for five minutes and drop off a few things for your file." No big deal. I've picked up several new clients because I was "waiting in the wings" when their regular writer moved on, moved away, or irritated them one too many times.

Don't Send It Unsolicited That brings up a good point. If you're just *really* not looking forward to the phone calling part of the prospecting process, you may be tempted to skip that step altogether, assemble a list of creative directors, communications managers, and marketing folks around town and just send out unsolicited packages of info with résumés, samples, etc. You might even convince yourself that if you do enough of this, it'll be just as effective as contacting them first. And you'd be wrong.

If people aren't expecting your correspondence, chances are excellent it'll go into the trash unopened. You really need to establish that connection with prospects so that they know what your package is when it shows up on their desk. Even then, there are precious few guarantees that it will turn into real paying work, but at least you've established a rapport and a potential need on their part before going through the time and expense of sending them something.

One of my clients, a local communications director for a technology company indirectly echoes these sentiments and goes a little further when she says, "For those writers sending out unsolicited samples, make sure the envelope and pieces are eye-catching and designed well. White envelopes with typed or laser printed labels go straight to the circular file. Find a designer or graphics student and barter services."

So, if you're going to send out unsolicited literature, you have to make it attractive enough to catch the eye of someone who isn't expecting it. Swapping services with a designer or graphics student is a good way of going about it. If however, you don't plan on spending the hours and the bucks to generate graphically impressive mailings, you need to qualify your prospects in advance and have them anticipating the imminent arrival of your gems.

DIRECT MAIL—STAY TUNED...   At some point, you'll probably want to venture into the arena of direct mail, which is really not as daunting as you might imagine. Just get a good list, usually one you're compiling yourself over time, a good letter (or postcard) and you're in business. In Chapter Eight, I'll show you step-by-step, how to easily put together an effective mailing to 250 of your best prospects for about $60, including postage! Don't miss it.

CREATING A COMPANY BROCHURE   OK, so you've made all these calls and lo and behold, you've found a few folks who want to see some literature—a brochure, samples, a résumé, business card, etc. In the next chapter, I'll get into the specifics of making a request for information an easily handled task (hint: it's all about simple, repeatable systems). Until then... let's talk about a brochure.

Now, don't get me wrong. In the beginning, a brochure might not be as crucial to your success as résumés, samples, etc. By the same token, a brochure isn't very difficult to put together and can make a powerful subconscious impression on a client.

"Could You Send Me Something?" When someone asks for literature, you respond, "Sure, I'll get it right out," but what do you send? An introductory letter, briefly describing what you do, to which you attach your business card? For some businesses, it may suffice. For writers, however, it's a bit on the lean side. A brochure can do the trick.

Get Clear The Brochure. Scary thought? It doesn't have to be. A little secret about your first brochure. While ostensibly its purpose is to let prospects know who you are and what you do, you'll benefit as much or more than your clients will. The reason? Doing a brochure forces you to get really clear about your purpose, what services you offer (are you a generalist or a specialist?), and just as importantly, your limitations—what you don't do. Until you do this, you may be operating with a vague direction, and "vague" won't move you forward as you want to move.

The Sad Truth Don't get all wrapped up in trying to create a masterpiece. Why? Here's the unfortunate truth. Most brochures end up in the trash, or quickly filed and out of sight. It's always going to be more important to you than it ever is to someone else.

But remember: the mere fact that the client knows you have a brochure, whether or not it's seriously scrutinized, creates a subconscious impression of your business as more established, stable, and professional.

Concentrate on creating a simple, concise, easy-to-read source of information: an 8½″ x 11″ six-panel tri-fold, that slips neatly into a #10 envelope, along with a cover letter, business card, and possibly one other insert. No need to overwhelm on the first pass. Also, by so limiting the contents to less than one ounce, you keep the mailing cost to 33¢. This is important if you're talking about mass mailing on a budget (and who isn't?).

Look Good for Less If you have a good laser or ink-jet printer—or access to one—and haven't yet discovered "upscale paper" companies like *Paper Direct*, (www.paperdirect.com) or *Paper Access* (www.paperaccess.com), you need to. For about $100, they'll set you up with a whole kit of paper blanks for brochures, letterhead, envelopes, business cards, and more, in a veritable rainbow of style choices: classic, art deco, traditional, cool, funky, etc.

Design your brochure in a three-column, landscape format (In Word, go to *Format*, then *Columns*, click Three, then *OK*. Then click on *File*, *Page Setup*, *Paper Size*, *Landscape*, then *OK)*. Then run your paper through twice and you've got great results for peanuts. Another plus of this route is the ease of revising and customizing. Print them as you need them. Change them when necessary.

The Structure Let's look at physical structure and the flow of the piece. Check out the sample brochure in Appendix A as an example and follow along. Certainly not the last word in marketing brochures, but a perfectly serviceable model.

The front panel should be simple and uncluttered. A company name, and possibly a one-liner. Mine says, "WriteInc." up top, and then centered about ¾ the way down: "Offering the Southeast an array of professional writing services in the sales and marketing arena." Period.

As you open the brochure, you first see the back of the right flap folded in. Here's where flow comes in. This panel performs double duty. It's an intro to and exit from the main three-panel meat of the brochure. So it should hit on some general concepts that can serve as an introduction *and* a summary. My four headings in this section—followed by three lines of descriptive copy for each—are "Solid Writing," "Creativity," "Value," and "My Best Stuff"—a final promise of what I'll deliver.

The three inside panels tell your story. In the first panel, you might get into the specific services you offer, i.e., brochures, ad copy, video scripts, etc., as well as a mini-bio on yourself. Panel Two can highlight the advantages of using you, answering that all-important prospect question, "What's in it for me?"

Finally, panel three is a logical place for the nuts and bolts. How you work. Initial consultation. Terms and conditions of work and payment. Roughly put, these panels cover features, benefits, and logistics. What, why, and how.

The Power of Testimonials One final touch, which can be quite effective, is testimonials. The bottom quarter of each panel on the brochure is a client quote—three in all—with key phrases highlighted, along with their names, titles and organizations. You could actually devote a whole panel to testimonials.

Like the front panel, keep the back panel simple. Your name or company name, possibly an exit tag line (mine is "A powerful partner for your next sales and marketing campaign") plus address, phone number, fax, and e-mail.

SHOULD YOU ADVERTISE? Being the Lone Ranger that I am, I've always chosen to rely on my own prospecting and direct mail efforts to unearth the business. And you absolutely should too, even if you decide to run an ad here and there. Where are the best places? Well, one good place would be your city's aforementioned business publication. I chose the annual *Creative Index* of *Oz*, the local creative industries publication I mentioned earlier.

People just routinely hold onto this issue for the better part of a year, which is an absolutely ideal situation for folks like us—advertising with a long shelf life.

I received three calls from this little $75 business card-size ad within a few weeks. I met with three new prospects, one of whom was a solo graphic designer who called me sight unseen. I accompanied him on a three-hour meeting with his client two days later and in the next 10 months, that client put about $9000 in my pocket. Yeah, it was worth it.

ON YOUR BOOKSHELF Now, a writer needs good tools to do his or her job. Such as:

Dictionary THE happenin' dictionary out there these days is The American Heritage Dictionary—lively, topical, fresh. Yes, I am talking about a dictionary…

Thesaurus Your best friend (buddy, pal, mate, ally, comrade). It comes in especially handy when you're crafting advertising copy for the same product, and you need new and fresh ways to say the same darn thing you've said 50 million times before. This'll make you look good. I highly recommend *The Synonym Finder* by Rodale.

Unlike the two-step process typically necessary with Roget's, Rodale's is arranged alphabetically, all 1361 jam-packed pages.

Of course, if you're running *Microsoft Word,* you could just hit Shift-F7 for Thesaurus and save yourself the $13.99 plus tax, but I wouldn't recommend it. It just doesn't deliver the detail of Rodale's.

Strunk & White's *Elements of Style* The perennial favorite in style guides for a jillion years. Just a thin little volume that won't cost you much or take up too much shelf space, but generally has everything you'll need to know to answer those annoying, recurring questions about punctuation, the right time to use 'that' or 'which', correct footnote format, and so on.

Now, when you're talking about catchy ad/marketing copy, grammatically correct copy can sometimes be relaxed a bit. For the most part, however, when it comes to writing straightforward copy and its accompanying rules for commas, parentheses, quotation marks, etc., you better get it right. Find your answers here.

Dictionary/Thesaurus of Quotations While the most renowned one is *Bartlett's*, I have something called *The International Thesaurus of Quotations* compiled by Rhoda Thomas Tripp. Arranged alphabetically by subject: Ability, Absence, Absurd, Accomplishment, and so on, with a listing of anywhere from five to 200 quotes on each subject.

If you're writing speeches, a reference like this is a natural. And you'd be surprised how often a pithy little quote can spice up a piece of marketing copy, and add a very nice unusual touch to your work. Seriously, it's the sort of little thing that, in a client's mind, separates decent copywriters from exceptional ones.

Those four are your definites. Others that are optional but make for interesting and often very useful reading are:

The Writer's Market Now, after I've gone to great lengths to tell you about the pitfalls of trying to write magazine articles (time-consuming, highly competitive, low paying), let me amend that.

Good freelance commercial writers tend to be curious and opinionated about a lot of subjects, which we end up wanting to write about. We take a vacation and think, "Hmmm, I'll write about my trip, submit it to a magazine, and pay for my vacation." Good idea. Of course, you might only earn enough to pay for your parking at the airport…

So, when that urge strikes, it helps to have *The Writer's Market*—an annually published listing of virtually every single publication across the country that accepts submissions, broken down by category, with all the crucial information: what they look for, length, how many outside submissions they accept yearly, what they pay, (I recently read that the fees they quote in WM are usually half of what they really pay), contact info, dos and don'ts, etc.

Food for the Soul As far as I'm concerned, you do the magazine article/newspaper column thing for the jollies, the validation, and the thrill of seeing your name in print, and not the money. The money is gravy. I'd hate to have to count on it.

The profile of the freelance magazine writer fighting with editors over pittances, and staying one step ahead of the landlady is just a little too crazy-making for me.

When I first started writing columns for publication—which I'm still doing weekly—what a cool thing it was to open up a paper and see my work and my picture. I was just happy to be there. When the check came—usually enough for a trip to the grocery store—it was just the icing on the cake. Kind of a "Oh-I-get-paid-too?-Cool!"

Added Bonuses FYI, as I'll mention later as well, *The Writer's Market* also includes a wonderfully thorough fee schedule for every sort of writing project, including those in the commercial arena. In addition, they're devoting more and more space to landing various writing jobs (including commercial) through the Internet. Check it out.

The Chicago Manual of Style The reigning authority in style guides out there, this hefty bright orange tome makes *Strunk & White* look like an afterthought. Nearly 900 pages long, it covers absolutely everything that the most curious mind in the most mind-expanding drug-induced stupor could possibly ever want to know or imagine he'd want to know about punctuation, copyright law, spelling, names and terms, titles, speech, dialogue, captions, abbreviations, public documents, definitions, and a zillion other things.

Whack on the Side of the Head This fun, provocative, and quirky little volume from the '80s, written by California creativity consultant Roger von Oech, is a wonderful little tool to jump start your creative juices. While arguably it will help anyone out there think outside the box, regardless of one's profession, it's especially valuable to those who are writing the creative stuff—clever ad copy, edgy corporate identity stuff, in-your-face CD-ROM scripting, etc. We all need a different perspective from time to time, a new way to look at old ideas, products and directions, and this can deliver just that.

OK, now that you've got some ducks in a row, let's take a moment and talk about technology. As in, what are the electronic tools you need to do your job? And if you're a techno-phobe, relax—it's pretty painless. Let's go shopping....

Chapter Seven

Technically Speaking...

IF I CAN DO IT...   In case you've managed to dodge the high-tech bullet all these years, let me again repeat my mantra for this book in many arenas, but *especially* technology: **If I can do it, you can do it.** With every fiber of my being, I believe this. I didn't have a computer before I started this business. I learned it all from scratch and without even taking classes. It can be done.

I can hear you: "Well, you just don't understand how bad I am when it comes to technology." No, *you* don't understand. You're talking to a guy whose idea of technical proficiency is changing a light bulb or extracting burnt, stuck toast from the toaster.

And, yes, learning a computer can be a crazy-making experience. Since most of the world is cyber-literate, chances are good you've already wrestled with this learning curve. Regardless, you'll probably relate to the following piece I had published a few years back, especially when you realize how vast my ignorance of technology really was (and largely still is!) when I started out...

LIFE IN "CYBERIA"

WARNING: New computer owner on loose. Armed (with a little knowledge—very little.) and extremely dangerous. Slowly but surely, I've emerged from my technological stone age and have begun to walk erect. But, hey, it's been no picnic. The irony? All those violent *homo sapien* tendencies that we thought had been blunted by decades of mindless TV and the numbing suburban existence suddenly come back with a vengeance.

That little bit of knowledge breeds chronic frustration, which can suddenly and without warning erupt into homicidal seizures. Makes me wistful for my familiar and peaceful Neanderthal life: cave, clubs, word processor. Ah, the good old days.

Learning a new software program gets you in touch with new feelings. What it feels like, for instance, to be the stupidest person on the face of the earth. Computers have this uncanny ability to transform us into blithering schizophrenics. One second we're triumphant, a veritable Mighty Morphin Power Ranger. It's usually a result of figuring out something earth-shattering like how to load paper. (I'm almost there. Any day now. You watch.)

Of course, the next second, we're whimpering, tantrum throwing toddlers. This hunk of metal, glass, and plastic brutally reduces us to our most fundamental insecurities. One good session of being broken in by a new software program (don't kid yourself...it's running the show) and you'll be questioning whether you started potty-training a little too late. Course, the thing that really chaps your buns is that no matter how lost you get, you know it's your fault. There's always a reason why something isn't working. And you're it.

The other day, I almost tried to see if a dot matrix printer could fly. I didn't think it could. I just wanted it gone. Quickly. After spending a solid five minutes trying to feed paper onto those stupid little tractor wheels, I would have undoubtedly made Mr. Hyde look like Mr. Rogers. I deeply, earnestly wanted to kill something.

I'm told this really isn't difficult stuff. Oh well. Just steer me toward *Computers for Morons and Slow Learners* 101. The rest of the world is writing Ph.D. theses and I can't find my He-Man lunchbox for Day 1 of first grade.

But, even a blind squirrel finds an acorn from time to time. Every now and then, when I'm swatting a fly or picking cookie crumbs off the keyboard, I'll stumble my way to a few correct keystrokes. When I hit a hot streak, I sometimes actually put a whole article together. Once I'm done, I have lots of fun with *Spell Check* and *Grammar Check*. *Grammar Check* doesn't quite know what to do with me. Reason being, I often write in sentences like this. And this. Not to mention this. Really.

Take a sentence like, **"And this."** How does *Grammar Check* find this sentence offensive? Let me count the ways. Its opening salvo, predictably, is "This does not seem to be a complete sentence." Duh. Round Two is, "It is preferable to avoid beginning a sentence with **And.**" Thanks for sharing. Quickly followed up by, "This sentence does not seem to contain a main clause." And finishing up with, "May we suggest a good remedial English tutor?" So polite.

Since there's no effective way of explaining myself to this box of chips, I just keep hitting "Ignore." Boy, that feels good. Like telling your English teacher to go jump in the lake. Repeatedly.

Occasionally, the weight of one too many dangling participles, run-on sentences or passive voices finally takes its toll. Its chips start cracking and leaking vital "smart juice." I haven't actually witnessed this, but given its subsequent bizarre behavior, it's the only thing I can think of. Judge for yourself.

I wrote a sentence once that read, in part, **"...I really didn't mind that much (boy am I dumb)..."** Its suggestion: "Consider **is** instead of **am**." Hmmm...... "boy, **is** I dumb." I like it. The next one was, **"I tracked him down and found him safely tucked away..."** What say you, oh wise one? "Consider **he** instead of **him**." OK. "I tracked **he** down and found **he** safely tucked away." Cool. It's starting to think like I do. And who says computers can't learn?

Spell Check, while essentially useful, is always good for a few laughs as well. **Cuz**, times arise when I just **gotta** use words that it **ain't gonna** like. So, it complains...and suggests alternatives. It's only trying to help. Taking its cues, the sentence above would look like this: **Cuss**, times arise when I just **goat** use words that it **Ann's gonad** like. Much better. That's what I meant to say. I just need to put this puppy on autopilot, set it loose, and collect the royalties.

But hey, that's good news. Because, besides increasing the chuckle quotient, if that's typical of a computer's intelligence, we can quit worrying about ever being replaced by them. Small consolation right now, but I'll take it. One for the good guys.

Incidentally, always run "Spell Check" on your copy before submitting it to clients, but *never* rely on it to catch everything. *Our* instead of *out* and *hat* instead of *has* will slip on by.

OK, SO WHAT DO WE NEED?   The simple bare necessities... Remember the point I made a few chapters back about how little investment this business takes to begin, and how low the overhead is to sustain it? You'll recall that the list of "must-haves" was pretty short:

- *Room - or some dedicated space.*
- *Phone - with answering machine/voice mail capability, preferably with speakerphone.*
- *(Preferably late-model) computer and printer*

• Fax machine (or a fax program on your computer).
• Internet Access - mainly for e-mail
• Printer paper and floppy diskettes.
• A nice business card.

That really *is* all you need, but there are a number of other things implied here. So, let's get a little more specific.

Your Computer The optimum technical set-up for a prospective freelance commercial writer is a late-model Pentium computer. Pentiums are getting cheaper and more obsolete by the hour, so you're best off getting the most computer you can afford at the time.

At the time of this writing, the 800 MHz Pentium IIIs are hitting the street and there's talk of 1GHz machines on the horizon. We'll discuss software in more detail in a moment, but suffice it to say, you'll need word processing capability (i.e., *Microsoft Word*), fax, contact management, and invoicing programs, along with Internet access for e-mail and research. Your built-in fax/data modem should be 56K or faster.

Big Hard Drives, Big Waste If you'll be using your computer mainly for your writing business, don't pay extra to get some 15–20 gig hard drive. That's like renting a one-bedroom apartment with an airport hanger for a storage closet. Big hard drives are necessary only if you're going to be saving a lot of photo images, or you're getting into graphic design work, both of which take up a lot of disk space. But if you're not, it's a waste.

Just for fun, I went through my hard drive the other day and added up all the disk space taken up by ALL my writing for the past six years (including this book). It came to a total of just under 60 meg which is a little over 3% of my relatively microscopic 1.6 gig hard drive. Yes, software will take up a lot more than that, but even with all my software, I've still got well over 50% of my hard drive free after all this time.

PC or Mac? While most graphic designers you'll come in contact with are Mac users, for the most part, it's still a PC world out there, which is what I'd recommend. Translation programs make converting between PC and Mac very simple. Since often you're not even dealing with a designer but delivering your copy right to a client, having a PC will keep you in sync with most of the world.

But hey, if you've got your heart set on a Mac, you'll get along just fine. In fact, conventional wisdom out there has it that Macs are dramatically easier to use and have exponentially fewer problems.

Buy What Your Friends Have Another way to decide which computer platform to buy is cunningly simple: Do you have a computer whiz friend who's foolishly offered to be your unofficial technical support person? (You better hope they never come to their senses…) If the answer to this question is yes, then you simply buy whatever they have. End of discussion.

SOFTWARE

Which Word Processing Program? I use *Microsoft Word for Windows98*, the standard word processing program out there. I know next to nothing about *WordPerfect*,® so don't even ask. And frankly, I haven't run across a client yet who uses it, so just get Word. See my recommendations later in this chapter ("How Much Technical Expertise Do I Need?") about getting up to speed on *Word*.

Fax Programs Faxing documents can be done two ways: with a stand-alone fax machine or with fax software. Actually there is a third way: through e-mail, the new and upcoming technology. I use option #2, a fax program called *WinFax Pro*,™ which is very reliable.

Another quality program is *ProComm Plus*.™ Can't go wrong with either. They'll run you about $100. If you have a fax program like *FaxWorks*, which comes as bundled software with many computers today, find out if it's a 16 or 32-bit program. *FaxWorks* came with the Gateway computer I bought a few years back and it was a 16-bit program, running on 32-bit Windows 95. Because they conflict, about 10–15% of the time, other fax machines or fax programs can't communicate with mine. I wrestled with this for a few years, then finally bit the bullet and bought a compatible program.

Spring Cleaning… Just a little note about fax programs. Clean out your fax logs periodically. Every time you send a fax, your program saves a copy of it, which is an image, not just text, which means it takes up a lot more disk space than a few pages of text would. You already have those documents on your hard drive, so you don't need them in a fax log.

Once, back in my 386 days, I reclaimed 47 meg of space instantly by cleaning out fax logs that had built up over two years. While 47 meg today is nothing, at the time it comprised about 25% of the teeny-weeny 210 meg hard drive on my 386, the machine, incidentally, that built my business.

Do You Need a Stand-Alone Fax? The obvious downside of a computer fax is that you can only fax documents which you've generated on your computer.

In my case, that's been the overwhelming bulk of faxes I've ever wanted to send. External documents must be faxed from a stand-alone machine, or scanned in using a scanner ($100-250) and then faxed.

Incidentally, the print quality of computer-generated faxes as they're received on the other end is significantly higher than those sent from a regular fax machine. While I have never owned a stand-alone fax, there are times when I wish I did (though apparently not enough to make me actually go out and buy one). Of course, these days, for a pretty reasonable amount of money, you can get a combo machine that faxes, scans, and copies.

Contact Managers (CM) A CM program is essentially a computerized address book on steroids. It's a system for staying on top of your clients: all pertinent info, the time, date, and content of all your communication with them, along with simple calendar structures for planned and periodic events. You can generate mailings, schedule regular follow-up calls, and make a well-organized marketing campaign a natural, somewhat effortless (it's never completely so!) by-product of the system.

A good CM program will not only dramatically simplify your life, but help you be tremendously more effective, productive, and organized as well, while generating little additional work. It's a great tool for lazy people like me. If that's you, get a CM. Trust me.

"Maximize" Yourself The most popular contact management program on the market is, of course, *Act!,®* currently in its 2000 release version. *Act!* is very powerful, and for my purposes, had a lot of features better suited for heavy marketing, mucho mailings, etc. What would I recommend? I chose another very popular one called *Maximizer,®* which is totally customizable, boasts relational databases (change one, others automatically change), makes it amazingly easy to keep up with your client follow-up, and still has all those great mailing features. FYI, *Maximizer* costs about $70-80, while *Act!* will run you closer to $200.

Pointless Technology Though the electronic rolodex portion of a CM is infinitely superior to its manual spinning counterpart, the calendar portion is another story. For logging appointments and follow-up calls, deadlines, etc., I've found over time that I much prefer a plain old-fashioned book-style *Day-Timer* or *DayMinder* for scheduling appointments.

I assert that the calendar feature of CMs is a classic case of JBWC (Just-Because-We-Can) technology, which ends up being significantly more cumbersome than doing it manually.

By the time I open the program and then the calendar portion, scroll to the day, fill in the information and close it out, I could have jotted it in my book, had a cup of tea, taken a walk around the block, cleaned the lint out of my belly-button…you get the idea.

Electronic calendars do have one nice feature—they can alert you to upcoming appointments with an alarm. If you're not one to regularly check your calendar, it's something to consider.

Invoicing Programs While most of the contact management programs have some invoicing capability, I'm only familiar with the arrangement on mine, which is not very handy. Others may be better. Instead, I bought a very simple program called *My Advanced Invoices (MAI)* that cost about $40, is very easy to use, and instantly generates all sorts of nifty summary reports.

When you've got money in the bank, your mortgage is paid for next month, and your invoice program is telling you that $8,465 is still coming in, life is good. *MAI* has customizable screens and templates to make your invoices classy and professional looking. It's all you'll need.

Back Up Everything, Always, Constantly This is *very* important. Get into the automatic, don't-think-twice-about-it habit of backing up your work on diskettes or a Zip® drive constantly. Not just occasionally. Every single time you work on a document. The only thing worse than losing your last two hours of work to a mysterious system crash or power-zapping thunderstorm is losing your whole last year's work to the same nasty things.

Tape back-ups or Zip Drives are built-in or external storage devices with anywhere from 100–400 MB that allow you to save all your files at once. While it'll make rebuilding from a crash that much easier, their value as peace of mind enhancers is priceless.

I've had three system crashes and each one necessitated wiping my entire hard drive clean and rebuilding it from scratch. Even though I had everything backed up, it was still a nightmare. Without back-up… I don't even care to ponder that scenario. Suffice it to say, if it happened to you, you'd be hating life in a very big way.

If you're at your computer for many hours at a time, always be saving your work. I just set my computer on an automatic save every 10 minutes or so but of course, that's just to the hard drive.

If you're using Windows95, while undoubtedly you know how to save to a diskette, here's (probably) a new way to do it and one that doesn't end up risking those weird screen blackouts and system shutdowns that often happen in this program:

- *Close the document*
- *Put in your diskette*
- *Go to Exploring (which I always keep open)*
- *Find the file and click it once to highlight it*
- *Click on File, then Send To, then 3½" Floppy (A:)*
- *When it's through saving, just hit Enter to reopen it.*

MISC. GADGETS & GIZMOS

Do You Need a Laptop? You'll get by without one, but once you get one, you'll find plenty of opportunities to put it to use. In fact, if you haven't bought a computer yet, you might want to consider buying a laptop as your primary computer.

Remember, you can always buy an external keyboard and monitor (even used) for just a few hundred bucks more, plug them into this smaller computer and convert it into a bigger and more user-friendly machine for your home use.

A laptop is a second-tier purchase and with technology changing as much as it is, you can pick up a used one for very little—$250–$300. Remember, we're talking about copywriting here. Words. You don't need much. I have *Word*, fax, and Internet programs loaded up and it easily handles all my mobile computing needs.

On-Site, It's Outta Sight It's perfect for on-site jobs—where you're actually working on a client site for days or weeks at a time. Doesn't happen a lot but when it does, you're set.

It's also invaluable for project planning or copy revision meetings. If you're creating or revising as you go, you can stay an extra 10–15 minutes after the meeting by yourself and get your clients a copy of the outline/revised copy before you leave and essentially shave an extra day off the project. However, always make sure you take the time you need to get something right as opposed to being enamored with getting it done then and there.

Buy a Microcassette Recorder That's an order. I get a lot of work done in my car. If you end up getting a lot of creative work, such as ad copy, sales promotional material, headline concepting and the like, mindless driving time can become instantly productive. If I'm heading out to run errands, to a meeting, or taking a day trip and I have a creative job I'm working on, I'll bring my notes attached to a clipboard, a pen, and my microcassette recorder. As ideas occur to me, I record them until I can get home and transfer them to the screen.

REMEMBER: *Make sure you always have fresh batteries in your recorder, and test it before leaving home.* On more than one occasion, especially at night, when I couldn't see as much, I've gotten home, only to realize that I'd spoken all those incredibly lucid, wildly creative, and dead-on perfect gems into one lifeless little hunk of plastic and metal. Talk about depression. And don't forget—these little gizmos are perfect for phone interviews (See Chapter Eight).

New voice recognition technology like *Naturally Speaking* actually allows you to capture your thoughts on a small portable recorder and once loaded into a special deck hooked to your computer, have those thoughts automatically print to your computer screen. Now, if they could just figure out a way to automatically generate the thoughts and ideas ... I could spend more time at the beach. It's coming, I'm sure ....

A FEW PHONE TIPS

Get a Speakerphone Or even better yet, a headset for your phone. Anything that allows you to communicate hands-free is a big help with phone interviews, allowing you to type while you're talking. Or when you're on hold, you can still be productive.

Calling Features If you live in an area where you can get your local phone company's voice-mail service, get it, along with *Caller ID Deluxe, Call Waiting,* and *Call Forwarding Don't Answer.* While most people who get them for their personal use just like having the flexibility to be anti-social if they'd just as soon *not* talk to their caller, for businesspeople, these services offer some different and very significant benefits.

In addition to *MemoryCall* professionally capturing all your calls—without that tacky staticky answering machine background sound—and allowing frequent callers to bypass your message by hitting #, *Caller ID Deluxe* lets you know who's calling in, whether or not you're on the phone. If you are talking, and your *Call Waiting* beeps in, a quick glance at your box lets you know whether to take it or let it roll right over to voice-mail.

Prospect Confidently This is especially important when you're cold-calling. You've just made 35 phone calls and finally that afternoon, you get a call back from a prospect, who's possibly interested but very curt and gruff on the phone. Murphy's Law has it that at that precise moment, your *Call Waiting* will beep.

Without *MemoryCall*, you have to stop—you don't want to miss a call—and feeling like a total dork, ask "Could you hang on for a minute" (heavy 'my-patience-is-dwindling' sigh on the other end) while you find out who's there, all the while certain your prospect will have split by the time you return. Too much anxiety for me.

Just as importantly for us freelancers, *Caller ID* leaves the names and numbers of all callers, including those who didn't leave a message. If I'm a client, trying to find a writer (and into instant gratification, as we all are) and I get voicemail, *and* I have a list of four other possibilities, I might just hang up and go on to the next name. If I know who it was soon enough, I might just salvage u job.

If it nets me even one small job a year that I wouldn't have otherwise had, it's paid for itself about 10 times over. Even if it doesn't, the certainty of knowing who called is wonderful soothing balm compared to listening helplessly to a bunch of hang-ups.

One last benefit. If you're on deadline and need to put your nose to the grindstone, knowing who's calling allows you to avoid answering non-essential calls and stay focused.

Pager and/or Cell Phone? After five years, I finally broke down and got a cell phone. Not because I absolutely needed it, but because they'd gotten so cheap. And they really *can* free you up.

On days when the four walls of the home office are closing in and I need to get out and see something different, I can forward the office phone to the cell phone and head to the library or coffee bar. With *Caller ID* on the phone, I can choose which calls to take and which to return later. Just don't give the number out to the world.

If you choose not to go the mobile route, you'll be fine. But in that case, I would absolutely recommend getting a beeper. The day I bought the pager was the day I missed a call for a $400 job that I could've easily knocked out in an evening. By the time I got back to my client, she'd given it to someone else. Since the pager and 12 months of service/voice mail cost a grand total of $99, that one job would have paid for it four times over. Oh well.

How Much Technical Expertise Do You Need? I have friends who like nothing better than cracking open new software programs and working into the wee hours of the night. Their palms get all sweaty, their breathing gets heavy, pupils dilate—it's scary. Not me. Remember, if I can do it... So, the following discussion applies to the true cyber-phobics out there, who know very little about *Microsoft Word.*

More Knowledge = More $ There are plenty of clients who will only want you for your wordsmithing prowess. If you just know how to use the less complex word processing capabilities of your PC, can save a file to a disk or e-mail that file, that should be plenty for about 90% of your clients out there. Today. However, I see storm clouds gathering on the horizon.

Put it this way. While it may not hurt you much to have limited technical expertise, especially in markets where there's plenty of work, if you can deliver copy in rough layouts like 3-column formats or tables, for instance, or use *Microsoft PowerPoint*® or *Excel,* you'll be that much better off. Bottom line: People like to hire people who make their lives easier and who create less work for them by their presence. Pretty understandable.

Not as Hard as You Think As for most of the basics of formatting, we're not talking rocket science here. And you've got a few options for getting up to speed. First, you can follow the technical manual on *Word* and teach yourself. Of course, most of these esoteric manuals are written by clueless techs who, because *they* spend their whole lives marinating in this stuff, think the rest of the world does too.

If you didn't know better, you'd think they were writing them as references for each other and not for people who might be new at this game. They are exercises in vagueness, obtuseness, and incomprehensibility.

Probably a better bet for the do-it-yourself-crowd is to get a copy of *"Word for Windows95/98 for Dummies"* along with the official *Microsoft Word* manual. Use the former as the lead guide and the latter for supplementation. THE best way to learn this stuff—if you've got a few bucks—is to take some classes. Check the Yellow Pages or local computer magazines (in computer stores) where you might also find ads for tutors offering targeted instruction.

With classes, count on needing to master the Beginning and Intermediate levels of *Microsoft Word.* Again, advanced level stuff will obviously make you more marketable, but probably isn't necessary for the majority of work you'll be doing.

Wanna Get "Graphic"? OK, let's take it a step further here—though purely optional. Learn a little graphic design—i.e., a good working knowledge of *QuarkXPress*™ (THE preferred graphic design software currently)—and you'll definitely boost your value.

Add to that *Adobe Illustrator* (THE drawing program) and *Adobe Photoshop* (for photo manipulation), and you'll be a dream come true for many clients. Someone who can competently do both design and copywriting—which, barring a life-altering religious vision, just isn't going to happen in *my* life anytime soon—will likely have a full plate.

What company wouldn't want to simplify matters by dealing with one person and eliminate any possible communication issues between copywriter and designer? And a freelancer at that, whose lower overhead translates to a very reasonable total project cost. Just know that going this route will entail a much greater investment of time, equipment and software.

Again, while learning design is not something I'm interested in, I'd never discourage anyone from double-majoring. If you're a good copywriter and feel you have a good sense of design, go for it. It will absolutely elevate your market worth considerably.

Project Management, Anyone? Add one more element—project management—and you'll be totally irresistible. Project management means offering a total turnkey package, from initial meeting to delivery of final printed product, for one fee. In most cases, your proposals would be little more than a one-page itemization of costs with a timetable.

Obviously, you'd need to know the ins and outs of the printing arena: the feasibility and costs associated with certain directions: 2 and 4-color process, paper types and sizes, and whether they're standard or custom, standard or PMS color (seriously…), how to get quotes, developing relationships with printers, etc.

It can be complicated stuff, but if you keep at it and ask a lot of questions of the right people, you'll learn. By adding project management to your list of services, you could take a project from start to finish with a staff of one.

Keep in mind, all these scenarios of multi-aptitudinal prowess are just possibilities, certainly not necessities to be successful as a copywriter. I'm proof of that. A more likely and certainly less involved scenario would be to team with a designer for turnkey projects, something I discuss in Chapter Thirteen ("Dos, Don'ts & Don't Forgets"). In the case of a teaming, the designer, given his or her expertise, would be the project manager.

How Much Design Stuff Do You Need to Know? Technically, very little, but you want to have a sense of how it all works, and more importantly, what's possible technologically—which means stylistically—so you can speak intelligently when talking to clients and working with designers. But technologically, the graphic design field is constantly changing.

Every few years or less, designers who want to stay competitive upgrade their equipment and software. That means more money and education, just to keep current.

That's the beauty of copywriting. With certain small exceptions like changes in the above-discussed technology, good writing is good writing, and given that there's precious little good copywriting out there, there will always be a demand for solid skill in that arena.

Not to say that writing hasn't or isn't evolving in certain arenas. It is, and I've seen it especially in the area of ad copy and corporate image pieces, where the writer and designer are working much more as a team to create a true integration of words and images. In these cases, the two components simply can't be separated, because one so intimately and critically complements the other. All of which makes for much more interesting and challenging work.

You're Not in a Vacuum To a certain extent, that's my point with this section. You need to know a little about design, because in 90% of your work, you'll be factoring in the design, in terms of knowing how much copy you need to write, where that copy will be positioned in the piece and the overall tone that the piece is trying to achieve as a function of the marriage of images and words.

It's here that you can become that much more valuable to a client and a designer if you have a feel for the visual. I always disclaim any design-related suggestions I make in meetings where designers are present—"Now, I'm not a designer, and I would never dream of telling you how to do your job…" That's usually enough to reassure them that you're not encroaching on their traditional turf and make them more receptive to your suggestions.

Don't Be Shy As a writer, knowing that your words will be put into a certain layout, it's only natural that good ideas for powerful graphic images will occur to you. A confident designer will generally welcome your input, always open to good ideas, especially from a teammate intimately involved in the project.

A few months back, in conversation with the graphic designer with whom I was teaming on a direct mail package for a credit card company, I suggested a certain image for the envelope concept. She loved it, went with it, the client flipped, and everyone was happy.

Suffice it to say, your best bet is to learn by exposure. Make friends with some graphic designers along the way and when you team with them on projects, pick their brains about the process. But rest assured, you won't be terribly hobbled without this knowledge in the beginning.

WHAT ABOUT THE INTERNET?

Just Do It If you're not already wired to the Internet, do so. If for no other reason, e-mail. Which also means file transfer. The days of having to mail, FedEx, courier, or personally deliver a diskette with a project's files are numbered.

Now when I'm done with projects, I just e-mail the files right to the clients. They can download it and we're done. Back-and-forth edits are much easier with e-mail. More and more clients want me to be able to communicate electronically. Again, like anything new, there's a little learning curve, but, trust me, it's very little. And it will make your life much much easier.

While e-mail alone is a swell reason to be on-line, as a writer, the 'Net pays much bigger dividends. I recently did a newsletter for the huge hometown telecommunications firm and needed a few bits of info for one of the articles. Five minutes after logging on to their web site, I had everything I needed and the article was finished—at 1:00 a.m. No playing voicemail tag with overworked corporate wonks, which would have dragged out a simple 10 minute process into a week and a half.

Research Pays Off It also comes in mighty handy if say, you're doing a brochure on ABC Manufacturing, with whom you have your first meeting tomorrow morning. By visiting their web site, you know who they are, what they do, and are in a much better position to speak intelligently and recommend creative directions.

In this case, using the Web is an amazingly easy way to make a tremendous first impression. For professional research, it's an absolute boon, like having the resources of the world's most extensive and current library a few mouse clicks away.

Offering anything you want to know about anything, the 'Net is a quick, cheap, effective way of getting the answers. With unlimited use running about $20 a month these days—and sure to come down even further over time—it's the mother of all bargains. Of course, always double-check the accuracy of material you find on the Internet. This may be a shocker, but not everything you read is true.

Just Saying No to "Chat" Afraid you'll turn into a "Net-head", spending great chunks of time surfing or cyberchatting? Fear not. I mean, I can't speak for you, but in my case, I went through the usual initial fascination, which very quickly wore off.

The chat rooms, by the way, *are* interesting—for about five minutes, and strictly for observing the dynamic at work. The conversation is so insipid and vacuous for the most part, you'll quickly think of better ways to spend your time. Unless you happen to be insipid and vacuous yourself, in which case, you will have tapped into the mother lode of kindred spirits.

Where to now? Now that you've got all this wonderful technology, how can we best put it to use? There are lots of ways to streamline this business so you can accomplish the most amount of work with the least amount of effort. Let's talk about "Systems," shall we?

Chapter Eight

The System Is the Solution

MAKE IT SIMPLE, AND YOU'LL DO IT   Being typical human beings, we're always looking for the easy way out—getting the work done with the least amount of effort.

When we started out, I told you I'd show you how to make a healthy living and still have a life. That means making the most of our time and spending as little time as possible doing the busy work of creating direct mail campaigns, assembling and sending out marketing packages, marketing by fax, etc. The key to all this is…

Simple Repeatable Systems   In this business, you have to get your name and yourself in front of a lot of people to get the business. The cold-calling, sending out of information (mailed, faxed, or e-mailed) and follow-up has to happen. Leaving it to chance or worse yet, our "best intentions," is simply not wise.

By systematizing the process, however—thanks to your wonderful computer—it becomes a simple matter of a few mouse clicks to get information together and in the hands of your prospects and clients. In the process, we can actually make this potentially grueling process quite bearable and even (dare we say it) fun!

And the easier the process of prospecting for business is, the more likely you are to consistently do it. Logical. As we discussed earlier, if you do your personal marketing on a consistent basis, you will put yourself ahead of about 95% of your competitors.

In Chapter Six, we discussed some very formulaic ways of going about the prospecting process, making it a series of simple steps, not some unpredictable, anxiety-filled process, fraught with unknowns and "what-if's." We'll apply the same philosophy here.

Mental Prep 101 To a large extent, what's really behind all this talk of systems is the whole notion of being mentally prepared to receive the gifts (interested prospects, more business, etc.) that the universe is waiting to bestow upon us. Now, while this discussion strays into some semi-spiritual territory here, which may or may not strike a chord with you, concentrate on the inherent logic of the strategy. We're talking about the nitty-gritty of business-building here, from personal experience.

If It's Painful, You Won't Do It… When I started out, embarking on a phone prospecting campaign *without* having any systems in place, a funny thing happened. Every time I got someone on the line who was interested in seeing a package of my work, I quickly realized that between typing the cover letter, putting together an appropriate résumé, and assembling the right samples, I could easily spend an hour putting together one mailing.

After slogging through this excruciating ritual 15–20 times, how excited do you think you'll be about getting a "hot one" on the phone, knowing what's next? And yet, isn't that the whole point? Every job starts with a "hot one" on the phone. You'd better be excited about it. So, if I could show you how to reduce that 45–60 minutes down to 5–10 minutes max, might you rediscover your enthusiasm?

Be Open to Receive When you get on the phone to prospect, you'd better be excited, enthusiastic, and absolutely certain that your future customers are only a few phone calls away. In other words, you need to be expectant and *open* to receive. If you're dreading the process, you're probably going to unconsciously be putting out some pretty serious "Go Away" vibes, and your efforts will bear that much less fruit. And you won't even realize that it's happening. Believe me, it makes a difference.

As we discussed in Chapter Six, you still need to be very careful about who gets a package. Make sure they truly are interested and not just trying to get you off the phone. Let them ask for it. Don't offer first—because frankly, anyone will take your information.

If you dialed any phone number at random and talked to whoever answered—butcher, baker, candlestick maker—and were persuasive enough, any of them would take a package of information from you. We need to be a little discriminating.

OK, the client/prospect says, "Yes, I'd be very interested to see your work. We're looking to beef up our stable of writers." And let's say you can't get in the door for a meeting right away so you need to put a package together. What will you send them?

EASY LETTERS, RÉSUMÉS, AND SAMPLES

Follow-Up/Cover Letters Every time you meet with prospects or talk with them on the phone for the first time, if there's potential business down the road, send them something to get your name in front of them again.

Letters for Every Occasion At some point early in the going, you need to sit down and create about a half dozen versions of form follow-up/cover letters. Each letter should be a separate file with its own distinctive name and should address the following situations:

1) You have met with a prospect and introduced yourself and your work. He's excited about working with you, but no work is immediately pending.
2) You've met with a new client and will shortly be starting work on a new job.
2a) An expanded version of the above letter where you feel it's important to review a few key points about your skills that were discussed in your meeting as being particularly important to the client.
3) You've talked to a prospect, who will probably be a long shot for work in the future, but you're sending out a letter, résumé, and business cards.
4) You've talked on the phone with a new prospect who hires freelancers on a regular basis, and this letter will accompany the package of samples, résumé, client list, etc.
5) You've received a call from an assistant to a creative director or communications manager with the request to send his boss a package, and this letter accompanies that package.
6) Slightly different versions of the above letters for video/CD prospects vs. print/collateral prospects, where references to "copywriting" change to "scriptwriting."

Samples Enclosed Now, I'm going to make your life really easy here. I've included samples of my versions of all these letters in Appendix A. You're welcome. You'll notice they all have some common components. Why reinvent the wheel each time? As long as they're strong reminders of your meeting and drive home points that are important to the client, they don't all have to be wildly original. Remember, it's the only one they'll probably ever get. As you'll recall, my standard opening is:

> *As a freelance writer, my goal is to enhance your image, improve your profit picture, and make your life easier. If it carries your name, shouldn't it be the best reflection of you?*

These are guidelines for different possible letters and the points to cover, *not* the last word in letter-writing. Please don't copy them verbatim. With a little thought, you can probably come up with additional versions as well as different forms for these letters that are at least as effective, if not more, than mine.

Once you've created the letters, when you need one for a particular situation, call it up on your computer, fill in the name/company/address info and send it out. It's not this onerous chore that needs to be created from scratch every time.

Try to customize them as much as possible, making a reference or two to specific points discussed in the meeting/conversation so it doesn't look too shamelessly boilerplate.

The Right Greeting Depending on the rapport you have with your prospect/client, use your discretion as whether to address them Mr. Jones or Tom, Ms. Taylor or Mary. If you've connected nicely with them, the informal first name is probably safe, and will be appreciated. Your clients/prospects all want to be respected, but most also appreciate the human touch and the fact that you felt comfortable enough to call them by their first name. Though, when in doubt, stay formal.

Résumés As with letters, given the capabilities of computers, there's no excuse not to have multiple versions of résumés tailored to different clients' needs. In the beginning, before you have a large body of work to show, you'll be delighted to add any new completed projects to a single but growing résumé of credits. After awhile, you can start creating different résumés for different areas of specialty.

I have different résumés for ad copy writing, video/CD experience, technical projects, brochure/collateral work, speeches, articles/editorial, public relations, as well as several general versions to send to someone who may have different needs or wants to see the scope of my abilities. Given that you'll be tailoring a résumé to a particular specialty, always keep it to one page in length.

Tailored To Each Client Each of these specialty résumés won't consist solely of projects in that genre, especially in the beginning, but if they lead with two or three items in that arena, you'll be putting the appropriate emphasis where it goes for *that* particular client. I create separate files for each résumé and name them Resvid (video), Resad (advertising), Respch (speeches), etc.

Once you've done work for a healthy array of clients, create a client list to include with the résumés you send out. I use the same one, make it page 2 of *all* the résumé document files and then print it out on the back of the résumé. Your first contact with a new prospect is no time for modesty. Put your best foot forward. It can be an impressive snapshot to show clients that a lot of high-profile firms have been satisfied with your work.

Even if you've only done one job with IBM and that was a year or two ago, by all means, include their name. They don't have to be a regular, "call-you-every-week" client to make the list.

You might include several references (three ought to do it) on the résumé or client list—folks certain to sing your praises to the heavens. Include name, company name, title and phone number. Needless to say, only include those companies that you could comfortably send your prospect to for a reference (by the way, they almost never check, but pretend they will).

Keep 'Em Fresh Periodically replace these references with fresher ones. As mentioned, while your prospects will rarely ask for or call references, the fact that you offer says something about your abilities and confidence.

Also, update your résumés regularly, adding newly completed projects to a particular client's listing and newer projects to a particular type of résumé. I print my résumés out on a piece of letterhead, saving the need to type all the contact information. My résumés generally take the following form:

PETER BOWERMAN
(770) 555-6543

SELECTED FREE-LANCE WRITING CREDITS
1) CLIENT: **ABC Corp**. - Atlanta, GA
   PROJECT: Corporate Sales Brochure, Rate Book, and Customer Newsletter for
            Mexican Operation

2) CLIENT: **The Biggie Snack Company** - Atlanta, GA
PROJECTS: Program Guide for Boys & Girls Club/Biggie Snack Alliance,
           Concepting Projects (Est. 35+)
           Misc. Product Marketing Brochures
3) CLIENT: **MegaPhone Corporation** - Atlanta, GA
PROJECTS: Monthly Internal Newsletter **(CommTalk On-Line)**
           Eight-Page Small Business Division Newsletter
           Descriptive Product Brochures (4) on calling features

Samples of Work The next thing you'll be sending out to clients is samples of your work. Now, given how precious samples are (See Chapter Thirteen— "Do's, Don'ts & Don't Forgets"), you probably won't be sending out originals, but making photocopies of your better pieces. The only exception would be if you have a healthy number (a dozen or more) of a particular piece, *and* it's a big important prospect who could mean lots of business and you want to put together a killer package.

Doing a "Copy Day" Get in the habit of making copies of your samples as soon as you get them—at least the ones that you'd be proud to show. It's worth it to spend the better part of a day copying a bunch of your best pieces. If a particular sample is a long, multi-page masterpiece, unless it's all fabulous, pick out the key pages that would fall into a logical sequence and copy them.

Wherever possible, make double-sided copies, which saves you postage when you're sending out packages. Make 25–30 copies of each one that you plan to send out regularly. Keep them all filed in separate file folders or even better, in one of those cardboard racks with a bunch of stacked sheet-sized compartments.

Check the office supply store circulars in your Sunday paper for one or two cent per copy specials that run occasionally and save a bunch of money.

From One Hour to Five Minutes *Now,* when you're talking with a client, for instance, in advertising, and they want a package, all you've got to do, after making sure of what type of work they want to see (let's not guess), is go to your file cabinet or rack, grab one of these, one of those, and one of the other, spit out the appropriate form cover letter with minor customizations tailored to the conversation, the advertising-oriented résumé/client list combo (or just grab one if you've already printed out multiple copies), two business cards, and you're done.

No hour-long agony of putting a package together. 5–10 minutes and you're on to the next one. It's a beautiful thing.

THE FAX (OR E-MAIL) AS A POWERFUL MARKETING TOOL While typically you'll be mailing informational packages to clients, faxed or even e-mailed information will often do nicely. You won't know if you don't ask. If you suspect that the client is a long shot for business, ask them if you could go ahead and electronically send them a résumé, client list, and a few samples. You'll be surprised at how often they say, "Oh sure, no problem." Again, we're talking simple, repeatable systems that get your name in front of as many people as possible in the shortest period of time with the least hassle.

Let's talk about faxing samples. If you have a stand-alone fax, you can usually fax copies of your actual samples to the client. If your fax is built into your computer, unless you have a scanner to scan in the originals and then fax them out (or better yet, e-mail them as graphic files), all you can fax is the copy (minus the graphic layouts) that you generated on your computer.

Small Downside, Big Upside Now, you'd probably imagine that only having a computer fax would be a great disadvantage. Certainly, if you have a nice sample that faxes well, that's preferable to a page of text. And as discussed earlier, when you're dealing with graphic designers, the aesthetics of the piece, not surprisingly, become that much more important. But many printed pieces today, given their complexity not only in structure but colors as well, when photocopied, just don't fax very well, and so a clean sheet of text can be just as, if not more, effective in conveying writing ability.

Your Best Stuff The other big advantage of faxing or e-mailing computer-generated text samples—and anyone in my field can *so* relate to this—is that you can send out the copy you feel is your best, and not be limited to what ended up in the final piece. Because from time to time, a finished project will look beautiful from a design standpoint, but what the client did to my copy made me cry.

In cases like that, you've got two choices. Don't send the piece, even though it looks great and has some big corporation's impressive logo at the bottom. Or send it along with a note telling them how badly the client butchered your copy. Kidding. Not cool. You'll come off as a whiner, even if you're right.

But if you're going to simply fax them text from your computer, you can send them anything your little heart desires. You can put back all that wonderful copy that the client ultimately replaced, and show your prospect what you're really capable of. Seriously, you are the professional, and because of that, much of what ends up getting changed by the client won't be as good as it was before. Here's your chance to make it right.

If the filename of the original good draft is "abccorp.doc" (in Word) do a *Save As* "abccorp2.doc" and make their unpleasant revisions on the new document. Your original will live on and perhaps live again as part of a package to a future prospect. Now, you need to do a few things to your computer text samples before sending them out.

Creating Sample "Frames" First of all, as much as possible, try to keep samples to one page. Cull the piece down to a manageable size and include enough to give the client a good sense of the logical flow of the piece. In the case of multi-page video/CD-ROM scripts, include one particularly good representation of your writing ability, even if it doesn't tell the whole product story.

Secondly, at the top of the page include an intro line that has the same font, point size, and style on all samples. In the examples below, note whether it's a *Sample Excerpt* or in the case of a sales letter, (where you can include the whole piece), just a *Sample*. Examples:

Sample Excerpt:

Script for *Junior Achievement* Atlanta Business Hall of Fame Awards Ceremony and Dinner

Sample Excerpt:

Product Brochure for *Formula One* Electronic Printing Software

Sample:

UPS Marketing Letter Introducing Service Enhancements

Complete Faxable/E-mailable Profiles Want to take this system thing to even greater heights, and further simplify your life? Here's a common scenario.

You talk to a prospect by phone and she wants to see a little info about you.

By pre-assembling ready-to-go faxable/e-mailable packages (each on its own computer file) tailored to a specific type of work—ad copy, collateral, video/CD-ROM, technical, PR, or general—it's a snap to give them the info they need to make hiring decisions. What's in one of these packages?

Form follow-up/cover letter version #4 (the "Spoke-to-interested-client-on-the-phone-who-wants-information" version), the correct résumé/client list, and a few appropriate text samples of your work. It's all together in one computer file, you just tweak the letter to fit the conversation, and it's on its way to a prospect. Yes, it'll take a day or two to put the above-described system pieces together. But, knowing how easy it is to get a powerful package out to a client quickly might just turn you into a prospecting machine.

DIRECT MAIL

Keeping in Touch   Unless you're blessed to be in a market where you're the only copywriter and hundreds of firms are vying for your time (in which case, you better keep it to yourself, or I'll move there), chances are good that you'll periodically have to remind your market that you're out there. As discussed, this can be accomplished by phone calling and a follow-up with brochure, business card, résumé, samples, etc.

At a certain point in my business' development, however, I ended up with a core of clients and prospects—people for whom I'd either done work, or who had expressed the possibility of needing my services in the future. I do call these people up occasionally, but if they're busy, and the phone call's quick, they will have forgotten all about me approximately five seconds after they hang up.

So it really makes sense to send them an actual physical reminder from time to time. Something that sits in front of their nose for a minute or two—like a postcard, for instance. And there's a way of creating these simple little marketing devices for far less than a nickel apiece (plus postage). How?

Easy, Even for Me…   Well, I have to warn you that what I'm about to suggest may entail becoming mildly proficient with a desktop publishing program such as *Microsoft Publisher.*

By itself, *Publisher* will run you about $70, though these days, chances are good that it will come bundled with a bunch of other Microsoft programs like *Word, Power Point, Excel,* etc.

It took me all of about two hours to create the front and back of a marketing postcard using *Publisher*. They have all kinds of neat clip art that's easy to add and makes your presentation a lot more interesting and engaging—key to getting noticed. Though, within reason, *anything* that gets your name in front of your market is better than nothing at all. (See sample in Appendix A)

The reason I am suggesting *Microsoft Publisher* is that you—that is, someone who's not a professional designer—can create professional looking pieces. Not that a real graphic designer couldn't do a better job, but it will serve your purposes admirably. Now, if you're just a genetically wired software-phobic, you might be able to do a passable job with *Microsoft Word* and the clip art library that comes standard with *Word*. But *Publisher* will definitely make a better impression.

About Three Cents Each I then bought a ream of fluorescent yellow 8½" x 11" 65 lb. cover stock, which is the thickness of post cards (Astro-Bright is one brand), laid out four clean laser copies of each side of my 4¼" x 5½" card on two 8½" x 11" sheets of paper and with the help of a friendly employee at the local quick copy place, did double sided copies on my stock and chopped the sheets up in fours on their paper cutter.

Voila! 260 postcards for a total of about $7.50 and about four hours of work in all including the design process. The one ream of cover stock paper ($10 for 250 sheets) will yield 1000 postcards, about four 250-piece mailings.

Oversize Variety? Of course, you could put just two postcards to a page (8½" x 5½") which is bound to stand out more than one half its size, especially on Astro-Bright paper. Of course, you'll pay 33 cents each for postage, as opposed to 20 cents for the smaller one. Your call.

I did an oversize postcard mailing early in my career, enlisting the artistic talents of a young illustrator I found at one of the local art schools. I paid him $100, a relative pittance. But he was glad to get the money and more importantly, the sample for his book.

Now obviously, 250 pieces isn't a lot of mail. But as a way to keep your name in front of steady clients and interested prospects, or do some "cold" mailings to those who've never heard of you, 250 postcards can easily unearth two or three new customers or breathe new life into an existing client or previously-contacted prospect.

Remember what your stakes are here. If you get even one $500 job out of the mailing, it was more than worth it, though chances are you'll do much better than that, especially if you're doing them regularly (i.e., four times a year). With postage 20 cents each on the smaller card, the whole mailing cost less than $60.

Do this and you'll be way ahead of the competition. Very few people in this business do any sort of regular, organized, direct mailing to clients. Keep it simple and you'll keep doing it *and* keep getting new work.

Timing is Everything A little suggestion about the timing of these mailings. If you plan on only doing two a year, schedule one for January and one for June. If you're going for four or more, make sure at least two of them are around those months. Why? January can be slow just because… well, it's January. Not always but by no means unusual. Drop a mailing right after New Year's so it's waiting for them when they get back to work after the holidays, and you'll be one of the first names they think of when they need a writer.

Mid-June is a fine time for a mailing because typically in this business, the summers are slower due to vacations, ends of fiscal years, projects being back-burnered, budgets running out, etc. So in anticipation of that, it's not a bad idea to remind your market that you're out there so you can get your share of what will be a somewhat reduced workload, industry-wide, during July and August.

Get Creative Besides just creating a general, "This-is-who-I-am-what-I-do-and-who-I've-done-it-for-call-me" mailing, use your imagination to design a variety of other messages. Target a specific industry with a listing of recent work you've done in that industry, and who for. Remind your market of a specific type of work that you're aggressively pursuing.

Invariably—and I mean *invariably*—within a few days after I send out a mailing, I'll get a few calls and at least a job or two, sometimes off of the mailing, sometimes not, but it always happens. It's called synchronicity. Someone who forgot about me just had a need arise for copywriting when my postcard crossed their desk and their regular copywriter wasn't available. Bingo! I get the call. If I do a good job, guess who they're going to think of the next time they need a writer?

"Cause and Effect" in Action Once you've gotten proficient with your desktop publishing program of choice, spend one evening or weekend afternoon and create two to four different designs for different messages. Put together some "shells"—the basic structure with layout and clip art in place, with only the text to input at a later date, tailored to a particular market, or focusing on a particular message.

Then, whenever it's time for a mailing and assuming you've got paper on hand, you know that with just an hour or two invested, you have another mailing ready to go out. Once you discover for yourself that you indeed will get new business from every mailing (don't take my word for it, find out for yourself), you'll actually look forward to the process, knowing that your income will soon rise.

Direct Mail to New Prospects Obviously, creating a postcard is just one very simple way to skin the direct mail cat and is perfect for keeping your name in front of your existing client base. Some would suggest putting together a direct mail package with a cover letter, a few clips, and a reply card. Do I think it's necessary? Depends on your market, how competitive it is, and how ambitious you are. If there's plenty of work to be had, it's probably not necessary.

Sure, it would be effective, but considering that you're going after a miniscule slice of the pie here, I think a colorful post card that lists some more high-profile clients, some of the types of work you do, along with a call to action, and all housed in a catchy layout, is plenty effective.

Remember, the typical individuals who can hire you get tons of mail and they'll notice the stuff that stands out, as opposed to an envelope they need to open, something they may or may not do, especially if they're not expecting it. (You *did* call first, right?) If he/she is interested and you tell a good story in a quick read, I say you've got at least as good a chance if not better, of getting their attention than someone sending a more complex mailing.

If they're interested, they'll call or keep the card handy. If you're going to do a more comprehensive multi-part mailing like the one described above, at least use colored envelopes, or some other attention-getting feature such as personalized handwritten envelopes—things to help it stand out.

Again, keep it simple and you'll do it. Four postcard mailings that are simple to put together and which for that reason you actually do end up mailing, are vastly preferable to one really involved mailing that was so labor intensive that you only end up getting one out.

A Different List With new prospects, obviously you need to get a different list. I'd go about it the same way I compiled my phone calling list in Chapter Six. Check with a company like *BusinessWise,* where you can rent lists of local businesses on diskette, or as printed labels for particular categories you want to pursue: e.g., banks, insurance companies, architectural firms, advertising agencies, and so on. Or try the *Book of Lists,* which as you may recall, has probably equivalents in about 40+ major cities, published annually by the "…*Business Journal*" family - *www.amcity.com.*

Promote Your Web Site Now, while this probably isn't something you'd be doing right out of the gate, as soon as you've got some good clips to show, why not create a web site? You could put it together yourself or pay someone experienced to do it, a service that's becoming more available and less expensive every day.

It's the perfect way to showcase your work, and becomes incredibly easy to promote on a direct mail piece. How much easier could it be for a prospective client to get some samples of your stuff than on the web?

You're busy doing other things and your direct mail postcards or e-marketing campaign is circulating in the creative community promoting the heck out of www.kickbuttwriter.com. You get calls from prospects ready to hire you and it's the first time you've ever spoken to them. Cool, huh?

MISC. TIPS FOR MAXIMUM EFFICIENCY

Use Project Folders Get some enclosed folders, which look like regular manila folders except that they're closed on the sides and are accordion-like to accommodate a healthy stack of papers. Get a wire rack with 8-10 slots. When you start a project, grab a folder, scratch out the last project name on the front of the folder, write the new name on it, and keep everything related to that job in the folder.

When the job is done and billed, chances are you now have this folder stuffed with papers. Unless you know for a fact that you'll be needing some of the source material again, dispose of it (recycle if possible). Be ruthless about this or paper *will* take over your office.

Organize Your Computer Set up your computer into a Main Directory for your business work (mine is WriteInc.) and sub-directories for each of your regular clients. You'll always know where to find any project you've done for XYZ Corp. If you pick up a new client that you suspect might be a one-shot deal, keep their project in another sub-directory called Misc. If they become steady, give them their own sub-directory. Create a second main directory for your *other* writing—the creative stuff that your dreams are made of. I call mine Soulfood.

Create "Leave-Behinds" To have something to leave with new clients or prospects, take a regular manila file folder (or better yet, a colored one to stand out) and on the tab, affix a printed label (in *Word*, go to *Tools*, then *Envelopes* *and Labels* and then *Labels*) with four lines: your name, "Freelance Copywriter" in big letters, your company name, and phone number.

Into the folder go a résumé/client list, three business cards, and appropriate samples. Now they have your stuff all in one place, in a folder that's ready for easy accommodation into their system. And you'll instantly impress them with your organizational skills.

HOW MUCH MARKETING IS ENOUGH FOR YOU?   I assert that in typical markets, if you follow the marketing steps I have laid out here—prospecting, regular (and simple) direct mail campaigns, the systems, networking, etc.—you will be plenty busy. The key to this system is to figure out just how much marketing is enough to keep you—one person—steadily working, and then do a little more.

By the way, if you're doing steady marketing, there will be times when things get too busy and you've got to turn down work. The best strategy here (and one I discuss in more detail in Chapter 13: "Dos, Don'ts and Don't Forgets") is to develop a referral network of fellow writers—people whose work you've seen and know to be good. You turn over work to them and they'll do the same when they're busy and you're slow. Everyone wins.

The "Right" Work   If you do choose this line of work, in the beginning, you'll be focused, as I was, on simply getting work—*any* work. As time goes on, and your income rises, you'll naturally gravitate towards projects which bring you joy and pleasure and away from those that make you grumpy and sour.

So once you've done enough of a certain kind of work to know you like it, you're good at it and have enough samples to prove it, create some direct mail pieces like we just discussed that position yourself as an expert in that niche and then research which companies are your best targets.

Bottom line, within a few years or less of beginning, you should absolutely be able to steer your career in the direction of your writing "fascinations," and in the process, turn your work into your bliss. The fact is, even on a bad day in this business, when I'm doing work I don't really enjoy, I wouldn't trade it for a good day in corporate America for anything.

CLIENT MEETINGS

Always Push for a Meeting   Remember the point I made earlier (about eight times), that while one in ten prospects who get your information will hire you, one in three who you meet will hire you. So, once you find someone who is interested, always press for a meeting.

Make it sound very non-threatening: "I'm going to be in your area a good bit this week (even if it's a stretch) and if it makes sense, I'd love to stop by for 10 minutes, meet you, find out what you're up to, where your needs lie and show you a few samples."

Let's say you get your meeting. Now what? For starters, set up a time as soon as possible. Find out if there is anything he'd like to see in advance, such as résumé and client list, to give him an idea of what you've been up to and with whom.

I may send out samples if he specifically asks, but don't offer it, because being able to present your samples in person will be much more effective and it'll save you a lot of extra work. Find out the kinds of projects for which he typically uses copywriters and file that away for the moment.

Gather Info Should you call the day before to remind your client of the meeting? That's what most business etiquette books might say—and usually what I'd recommend—because it establishes you as a professional.

Others say that calling prospects gives them an easy way to cancel. That is a good point, and it has happened to me. If you set the appointment just a few days in the future, you could probably get away without a call. If you made it a few weeks ago, your best bet is to leave a message after hours the night before. By the time they get it (on meeting day), it's usually too late to cancel. Sneaky, but effective.

Pre-Meeting Prep Before the meeting, find out anything you can about their firm: gather brochures, check their web site, talk to people in the industry, etc. The more you know about who they are, what they do, and where you might fit into their needs, the more professional an impression you'll make.

Not a lot of your competition will do this. It's an easy way to set yourself apart from the pack right from the get-go. Do I always do it? No. Have I done it plenty of times? Yes. Has it made a difference? Absolutely.

Before the meeting, look through your portfolio and pick out the five or six pieces that you'd like to show your prospect, based on the info you received from him about his typical copywriting needs.

Better to be targeted than show everything, which, in all likelihood, will tire you and bore him. Whether or not you've already sent him a résumé, put one together to bring with you. Chances are good there'll be someone else who could use it.

Speaking of that, in addition to your main prospect—usually the creative director, communications manager, director of development, or similar—it's very common *and* preferable to meet with several people at once. Graphic designers, account executives, and executive assistants are typical support people that are good to know—and good if they know *you*. In fact, if your prospect doesn't mention it, suggest that he try to assemble "the troops." He'll probably think it's a good idea and you've just made your outing that much more productive.

On meeting day, make sure to allow yourself an extra 10–15 minutes to get where you're going, if you're traveling outside rush hour and more like 20-30 minutes extra if you couldn't swing that. I'm assuming that you wouldn't deliberately schedule a meeting before about 10:00 a.m. or after about 2:30 p.m. unless you couldn't avoid it, or if you could actually walk to their office from your house.

Dress Safely As a rule, you can't go wrong by dressing up, whereas you could definitely goof by not. If you're meeting with a Fortune 500 company, professional dark suit and tie, guys, or dark suit, ladies, is always appropriate.

If it's a more creative setting, like a smaller ad agency or graphic design firm, then men can shift to slacks, sportcoat, and tie, and ladies, slacks, blouse, etc.

I can primarily speak for the Southeastern U.S.—Atlanta in particular— where it tends to be a little more casual, and even more so in the mean, beastly hot days of summer. In the south, the "Southern Uniform" for men always works for casual occasions (and some more formal ones as well): khakis, navy blazer, button down, rep tie, loafers. Having lived in the Northeast for years, I also know that that part of the country tends to be a little more starched.

When scheduling the appointment, go ahead and ask them what's appropriate. If it's UPS, IBM, MCI, Coca-Cola, don't even ask. If it's one of the smaller, artsier firms out there, they'll probably laugh at the suggestion of a suit and tie, along with the predictable mock threat of never hiring you if you *did* show up so attired. Of course, casual is becoming more and more the rule today even in some of the straightest-laced corporate settings out there.

In many places, Casual Day is now every day—a totally civilized concept— except those days when ... you're visiting prospects or clients! But don't assume that just because they're all in open shirts, you can be too. Let them razz you gently when you show up and let them tell you that *next* time, lose the tie or suit.

Two Business Cards for Everyone Bring plenty of business cards, keep them in a handy pocket or case, and get into the "2+ Card" habit of always giving each person at least two cards. Follow this rule with absolutely everyone you meet anywhere. Think about it. If the person only has one, she'll stick it in her desk drawer or card file and use it only when she needs it, which might be never.

Give her an extra or two and the next time anyone mentions copywriters, she's got a spare to pass on. This is especially important when meeting with prospects, because there's always a bunch of people who aren't in the meeting but who would definitely be in a position to need your services at some point.

Show 'n' Tell?   Once in the meeting, while you shouldn't turn it into a dog 'n' pony show, sometimes that's exactly what the client wants. Some writers feel that samples should be the last thing you show, that you need to walk in, asking, "How can I help you?" then get them talking and be there with the solution, i.e., you.

I wholeheartedly agree that the client ultimately wants to know how you can help make his life easier, but at the same time, he won't know whether he wants to even consider you in that role until he knows how good your work is.

The other approach makes more sense in a corporate setting, where you're meeting with someone more geared towards overall solutions. When dealing with creative folks, however, the portfolio is usually the first step. Always be alert to the moment when a prospect has had enough. It's easy to get on a roll and start giving the inside story on every piece in your book. In your mind, it's all so fascinating. Not so to a prospect.

Nice Looking, But … As discussed, there will be pieces in your book that look very nice, graphically, but which you really don't care to show because the copy ended up being edited into mediocrity.

If it's a big name company, there's something to be said for having them in your book (with logo prominent) and pointing it out without pulling it out. At least then the prospect gets to see the professional circles in which you're traveling. Just steer them away from looking at those and towards the ones you want them to see.

First Things First At the end of the meeting, get his business card along with a feel for the next step, upcoming projects, etc. If no work is immediately pending, find out how often to follow up.

THE first thing you do when you get home, before you pass Go, collect $200, or even go to the bathroom—OK, go do *that*—is sit down at your computer and bang out a quick thank-you note on a nice piece of letterhead, insert a business card and get it mailed that day. Or, better yet, send out a handwritten note.

Again, this is a simple way to distinguish yourself as a real pro *and* get your name in front of him yet again. Put a reminder in your *Day-Timer* to follow up on the agreed-upon date and do it.

Respond Quickly If you decide to run an ad as I did, you're going to get a few calls. As discussed previously, many of them will ultimately be a waste of your time (companies "updating their files" never to call you again in this life-time) but some will pan out. How quickly and thoroughly you respond to these calls can go a long way toward getting the business. I'll give you an example, one which is instructive regardless of whether they're coming to you or vice versa.

Often, the calls you'll get are from companies wanting a price quote on a particular job. Now, as we'll get into shortly, while you should always avoid "pricing-on-command," sometimes you can't get around it. The prospect has a list of writers he's calling, he needs answers right away, and if you don't have one, he'll find someone who does.

The Quadruple Whammy So imagine you're this executive whose company needs a writer. You call up one writer off an ad and you get a quote on a project, period. The writer (typically not exactly being a crack marketer) will likely just sit back and hope to receive a call back. The same prospect calls me. Note the four quick contacts.

He sees my ad (1) and needs a quote on a brochure. After I give it to him, I ask for his fax number and 10 minutes after we've spoken, he has a faxed or emailed client list and résumé (2) tailored to that project I've just quoted.

I call him the next day and ask if I can swing by and drop off some samples. He says "C'mon down!" I meet with him the next day, get my work into his hands (3). The "1 in 3 Rule" says I've just dramatically upped my chances of being hired. Even if he can't meet with me, at least I get to confirm his receipt of my client list and résumé and talk to him again.

If I've met with him, as soon as I get home, I send out a thank-you letter, reaffirming my skills for his needs. It's late afternoon, so I carry it to the post office, making sure it gets in the last pick-up of the day, and he has it two days later (4). I've shown up four times in four ways over the course of about four days, and because of all the information with which I've provided him, I've made it very easy for him to hire me confidently.

Provided my quote is competitive (and such professional follow-up on my part could keep me strongly in the running even with a higher quote), if you were him, who would you hire? Separate yourself from the pack. It's just not that difficult.

PHONE INTERVIEWS   OK, let's switch gears here and talk about phone interviewing, which roughly fits into the "Systems" discussion.

In the course of your career, you will undoubtedly be called upon to do phone interviews. It's something you should get good at and offer as a service, because it's one more way you can make your clients' lives easier, boost your value to them and make more money.

One of the most common reasons you'd conduct phone interviews would be to gather customer testimonials, very powerful sales tools. A line or two from a customer can sell more of a company's products than all the eloquent copy and fancy graphics on 10 slick brochures.

Easier If You Do It   If you've suggested to your client to include testimonials in the piece, follow that right up with an offer to conduct them yourself. There are at least three good reasons why. First, it's one less thing for her to worry about. And the less she has to do, the more pleasant the experience is of working with you, and the more likely she is to hire you again.

Secondly, and interestingly, it always seems to be easier for an outside party (i.e., you) to get good, positive feedback from a customer than it is for someone from the company.

It's just one of those paradoxical psychological phenomena—akin to why it's easier to bare your soul to a total stranger than it is to someone very close to you. People are just more likely to open up to someone not attached to the company. Sometimes customers don't want to gush to their business providers for fear that they might get a swelled head and become complacent. The third reason? It's that much more billable time and time equals money.

Understand Their Concerns   Now, FYI, it's not a given that a client will agree to let you do the interviews just because it makes sense. Rest assured, the main thing running through a client's mind is "Will this person handle himself professionally with my customers so that it reflects positively back on us?" After all, they'll obviously be picking their best and happiest customers, those who will undoubtedly give them high marks, and the last thing they need is for some-body to screw up any of that goodwill.

If you've made a positive, professional, poised impression up till now, and more importantly, can show them some pieces where you've done phone inter-views in the past, they'll probably agree to it.

The next step is to have her contact her clients and ask them if they wouldn't mind providing a testimonial for their new marketing material and if so, Joe Blow, an outside writer who's working with her company on the project, will be in contact with them shortly to get a few comments.

Stay on Top of Things OK, your turn. If you get the client's voice mail when you call, leave a low-key, professional, well-modulated message as to your intent: "Hello, Mr. Smith, this is Joe Blow, the writer who's working with ABC Company on their new marketing brochure. I'm sure John Doe from ABC has already contacted you to let you know that I'd be in touch with you to get a few comments about how you like dealing with ABC. My phone number is 555-6543 and I look forward to speaking with you soon."

On the off chance that John Doe never called his client or didn't get through, Mr. Smith knows who to check with first before calling you back. Give Mr. Smith a day or two at most to call you back, then call him again.

Count on having to re-call people who got your message but just hadn't got-ten around to returning it. Usually, they're glad you've called because now it'll get done and off their plate. You're the one who's on deadline. Take the respon-sibility for making it happen by being "intentional," but not pushy.

Better Yet…Set Appointments If you just have a few folks to get ahold of, and just for a comment or two, then tracking them down in the way we just discussed is probably your best bet. If however, you've got to reach a larger number of people for longer interviews, I *highly* recommend setting phone appointments. Ideally, have your client nail her clients down to a schedule.

I'm working on a project right now—a 12-page newsletter for a major telecommunications giant—which involves nine one-hour interviews with a bunch of senior executives. My client in the organization is setting up all these appointments for me, so I know that on Tuesday, October 27 at 10:00 a.m. I'll be talking to Harry Schmoe.

Sure, even with such planning, you're going to have people cancel on you and then reschedule, but it's still light years ahead of the alternative—track-ing them down haphazardly. I've done it that way and if you've got a lot of people to reach, it'll make you crazy. You end up chained to your desk for days, which for us free spirits, is just about the worst torture we can imagine.

When you call them, you get their voice mail. If you step out, Murphy's Law clearly states that they'll call back while you're gone, even if it's just for two minutes. Then you start all over again. You end up afraid to even leave the house or office. Or they'll return your call at 7:25 in the morning, the sneaky way to drop the ball back in your court, and it starts again. A huge time waster.

Do Your Advance Work Take it a step further and do what I do for these interviews. Come up with your questions in advance of your call, have them approved by your contact person, and have her get them into the hands of your interviewees prior to your phone meeting. A few people have actually filled them out before the interview, but at the very least, they're thinking about them and the process will go that much smoother.

In addition to the questions, seriously consider attaching a cover letter to the questions, such as the one below. The letter is "from" your contact person to her colleague interviewees, giving them a sense of what to expect, how the process will go, and reminding them of the importance of the project, so they're less likely to treat you and the slot of time as expendable.

Have your contact e-mail them the letter and questions. Adjust yours to the specific situation, especially the first paragraph.

Dear Interviewee,

The Benchmark newsletter and the accompanying web site are the main conduits of information to the field about the new ABC Corp. strategic direction and its implementation. Through your interview input, you have the opportunity to make a significant contribution to overall employee understanding and buy-in of the coming changes.

Please give these scheduled interviews the same consideration and attention you would extend to any high-level meeting. Please take a moment to review the Interview Guidelines below. We thank you in advance for your time and cooperation!

Interview Guidelines

- In the interest of expediting the interview process, please review the question list below and given the unique profile of your team (division, region, district, etc.) feel free to add additional questions and answers that would enhance the audience's understanding of your message and mission.
- Interviews will take no longer than one hour, but please allow the full hour.

- Because this issue of Benchmark will provide an "overview" sense of the new initiative, and given the limited amount of space per team in the issue (approximately one page, including any charts and graphs), please gear your answers towards generating a "topline" sense for your mission.
- Within seven days of the interview, you will be provided with a completed first draft for approval. Please return the draft with revisions within 24 hours.
- Due to the extremely tight timeframes for publication, please address your revisions to factual inaccuracies and/or key omissions, as opposed to style issues.
- If you have any questions or concerns about the interview process, please contact Mary Jones at 404/678-2345.

The Interview Process When you finally connect with Mr. Smith, start out by telling him you'll only need about five minutes of his time, which should do it in the case of a testimonial, more for larger projects. Setting the time parameters at the outset will relax him. Ask him if you can put him on speakerphone (if you don't have a headset—you do have one or the other, right?) so you can type while you talk.

Don't get too buddy-buddy with these folks. Walk a fine line between friendliness and straight professionalism. This is no place for your incandescent personality. Come across too strong and you can suppress their eloquent inclinations. You need to essentially disappear from the process except for playing a role as a facilitator of their thoughts.

Reliable Backup Have a tape recorder or your microcassette recorder (with a numerical counter—*very* important) handy and cued up next to the phone's speaker. You just type away, confident that you've got the tape in case you miss something.

Explain to the customer how the process will work: "Since most people don't speak in perfect sound bites, Mr. Smith, simply answer these questions as best you can and don't worry about it being perfect. I'll put a quote together from all your comments. Then I'll call you up, and run it past you (or fax or e-mail it, if it's more than a line or two) and make sure you're comfortable putting your name to it, OK?"

Once he's answered your questions and you feel you've got enough to use on the tape, let him go. You've got the tape if necessary to refer to in order to finish the job. If he says something key that you don't completely catch as he's speaking, type the counter number in your notes so you know where to go back to find it.

Typical "Testimonial" Questions to Ask:
What do you like about dealing with ABC Company?
Why do you do business with them and not the competition?
Any stories come to mind of "service-above-and-beyond"?

After you hang up, put your quotes together and run it by him for his approval. Discuss with the graphic designer on the project in advance how much space is going to be allotted to testimonials, and how many they want (I suggest three to four). On that basis, figure out together how long they should be. Quotes can vary in length but should fall somewhere in the range of the following:

Example Testimonials
"With ABC, I can place an order and not worry about it. Great follow-up and great follow-through. I don't have time to babysit orders and with ABC, I never have to."

"GHI makes it their business to understand our company culture and they're very good at being able to tell whether someone will fit into that culture. Their judgment in this regard is more refined than competitors of theirs with whom I've worked. In three years, GHI has never brought me a candidate who I felt was a waste of time, and that, to me, is the single most important benefit of working with them."

"XYZ places a lot of emphasis on the personal relationship with me, and works hard to grasp my needs. They understand my business, are good at quantifying what I need, and what systems would be the best fit for my situations. They've been very successful in anticipating my growth and recommending the right solutions to keep me running at maximum production and make best use of my resources. Results are everything. And ever since we've started using XYZ, we've consistently surpassed our previous numbers. XYZ helps me be successful in what I do."

Longer Phone Interviews Of course, most phone interviews won't be five minutes. If you're doing a trade article for a company, you might need to interview four or more different people. Some of them may be providing a good chunk of input to your piece, in the form of source material about the company—processes, procedures, products—or they may simply be providing a few quotes.

Do your homework in advance. Have a game plan for getting everything you need. Make up the list of questions on your computer screen. Again, figure out how long you'll need and let your interviewee know up front. Use your tape recorder to keep within the alloted time and to capture everything she says.

Good Questioning Skills Getting good at phone interviewing is a combination of preparation and flexibility. Use your questions to stay on track. If you get a cold fish—someone who's hard to draw out into conversation—it's usually not going to work to just ask your questions, take what he says, and be done with it. You won't end up with much.

With tough nuts like these, keep encouraging them with "that's great … just what I'm looking for..." while at the same time probing for more with things like, "Say more about that … that's interesting, can you elaborate?..." Make them feel like they're really delivering the goods and believe me, there are few people who won't really open up and give you everything you need.

People like to know you're with them, you're listening, that you care about what they say. Remember, you represent the company you're working for and that's important whether your interviewee is a customer or an employee of that company. Make them feel special, whoever they are, and you'll get good strong material.

Stay Loose, Get Lucky Don't be rigid. Use your question list as a guide, not the end-all-be-all. Don't be too sure what someone is going to say or even what you need. Have an idea, but be open to interesting developments along the way. The more open you are, the better, richer, and more interesting your copy will turn out to be.

For Good Measure One last tip: At the end of phone interviews (and in-person ones for that matter) with your key information source, ask him what three things he's going to want to see front and center in the finished piece. It's your last opportunity to take his pulse, make sure you're both on the same page and that there'll be no surprises. It may seem academic after spending say, 45 minutes on the phone with him, but I promise you, he won't react that way.

He'll be glad that you're taking the time to make sure he's gotten his points across. Think of it as nearly surefire insurance against "missing the mark."

OK, now that we're brilliantly systematized in every way, let's switch gears and talk about a favorite subject—money! As in how much to charge for the work we'll be doing and everything related to that pleasant topic—information you can take to the bank....

Chapter Nine

How Much Do I Charge?

AH, THE AGE-OLD QUESTION ... In the beginning of your career, within reason, you need to take virtually any fee you can get in order to build your business and reputation. I look back and have to smile at what I settled for at the outset, but that's just reality. Those with too much pride or too big an ego might just starve.

About three months into my career, I was hired to write a seven-minute video script. A project like that should've commanded about $700–800+ (not to mention a rush fee of another $100 or more, since they wanted it back in about 36 hours). I did it for $300.

Did I feel like I should've been paid more? Absolutely. Was I glad to have the work? You bet. Since I turned it around in 24 hours, I made $300 for a day's work. On most days, I'd make that trade. So what that I made about $20/hour instead of my $50/hour rate at the time? I did good work, impressed the heck out of the client, and picked up a bunch more work from him—at more fitting rates. And given that they did a beautiful job of producing the video, I now had a great sample to show.

Keep Your Pride Level Low When starting out, it's best to keep your SRT (Self-Respect Threshold) pretty high. There'll be plenty of opportunities down the road to get righteously indignant at clients who don't have a clue what good copywriting costs… when your phone is ringing off the hook and you're backed up with work for the next four months.

In the beginning, think of it as paid on-the-job-training. Learning new skills often involves *paying* for training. In this business, however, you'll actually get paid to learn new types of work, and payment will increase as time goes on and those skills grow. Approach this business from that angle and you'll have more enjoyment, less anxiety, and lower blood pressure.

YOUR HOURLY RATE   While you'll ultimately be pricing most of your work by the job—i.e., a flat rate—(few clients will give you a blank check), the first step is to determine your hourly rate. For creative writing such as marketing work, ad copy, descriptive collateral, the range is about $50–$125/hour. Rates for technical writing run generally lower than other copywriting: $35–60/hr.

I started at $50/hour. You won't make anyone flinch—except yourself—with a $50/hour rate unless it's someone who's never hired a writer before. While there are a lot of those out there, just because it may seem high to them doesn't make it so. $50/hr. is actually going to sound too low to seasoned copywriting-buyers, to the point where they may wonder how good you really are.

Give Yourself a Raise   So, start out at at least $50/hour if you plan to be in the more creative writing arena. The size of your market and the amount of competition may allow you to command more, or in some cases, less, but this is where talking to others in your field can give you a good idea.

After you've been at it awhile, you'll know when it's time to bump your rate up. If you're getting absolutely no resistance to your rate, and your portfolio is growing along with your reputation, give yourself a $10–15/hour raise.

Again, chances are good that the only person who will balk at your higher rates will be you. Call it "self-imposed sticker shock." Especially with new clients who don't have any idea of your rates, as long as you're competitive in your mar- ket *and* they're familiar with buying copywriting (certainly not a given), they shouldn't flinch.

You, on the other hand, may develop a stuttering problem as you deliver the new price: "My rate? Se-se-se-seventy five an hour. Yeah. That's right. You gotta problem with that?" Very smooth. Practice saying it a few times in front of a mirror. I'm totally serious.

Resistance From Your "Regulars"   It's always a little trickier with existing clients, who get used to things being a certain way. If you're doing really good work for a client and they know it, they might grumble a little bit and issue all sorts of grand mock threats, but it shouldn't be too much of a problem. Usually.

Some time back, I went to one of my regular clients for whom I'd been working (and doing great work) for about two years and asked him if he had a problem with me raising my hourly to $75, and he looked at me with a *very* concerned and firm expression on his face and said, "Yes, as a matter of fact, I'd have a very big problem with that." So, I kept them at $65.

I've got colleagues who might say, "You don't really know what a client would do until you do raise your rates. He could be bluffing and if you're that valuable to him, he probably is, as any halfway decent negotiator would." Maybe so.

In the end, however, I did finally get to raise them—to $85! It wasn't easy but the key was that I was ready to walk. As the old expression reminds us, "He who cares least wins."

Don't Miss Out on Money What you'll agree to on a project will often depend on your workload. If things are quiet, and someone's offering you $400 for a brochure you figure will take you 10 hours, $40/hour beats flipping burgers or waiting tables, though it might be time to start prospecting for higher paying work.

Now, if you've got a lot on your plate and more waiting in the wings—a writer's dream—*then* you can politely decline their offer and go back to that full plate.

Speaking of hourly rates, before you get all jazzed up and whip out your calculator, multiplying $50/hour x 40 hours, it doesn't quite work that way. If you're billing half that—20 hours or so—you're doing well and chances are, you'd be happy with it, at least for the first year or so. In a few years time or sooner, depending on your market (and your level of ambition), when you're at $75–85/hour—billing 20 hours starts looking awfully good.

Consider this: If you can bill about 20 hours a week, then your hourly rate times 1000 is your approximate annual income (20 hours x 50 weeks). $50/hr. = $50K. $60/hr. = $60K. When the time is right, don't let your own hesitance in bumping yourself up a mere $10 an hour take ten thousand dollars out of your pocket.

Big Jobs? Give 'Em a Break Now and then, big jobs come along where you're billing at $65-75+/hour for say, 30–40 hours a week for 4–5 weeks running. We love those. They're more typical in the technical writing arena, where you're working on huge documentation manuals for months on end (and at lower rates), but certainly not unheard-of in the more creative circles. Huge web sites, CD-ROM projects, major multi-piece marketing campaigns and major event speaker support are all examples of long-term projects.

On large jobs, it's not at all uncommon for a client to request a break in your rate. Don't consider that some kind of a slight. If I have a 100+ hour job on the line and I'm at $85 an hour, and the client asks for $75 an hour, I'll probably give it to him. Still not too shabby for less than three weeks work. To work with people, you've gotta work with people.

THE FLAT FEE   As mentioned, the hourly rate comes into play mainly as a number to share with the client, and as a basis for calculating a flat fee for a project. A flat fee, incidentally, is how you'll price about 95% of your work, especially in the beginning.

The only time a client will give you *carte blanche* and let you bill by the hour on a project is when they've worked with you plenty of times before on an hourly basis, and it's always worked out fine, *or* if it's a project that's impossible to estimate because no one knows how big it could end up being.

Consequently, it will only be on very few projects that you'll be able to charge by the hour—usually a big Fortune 500 company with large budgets. As you progress through your career, build up your client loyalty and trust and get into those Fortune 500 doors, you'll find your hourly rate jobs are increasing, as mine have. Smaller clients will naturally be more budget-conscious and will definitely want flat rate pricing, but the smaller jobs are also easier to estimate.

"Bonus" Bucks   Let me clarify one thing here. Let's take a typical scenario: You quote a flat fee for a brochure project of $900 (12 hours @ $75/hr.) Or alternately, you've been given a $900 budget for the project, arrived at similarly. In either case, you have set a mutually agreed-upon figure for the job.

Now, let's say the job only takes you nine hours. No, Virginia, it's not necessary or standard to only charge them $675 now (nine hours @ $75/hr). Once you agree on a price, even though you undoubtedly used your hourly rate to calculate the flat fee, the hourly component disappears and the flat fee takes precedence. Conversely, of course, if that 12-hour job ends up taking 15, you eat three hours.

The only time when you really should bill them for $675 is if the arrangement was to quote by the hour, and you only used nine hours, even if you told them you thought it might take you about 12. That's different from a flat fee based on 12 hours.

If You're Fast, Go Flat A flat rate is the best strategy when you know you work fast. If your hourly rate is $65 and you realize that the fair market price for a small trifold brochure is $750 (don't take this figure to the bank as it depends on your market) and you know you can knock the piece out in 7–8 hours, when it might take someone else 12, then clearly you're better off with a $750 flat rate, and effectively bumping up your hourly rate to $100.

A few years back, I remember doing a quick ad for a solo graphic designer. The ad was very similar to several others she and I had previously done for the same client. It needed to include almost the same information as the others with only headline and subhead changes.

The fee I'd gotten for the other ads with this client was $325 (5 hours x $65), and had become standard. So even though this ad probably took me two hours to do, I got paid for five. Good deal. Once you develop long-term working relationships with your clients, this type of thing will happen more and more.

Pick The Brains of an Expert If the client insists on a flat rate for a type of project with which you've had limited experience, it may be tough to estimate the job. At times like these, find a friendly and more seasoned writing colleague whose brains you can periodically pick about these and other issues.

I came across just such a 'simpatico' guy early on, and rang him up every three or four months, mostly about estimating rates. I promise you, most fellows writers won't mind at all, and will probably be flattered. He's now a valued member of my writers group.

HOW ARE FEES DETERMINED? So how do you and your client arrive at a mutually agreeable figure for the job? Well, for starters, I strongly recommend that regardless of how experienced you are—but especially if you're a beginner—that you never get roped into estimating "on-command."

Always gather the necessary information regarding the parameters of the project, then go away and get back to them later when you've had a chance to consider it all.

That said, the most common way fees are determined is for the client to simply ask you what you would charge for such a job. Not surprisingly, this is most common with clients that haven't purchased much or any copywriting ... or the smart ones who have. The first group just doesn't know—they need to follow your lead.

So you give them a figure, *after*, of course, you've had a chance to review what it is you'll be doing and think it over. The second group of clients—the smart ones—know what it should cost but want you to talk first in case you give them a figure lower than they were willing to pay.

The second manner of determining fees, more common with experienced buyers of copywriting, is the client simply telling you what their budget is for a job. Find out specifically what's expected from you for that fee, then go away and put the numbers together. If it sounds about right or something you'd be happy with, go for it.

If after you've thought it over, you feel that their estimate is a good bit lower than what it's going to take, politely say, "With all due respect, that seems a little low. Typically, a job like this will take between __ and __ hours, which at my hourly rate of __ , means closer to range of __ to __."

If they're inexperienced or were just trying to see how low they can get you (and trust me, they will try), they may simply say OK and you move on to the next point. If they respond with an ultimatum of sorts, like "Well, that's all we have for this job," then you need to make a decision.

Is their figure acceptable? If not, decline and walk. Who knows, they might surprise you with a counteroffer. But walk away because you truly aren't willing to do it for that amount, not because you're trying to keep the game going. If you can live with their number, then it becomes doubly important that you make sure both sides understand what the project will specifically involve and stick to it.

With a BIG Grain of Salt One more note about estimates. I met with a client a few weeks back for a new project. Up till now, his staff had been writing web site copy in-house for the company's clients, but didn't have the time anymore, so decided to outsource it (an increasingly common scenario these days, by the way). At the first meeting, I was told that, based on their experience writing a similar-sized project as the one we were discussing, it should take about 30 hours.

Hmmmm. Gotta be careful in situations like these, because your ego is involved. After all, as a "professional writer," it certainly shouldn't take me even the same amount of time, much less more than it took an "amateur." But how did they arrive at that figure? Are they factoring in time for meetings, concepting, travel, and other intangibles? Are they experienced enough to be able to competently estimate? Might they be lowballing you to keep their costs down, thinking a pro would balk at estimating higher than them?

Regardless of how sinister or not you interpret their motives, the best advice is to use their "estimate" as simply a mildly interesting but not terribly relevant piece of information. Rely on your own tried and true estimating guidelines, avoid getting sidetracked by their input, and keep your ego out of it. More to the point, as a colleague (who was also brought into this deal) so accurately put it, what's ultimately most important is that the professional writer do a better job, not necessarily a faster one.

You Go First … No, You Go First Clearly, the ideal situation is for the client to speak first, because it gives you the most room to move. I'll always shoot for that position by asking, "Do you have an idea of what you'd like to keep this to, money-wise?" In response, they might just give you a number, or say something akin to, "Well, the last time we did a similar project, we paid the writer $___." Again, use your own guidelines. If it's too low, respond as above.

If after you've gone away and crunched the numbers, their figure is actually higher than you figured it would take, then go back and in your best cautious voice (hey, they'll play games with you, so don't be afraid to return the favor) say, "Your number should probably be OK." If that should seem too insincere, consider this: If you answer too fast and too positively, "Sure, that sounds great!" he'll be thinking, "Darn, we could've gotten him for less." And that can set up all sorts of little unconscious resentments and raised expectations on his part, and make him more difficult to deal with.

Of course, asking them what they had in mind could get a response like, "Tell us what you think it'll take." Then you're back to the original scenario. If forced to quote on the spot, shoot high. You can always come down. Whether you like it or not, it's a game. The better you get at playing it, the more money you can make.

The point is this: you can go into the game just assuming people are going to be honest because you're willing to be and you hate the idea of playing games. Yet, the fact remains that, as businesspeople focused on their bottom line, your prospects will be trying to get the most for the least and many, not all, will bluff their way to the best possible outcome. Be prepared to meet them there.

Always Include Meeting Time When arriving at an estimate, always find out how many meetings the client expects and how long they'll be. Usually, there's one at the beginning, and barring a dramatic change in creative direction, anything else they need to discuss or get into your hands can be done by phone, fax, e-mail, etc.

If they ask for a flat rate for a particular job, make it clear that the figure you're quoting includes X amount of meeting time. They can have 29 meetings for all you care, as long as you know it and can figure an extra, say, 58 hours into your bid. If they say, "One should do it," there you have it, straight from the horse's mouth. Reply, "OK, then I'll factor that into my bid."—and put it in writing (See "Bid Letter" on page 135–6). Should they want another one, politely inform them that you'll have to bill them at your hourly rate for that.

Also mentally figure on a certain amount of phone time to review edits and generally discuss the project. It's hard to figure all of that but you'll learn by doing. Remember the "paid training" thing.

VIDEO IS DIFFERENT   While you base your fees for most work on an hourly rate, as a rule, you'll quote a fee for video scripts based on a "per finished minute" (pfm) rate, which can range anywhere from $80–$200. If you're new and untried, and the project's pretty simple, you'll be at the low end of that range, although I again want to emphasize the importance of taking whatever comes your way—within reason—when starting out.

I generally charge $125–$150 pfm. I'll be near the lower end for simpler, more straightforward "talking head" type training videos, while if the client is looking for more creativity and a fresh approach to their subject matter, it'll cost him more to get that.

It's Still Time   When pricing video, even though it's pfm, it's still your time we're talking about. To calculate your final fee, use your hourly rate and figure out how many hours you think it'll take to do the script.

THE "LOW FIGURE" LAW OF NATURE   Why avoid pricing a job on the spot? It has to do with the following immutable law of nature, which you'd better learn quickly. Let's say you've quoted the prospective client a fee range of about $500–700 prior to seeing the project (Mistake #1), but you felt you really couldn't avoid it, because he insisted on getting a feel for the bottom line.

Now, no matter how much you qualify that range by saying things like, "Now this is a rough quote … it could change once I see what's involved … please don't take this to the bank, etc., etc." (and of course he'll agree, "Oh sure, I understand; just trying to get a ballpark idea)" *he will only remember the figure at the low end of the quoted range,* and *will* etch *that* figure in concrete in his mind henceforth and forever.

Avoid Premature Estimation   Should you come back after seeing the project and say, "Well, it looks like it's going to be closer to about $750," his reply *will* be some variation of, "Gee, I thought you said you could do it for $500 …" And you'll curse and gnash your teeth—inside of course—swearing you'll never again be roped into premature bidding. And, of course, you will.

OK, so not everyone will do that to you. But until you know that a client has a firmly entrenched sense of fairness as part of his chromosomal make-up, assume he's a "typical client."

If he insists on getting an idea of fees, calculate a best guess of what the project will run and simply add about 25% or more to it. If it turns out that your unspoken mental guesstimate was on track, he'll be delighted when it comes in lower than what you told him.

NO WHINERS ALLOWED   Whatever you decide your fee will be on a particular job—and make sure you do your homework and calculations—make the decision that you'll be happy with that amount, even if you spend more time on it than you originally planned. This is the responsible, professional approach.

You don't do yourself or the client any favors by agreeing to a figure that's too low. Sure, you may get the business, but as soon as it starts getting a little sticky or more complicated than you pictured, (a lesser-known corollary of Murphy's Law states: The likelihood that a writing job will turn into a nightmare is inversely proportional to the amount of the fee), you'll start getting resentful and it'll show in your work. If it's that job you took for less because business was slow, tough. Suck it up and be a pro.

When it gets bad, just remember the OJT (on-the-job-training) thing we discussed before. The client doesn't give a rat's heinie that you miscalculated. All she cares about is that the job gets done well for the amount of money that you two agreed upon. Period.

Direction Changes = Fee Changes   Now, what I'm *not* talking about here is when the client changes direction from something already agreed on OR when she adds another component to the project that wasn't part of the original proposal and fee.

Say you're writing a brochure for the ABC Company. You decide on some directions for the piece along with a concept that the client likes. She gives the go-ahead and you get to work.

You write all this beautiful copy for the agreed-upon creative direction. Then, out of left field, she says, you know, we decided that we want to scrap that concept and do *this* one instead. "Sure. No problem, Ms. ABC. Let's sit back down and recalculate the fee."

If you've spent 4, 6, or 8 hours working on the concept that is now history, add that much more time to the original bid. This is non-negotiable. And frankly, anyone with even an iota of fairness and common sense will understand that.

In the second case, let's say you've given a bid for a project that includes brochure copy, a few testimonials that you'll gather by phone, and a small ad for a trade publication. Halfway through the project, the client comes to you and says, "I wonder if you could just include a few versions of a sales letter with that other stuff."

Your response? "Sure, Mr. ABC, my fee for a sales letter is $250 (or whatever it is) and provided the two versions are similar, I'll charge you $350 for both." OK, that's one possible response. Point is, it's completely unfair for any client to add more work to the original proposed project and expect you to do it for free.

Your Call What you ultimately decide to do is up to you. The $350 response is totally legitimate. If the client pays you generously and hires you regularly, you might want to be flexible. Maybe you do it for a dramatically reduced rate, or maybe you do it for nothing.

Should you choose one of these two options, make sure the client *knows* you're cutting him or her a break. The danger in *not* making that clear, is that you train clients to think that this is some standard, acceptable practice, which it most certainly is not.

Frankly, most clients know this and will rarely spring it on you. When it does happen, more often than not it's usually an inexperienced client who doesn't know how the process works. I'm being charitable here, since truthfully, everyone, regardless of whether they've hired copywriters before or not, should know how life works.

Eating Hours: "Food" for Thought That brings up an interesting point. I just finished working on a large Intranet development project. While I billed the client for 60 hours, the actual number of hours worked was probably closer to about 70. So, why didn't I charge for them?

This was my first project for this company, which was hired by a large telecommunications firm to do the work. At the outset, I estimated about 60 hours, even though it was understood that on a complex, longer-term project like this, it's always difficult to nail it exactly. Once I knew I was going over my original estimate, I had every right to go back to the client and say, "Well, it looks like it's going to be ten more hours." No one could fault me. But I decided not to. As the project got to the halfway point, my immediate client was getting pressure to cut their budgets so everyone was getting squeezed. Of course, I did let my client know I went over by ten hours but that I wasn't charging him for them.

By sticking to my estimate, doing a thorough, professional job (and charming the end client …) and not whining about hours, I left my immediate client with the impression of someone who is reliable, competent, and a pleasure to work with. Think he'll hire me again? You bet. And those "lost" hours will return many times over.

Revisions Are NOT All Included Into every estimate you give to a client, you need to mentally factor in time for revisions, and note on your estimate the number of revisions you've included. Consider how long revisions may take and add that number of hours to your flat fee quote. Count on 10–15% of what it took you to get that first draft done.

Don't think for a minute that if you say "Revisions are included in the price" without specifying how many (I'm assuming you wouldn't be so insane as to actually use that exact verbiage on paper or in conversation with a client), that clients *won't* just keep editing ad nauseum, soliciting the opinions of everyone from their vice-presidents down to the janitor along the way. They will. They have.

Some colleagues of mine suggest a specific line item on your flat fee estimate, with the exact number of hours dedicated to revisions. That's fine, except what happens if the copy is really good on the first draft, with only minor tweaking necessary, that perhaps the client can do himself?

You risk his coming back to you and saying, "Well, since you didn't have to spend any time on revisions, I'd like you to deduct those ___ hours from your bill," which essentially penalizes you for doing a good job. It may not happen, but arguably, you open yourself up when you get specific on the hours.

Some of my colleagues include one round of revisions, others two. I include two. Why risk having to bill your client for a few more hours on top of what he's already paying? In my mind, it doesn't leave a good taste. I've rarely gone beyond two revisions and if I did, it was usually because the client changed direction, in which case, we added more hours to the fee.

Make sure both sides understand what's meant by a "round" of revisions. If the copy is off from what he wanted or you missed something he said, then getting it right is included in the "round." If they're changing directions, then that's a different thing.

Occasionally, the client has wanted revisions beyond the two rounds and if it was only one or even two and they were very minor, I usually went ahead and included it. But that was a judgment call, as opposed to "how it's done."

If you've made it clear in writing that only two revisions are included and they want more, you have every right to request more money to do another round. Play it by ear. If you think it'll be minor, you may just go ahead and include it. If the client starts getting out of hand, gently remind him or her that only two revisions were included and if there are any more, you're back on the clock.

The "Endless Edit" There's a funny phenomenon about revisions which I came to realize early on in my career: When you stop and think about it, because there's no such thing as "perfect" copy (i.e., the "right" answer) one could technically revise forever, because each time you or a client looks at what's been written, there is undoubtedly some way it could be changed. Not necessarily improved. Changed. And changed again. And again. And again.

When you're preparing a first draft, put a limit on your own re-working of a piece or else you literally could go on interminably. It's like a sickness. Once you start, you end up obsessed, searching for the elusive perfect line or paragraph. Trust me, it doesn't exist. If it's good, leave it alone and move on. Generally speaking, the more I edit something, the less positive the outcome.

Of course, the same sickness afflicts clients, and unless you've set limits, they'll run you ragged with their new vision *this* hour. At least when you're doing it, you're only taking your own time. When the client does it and there are no limits, you're in trouble.

To keep revisions to a minimum, pay close attention at your initial client meeting. Sure, once or twice, I must have fallen asleep during that first meeting, judging by how far off the mark my first draft was, but that's extremely rare. As discussed in Chapter Three, pay close attention to what the client says and you'll probably nail it the first time, 90–95% of the time, about my batting average.

Lower Rates for Meeting/Research Time? The industry standard is to charge the same for research, background reading, or meeting time as for writing, and the overwhelming percentage of experienced clients know that. The ones who try to get you to reduce your rates either aren't experienced or are hoping you're not. That said, there just aren't many iron-clad rules about this business, especially in the beginning.

Certainly don't offer it, but if they ask (and believe me, it's rare they will), listen to how it's asked and respond accordingly. If a client asks it almost laughing, like he knows he has little chance of pushing it through, respond very matter-of-factly that you do get full rate for those times, and that little discussion should slink quietly away.

If he's a little more adamant about it, i.e., "I'd like to get a reduced rate for meeting and research time," then deal with it. I won't lie to you; it's not always easy to stand firm in the face of a direct challenge, especially when your money's on the line and you're trying to make a good impression.

By the same token, if you exude professionalism, and hence worthiness of your full rate at all times, clients will appreciate and reward that—the smart ones, anyway. While in some meetings, all you're doing is jotting down notes and saying "Unh-huh" a lot, don't let anyone convince you that that's less important than writing time.

Why You Shouldn't ... In fact, here's what you say to a client who's pushing for a reduced rate to explain (nicely) why you won't: When I sit in a meeting, even one where I'm not offering non-stop suggestions, I'm still deliberating, processing, and my mind is working. In fact, it's actually some of the most focused thinking I'll do on the project.

Lots of initial impressions are forming, ideas are sprouting, concept directions are popping, and all this is crucial. Don't think for a moment that I'm laying some clever BS on you here. It's the absolute truth. In many meetings, of course, you *will* be offering plenty of suggestions and input, and otherwise being extremely valuable. In those cases, there's not a reason in the world you should be paid less than your full rate.

Same goes for research time, which usually means reading the material they've given you and getting the "lay of the land." Again, it's inevitable that while I'm reading, I'm thinking, coming up with ideas and creatively percolating. That's worth your full rate.

If my clients could only see me when I'm in concepting mode, doodling in the dust on my desktop, making those funny drum-like noises on my cheek, or humming "I Can See Clearly Now" in hopeful anticipation of wildly creative visions, *that's* where they'd probably want a discount. However, as we'll discuss, those personal little M.O.'s are crucial to the creative process.

A marketing communications manager for an Atlanta-based technology firm graciously offered these tips when it comes to estimating one's hours: "Writers need to be very clear with clients that writing short copy can actually be harder and take longer than writing long copy. They also need to explain that reading corporate literature and research is on the clock." Thank you.

In other words, if someone is handing you a stack of stuff to read along with an hour-long interview with an article source, and expecting a one-page article, not only is research time billed at your full rate but writing one page might very well take longer than writing two or three. Make your life easier by asking enough questions of the client to get a solid sense of what they want to see in that one page.

Travel Time? Should you charge for your travel time to and from a meeting? Generally speaking, the answer is yes. I say generally speaking, because if I've got a steady client who hires me regularly, I'll probably cut him a break and charge only part or perhaps none of it. For example, a 1.5 hour meeting and 30 minutes of travel time each way might end up being a total of two hours. Your call.

The BEST Fee Info For a current and comprehensive fee schedule for all manner of writing projects, including commercial, pick up the latest copy of *Writer's Market*. You can't do a whole lot better than this.

DO WE NEED WRITTEN CONTRACTS? OK, you've figured out what you're going to charge for a particular job. So how do you deliver this bid? Call your client on the phone? Write a letter and fax or mail it off? Craft a multi-page contract, spelling out every possible contingency?

Well, yes. As in, all of the above may be appropriate for different situations. I know some of my "by-the-book" colleagues might take issue with me here, but I just don't believe in creating formal documents for every deal.

As mentioned, the situations in which it makes the most sense to create a formal contract are when you're dealing with a new client or if the job is fairly large, complicated, and multi-faceted. But for your average everyday, repeat customers with whom you've been working for awhile, I say it's not only unnecessary to use contracts but might very well be both irritating and insulting to them.

If you have a good working relationship, and you've always been paid, then why bother? Frankly, in six+ years, I've created less than a half dozen contracts of any kind, and I've only had one—that's one, folks—situation where I got burned on a deal and arguably, a contract might not have even helped.

The bigger and more established the company is (i.e., UPS, Holiday Inn, Coca-Cola, American Express, MCI, etc.) the less you really have to worry about it. They've got the money, they didn't get to where they got by hosing their vendors, so you're safe.

In all likelihood, the worst problem you'll have with the big boys (and it's not uncommon) is slow payment. Smaller firms—the "unknown entities"—are the ones you should be more concerned about.

Sorry to say, but the following has happened, though fortunately, not to me. You get a call from a company to do some work. The client doesn't want to pay anything up front, but you take the job anyway. You finish the job, bill him, and you never get paid.

You find out later that the bum's burned another copywriter before you and was trying to find another sucker (which he apparently did). It's not very common—companies don't stay around very long treating vendors like that – but it happens. Even more reason to be extra careful with new clients.

The Bid Letter For most small to medium-size jobs, if you feel you need a contract document of some sort, a bid letter might just do it. A bid letter simply spells out the basic parameters of the job: the fee for the job, the timing of payments, exactly what the project entails, what's included for that price, and optionally, time frames: when different phases of the job will be completed.

There's a place for the client to sign it at the bottom so he can't come back and say you never told him this, that, or the other. Send it as part of a follow-up letter to a meeting or phone call. You instruct him to sign it, make and keep a copy for himself, and send you back the original in a SASE that you provide. Here's a sample of a bid letter, with disclaimer at the end:

WriteInc.

October 10, 1999

Mr. James Smith - Manager, Field Communications
ABC Wireless Products and Services
1234 Perimeter Canyon Parkway
Atlanta, GA 33301

Dear James,

It was a pleasure meeting you today and I appreciate the opportunity to bid on the ABC Wireless sales brochure project. As requested, this is a formal estimate for copywriting services. For the discussed trifold brochure (8 1/2" x 11" with two vertical folds), I would like to offer a bid of $1,020, based on 12 hours at $85/hour.

This figure includes all concepting and copywriting, two rounds of revisions, and one additional meeting, if necessary. Additional revisions or meeting time would be billed at my hourly rate of $85.

1/3 of the fee ($350) would be paid up-front prior to the beginning of work with the balance of $670 due and payable upon completion and delivery of final approved copy. Assuming I receive the up-front deposit by October 20, 1999, I will turn in a first draft by October 27, 1999. Once revisions have been returned, I will turn around the subsequent draft within three days or less.

Should you choose to terminate the project at any time and for any reason, as the writer, I will be entitled to full payment for all time invested to that point.

With experience in both writing creative marketing brochures and for the telecommunications industry, I feel confident in delivering a quality product that hits the mark. Given 15+ years of sales and marketing experience, I bring the crucial "write to sell" mindset to the table, always focused on powerfully and effectively communicating to your target audience.

Please sign below, make and keep a copy for yourself, and return this original to me in the enclosed SASE. Thanks again and I look forward to working with you soon.

Peter Bowerman
I have read, understood, and agree to the above bid:

_____

James Smith
Manager, Field Communications
ABC Wireless Products and Services

_____

Date

THE PRECEDING IS NOT A LEGALLY APPROVED DOCUMENT. USE IT FOR GUIDELINE PURPOSES ONLY. I AM NOT AN ATTORNEY AND WILL NOT BE HELD RESPONSIBLE FOR ANY PROBLEMS, HASSLES, OR OTHER MESSES THAT YOU GET YOURSELF INTO OR THAT MAY ARISE FROM USING THIS DOCUMENT. CONSULT YOUR OWN ATTORNEY AND COVER YOUR OWN BUTT. I'M VERY SERIOUS. GOT IT? GOOD.

More in-depth contracts may be a good idea for much larger jobs and in many cases, those contracts will come from the clients themselves. I've signed more client-generated contracts than ones I created myself. In Appendix B, you'll find a more detailed contract with the same disclaimer.

"SPEC" WORK - YAY OR NAY?   "Spec" work (speculative) basically means one of two things: 1) doing a project for which you will be paid if the client is satisfied, or more likely, 2) you're one of several people "auditioning" for a big job by providing a free sample of work, typically giving a prospect an idea of how you'd approach a certain specified part of the project.

After the client has all the samples, he decides who gets hired (and paid) to handle the whole project, and if you're chosen, you usually get paid for the sample work you did as well. Those not chosen receive nothing.

Let me establish one thing right at the outset. While this does happen, such scenarios are extremely rare. The absolute norm is the "pay-for-work-regardless" scenario. But times arise …

Why Do It?   Why would any freelancers subject themselves to such indignity? Well, for starters, it's certainly not something you want to make a habit of doing. Furthermore, the creative industry is solidly against it, feeling that giving away anything devalues the work and makes it harder for everyone in the industry to be taken seriously. I can definitely understand that point of view *and* I have a few philosophical objections to their stance.

While, as mentioned, this rarely comes up, if it does, what will you do? And the answer is…it depends. Sure, it'd be easy to say, "Oh, I'll never do spec work because it devalues the profession." However, strong market forces are at work in the present business environment, creating opportunities that can't always be sacrificed for "the greater good."

If you're swamped, why do you need to do spec work? You don't. If business is slow and you've got a shot at a big project for investing a few hours of your time at no charge, do you take that chance or remember how the "bigger picture" of spec work devalues the industry for everyone?

Clearly, for many, bottom line considerations win out. Indeed, many will point to the existence of any speculative work as evidence of a basic economic reality: a greater supply of available expertise than demand. I object to the hard-and-fast stance of the industry.

As far as I'm concerned, you do your thing, I'll do mine, as long as mine doesn't bother yours and vice versa. If you don't choose to take the same path as me, fine. Just don't decide that for me. Realistically, of course, you'll probably never have to answer to anyone but yourself for making the decision to do spec work.

And for what it's worth, I've got the government on my side (a dubious honor...). In the late 1980s, the Justice Department, referring to the Code of Ethics of the American Institute of Graphic Artists (AIGA) which recommended that members not engage in speculative work, ruled that even if an organization doesn't have a history of enforcement, a written code is considered an intent to take such action, and that intent violates the Sherman Antitrust Act of 1890. So Justice made it clear that individual free choice to engage in speculative work was to be preserved, without fear of intimidation for exercising that choice.

You Decide   When it comes to eating, your business philosophy can shift. Anyone who's been in this business for any length of time has done spec work. It's not right or wrong. It just is. For me, by far the biggest issues are "How busy am I right now?" and "What's the upside potential?"

Go in with a positive attitude, but prepare for the most likely scenario that you'll end up with nothing. Like walking into a casino, don't spend anything you're not willing to lose. Be smart about it. Get a feel for whether the client is jerking you around and just trying to get a bunch of "somethings for nothing" or if it's legit.

KILL FEES   One note about the clause in the bid letter regarding payment in the event of project termination. While the concept of "kill fees" is more at home in the world of magazine article publishing, once in a great while it sneaks into the realm of freelance commercial writing.

When writing a magazine article, one for which the writer has already gotten the green light from the publication, if the magazine kills the story for some reason (change of the issue's theme, a hotter story, new editor, bad moon rising, whatever) the "kill fee" is the amount—anywhere from 15–40% of the original fee or some flat amount—paid to the writer as sort of a consolation prize.

You're Entitled In our business, if you've been hired to do a job for an agreed-upon fee and the project gets scrapped for some reason, you are entitled to be paid for the time you've put in thus far. In very rare cases, the client will establish a kill fee at the outset or even arbitrarily at the point of deciding to pull the plug.

It only happened to me once (the one time I ever got burned that I keep mentioning), where I just wasn't hitting the mark for my client's client, and they decided to get another writer. The original fee was $1500, I'd put in well over $1000 worth of work and I was paid $500 by the end user.

We hadn't signed a contract, so I was pretty unprotected. I was actually pretty ticked at my middleman client for not standing up for me and making up the difference. They knew how hard I'd worked, yet chose to hide behind their client's skirt, taking a *no hablo ingles* attitude.

Ultimately, I convinced *my* client to kick in an additional $250, which left about that much again as a final figure of lost income. This was a case of an arbitrary determination of a kill fee; in other cases it might be more established up-front, but as mentioned, it's usually an amount equal to hours invested thus far. Again, overwhelmingly, the norm is this: If the project gets canned at some point along the way, you get paid for all time invested up till then. If the project gets trashed after you've finished, you're entitled to full payment of the agreed-upon fee. Kill fees are rare, but just so you're familiar with the concept.

OK, we've talked about what to charge, how to discuss it and present it. How about once you finish a job? Onward to the process of billing and tracking down your money…

Chapter Ten

Happy Paydays!

BEING SMART WITH YOUR MONEY My first piece of advice about invoicing? Stay current! A friend shared a horror story about getting way behind on her billing because she was so busy. That, by the way, is one of the dumbest reasons I've ever heard. Sure, we're in this business for creative fulfilment and all that, but really, we're here to make money, so make collections a top priority.

Anyway, she finally got around to billing this one client for a bunch of work done many months before, but by then, the company was in financial trouble and her main contact had deserted the sinking ship. She went though hell trying to get paid and ultimately had to take a chunk less than was coming to her. All of which she could have avoided by timely invoicing.

When Are You Done With a Job? You know you're finished with a job when you ask the client if you can go ahead and bill it and she says "Sure." Pretty simple actually. Which brings up another point. Always ask. Don't assume you're done till you hear it straight from the horse's mouth.

As mentioned in the technology section, get yourself a simple little invoicing software program like *My Advanced Invoices (MAI)*, which will run you about $40 or less. When you're done with a job, print a bill, run an envelope through your printer (On *Word*, go to *Tools*, then *Envelopes and Labels*, then choose *Envelopes.)*

Once there you can customize your envelope copy with your choice of font and point size. If you're using custom envelopes printed with your company name, don't forget to click the *Omit* box by the return address window at the bottom), stuff it, and mail it.

Ask and Ye Shall Receive A little tip. On *MAI*, and probably on any invoicing program, you input the terms: how many days the client has to pay. I go ahead and put 15 days. Why not? If a company's system pays in 30 or 60, you'll get paid then. If it's flexible, you might very well get paid in 10. If you don't ask for it, you won't get it.

Invoice in Stages A little sidebar here about bigger jobs, which I would consider to be anything over about $1500–2000: it's pretty standard to invoice in stages, because the time frames are longer. It's not really fair to work on a project for 6 weeks, finish it and wait another 30–45 days to see any money.

Some (myself included) will bill in thirds, while others do halves. With thirds, you get a third up-front, another third once you submit a first draft, and the final third upon completion. With halves, you skip the first draft payment and get it on the front and back ends.

Three payments are usually more common than two and generally more comfortable for the client, who might be a tad nervous about paying for half a job before getting anything. And just for clarification here, while I have often walked out of an initial meeting with an up-front deposit check, you won't always have a check in hand before you actually start working. The accounts payable systems that most companies have—especially the large ones—are usually just not set up to write a check on the spot or even have one in a week. So, be flexible.

If it's a big company with a household name, don't worry about it. You'll get paid. If it's a new client but not well-known, better get your third up-front before starting, regardless of the size of the job.

Money on the Table Getting money up-front is fairly standard in this business, though mostly with new clients and for larger jobs. Here are the basic rules of thumb:

1) **New Clients** - Regardless of the dollar amount of the job, get a third to a half of the agreed-upon fee up-front. If they balk, politely explain that this is quite standard in the industry and that on future jobs, if they're small (under

$500), you'd be happy to bill them at project's end. Most won't have a problem with this.

Play it by ear. If it's a well-established company, and you've heard of it, follow your gut. I've let many slide on this and—knock on wood—it hasn't bitten me yet. If the client is acting a little weird, as if he's trying to hide something, think seriously about walking.

2) **Any Job Over $500** - Let your regular clients slide (it shows trust on your side) but again, get a third up-front from newer clients until you've gotten a good working rhythm going with them and have been paid regularly. Again, most should be agreeable.

3) **Large Jobs ($1500+)** - Even from your regular clients—and certainly from new ones—get a third up-front. Good clients are completely unfazed by this request. You may want to use a more formal contract, though a simple bid letter might be all you need.

TRACKING THE DEADBEATS   Obviously in this business, as a sole proprietor, you'll be wearing many hats. One of the least fun ones is your bill collector's hat. You mean, everyone doesn't pay you on time? No. Is it a common problem? Yes, but that doesn't mean it happens more than it doesn't or that it's always serious. Most clients will be conscientious about paying you on time. FYI, *I've always eventually gotten paid on every single job I've ever done.*

In this business, 30 days is the rule, though many writers I know ask for and get their money sooner. I've had plenty of clients who pay me sooner than 30 days, and a good number who quite shamelessly cruise right past that guidepost. For ad agencies and others—sorry to say—60–90 days is the rule. So, keep that in mind in light of the next discussion.

Cool's a Good Rule   OK, so what about those that ignore your 15-day terms as well as the 30-day industry standard? Well, let's have a reality check for starters. I'll admit right up-front—probably because I'm a classic conflict avoider—that I'm much more laid-back about this than some of my peers, and it's almost never come back to haunt me. You pick your comfort zone.

For starters, always tack on an extra week or more in your mind to any invoice. You bill it on a Thursday, your client gets it on a Monday. There's five days right there and if she sent your check out exactly 30 days later, you'd have it in your mailbox more than five weeks after the day you billed it. So, don't get all weird if the check doesn't show up exactly 30 days from the date that's printed on the bill.

It's a little over-anal to get all fussy with a client too fast about a bill. Might just irritate her, which if you're going to do, make sure it's for a darn good reason—like 90 days, for instance.

Second Notice So, now it's past 45 days. You've got a few choices. Send her another bill, highlight the invoice date with a marker and attach a very nice little note: "Thanks in advance for taking a minute to handle this. Look forward to working with you again soon." Or "Hope things are going well. When you get a minute, can you take care of this? Look forward to working with you again." In most cases that should get the job done.

Pick Up the Phone Option two is to give her a quick call. With a big company, your job is easier, because there's less emotion involved in dealing with a person who won't specifically be the one to hire you again.

Find out who handles accounts payable, and deal with it just like it's a little administrative matter, which is exactly what it is to them. "Hi, Mary, this is Peter Bowerman with WriteInc. and I'm just checking on the status of an invoice that's at about the 45-day mark. The invoice number is 12345 and it's dated 3/15/99." Mary should be able to give you a good idea when it's coming.

But obviously, big companies can lose invoices and screw things up in a bigger way than a smaller one precisely because they are big. I've fought with my share of accounting departments to get paid, but again, it's usually emotionally easier. When you're dealing directly with your immediate client for payment, it's trickier.

You can absolutely know you're being jerked around, but unfortunately, getting testy with the person who can bring you more business might just jeopardize that future, so you've got to be flexible in your principles. With big companies, stay on top of them and hold them to their promises.

Smaller is Trickier With smaller companies, you have to be more diplomatic. One excuse for late payment you'll hear endlessly from small companies—and it doesn't sound any more fair the hundredth time you hear it than it did the first—is "We can't pay you till we get paid."

Often it is true that a small company doesn't have the resources to front all their vendors' money before they've received their money. But by the same token, I've had one-person graphic design shops pay me before they got paid.

Life's Not Fair The general feeling among my colleagues is that it's a BS excuse and not your problem. When your work is done and you've billed them, you should get paid. That's how the world works. We're right. It's not fair. AND all that doesn't stop plenty of companies from still doing it to you.

So, what can you do? Well obviously, you have two choices. You can play hard ball, demand your money and run the very real risk of losing a client. Or you can roll with reality and expect that at least they keep you apprised of what's going on. Again, this is not the norm, but it happens enough to warrant figuring out in advance how you're going to handle it.

Can You Live with It? Probably ... I've got this one client—a 20-person graphic design firm—who unfortunately for the longest time has had most of their eggs in one Fortune 100 company's basket. The megacorp. in question keeps so many creative folks in this town busy with well-paying work that it's pretty much written its own payment terms: 90 days. If you don't like that arrangement, fine. Others will *and* do, and nothing changes. That, boys and girls, is the market system in action. It may not be right, but it's reality.

Of course, most companies adapt because if you're doing steady work for this firm, after 90 days, the checks are coming in regularly. Problem is, I'm not doing steady work for this client, so I end up waiting 60–90 days for my money. But in two years of working with these folks, I've always gotten paid eventually, so you know what? I leave it alone, do my work and wait longer for the money. Big deal. It's your call. You decide what you will put up with and what you won't.

I get together with my writers group every few months and the "We'll-pay-you-when-we-get-paid" subject often comes up. We rail against the inequity of it all, whine that it's an indefensible position, but I'm guessing that few of us walk away from these clients.

Over 60 Days? Once it goes over two months with a small company, the key is polite persistence. Be nice but stay on top of your client and pin him down as much as you can as to when your money's coming. If it's a client like the one I just described, where 60 days is a minimum, I won't even start getting concerned or involved until he's at 90 days or so.

What does have me lose patience really fast—and it will you as well—is someone avoiding me, not returning my calls, etc. I can forgive an enormous amount if someone's keeping in touch with me and letting me know the status of the payments.

If the client in question is a new one and one who isn't likely to keep hiring you (they needed a brochure but don't have ongoing needs), you can obviously get a little firmer with them, and you have every right to do that.

I wish I could say we live in a perfect world where principles applied equally to everyone (while we're at it, why not wish for a world where everyone did the right thing at the outset and avoid this whole mess to begin with?), but that's not real life. I don't treat all my clients the same and frankly, I'd be pretty dumb if I did.

"Live" Example I just called that (in)famous client of mine about an invoice that'd been hanging out there for about 100 days. Now, by any standard of decency or civility, that's clearly unacceptable. But he stayed in touch with me, let me know what was happening, and I knew I'd get my money. Today, a batch of checks, including mine, had just gone out. And in the past, he's never said "The check is in the mail" when it wasn't.

I thanked him, commiserated briefly with him over how long it took them to get paid by their client and left him feeling that I was a decent, understanding and easy-to-work-with vendor. I say people remember stuff like that. Others might call me a pushover, doormat, or sucker. And I'm OK with that. Pick your battles. There are worse things in life than well-paying, slow-paying clients. And I had my check in a few days.

Moving on, let's talk about the day-in-day-out life of a FLCW—the ebb and flow of work, the daily realities of this business that can simultaneously be some of the best and the most challenging parts of this business ....

Chapter Eleven

The Ebb and Flow of Work

THE UPS AND DOWNS OF BUSINESS—A PLOT? At times, you'll be absolutely convinced that all your clients have gotten together and decided that on a certain day, they're all going to call you at once, and then, again as one, not call you at all for the next month. And then repeat the process over and over until you've gone stark raving mad. Not so. It just seems that way.

Count on the feast/famine dichotomy being a pretty constant fixture of your professional life as a freelance commercial writer. It doesn't have to be that way, and if you're wonderfully disciplined about marketing yourself consistently, you'll probably have a pretty steady flow of work. Getting to a point where you have enough work that you can pick and choose is a very nice problem.

Unfortunately, human nature usually prevails, and we end up doing our marketing after things have slowed down, certainly not while we're cranking. The upshot is you'll have your alternating periods of being swamped and dead in the water.

Keep the Pump Flowing All that said, when work is flowing, it will follow a fairly consistent overlapping pattern. You'll get a job, and as you get into it, you'll get another and another. No need to finish one before starting another. Unless you're on-site at a client's office eight hours a day, five days a week for weeks on end and it's sucking out all your mental energy, keep adding new work.

Think about it. If you've bid a job out at $1200 (about 16 hours @ $75 an hour), and you've got a week to turn around copy, that leaves 24 other hours (in a hypothetical 40-hour work week) that you could be billing. Take whatever comes your way if you can work it in, since you never know when things are going to get really quiet.

If you've just come out of three straight weeks of $1500–2000/week, a two-week dry spell won't bother you much. You'll be able to play a little without freaking. Just get a good handle on how long it's taking you to get through projects so you'll be better able to gauge what else you can comfortably add to the mix.

In the beginning, it's best to err on the side of caution and bite off less than you think you can comfortably chew. Better to think, "Oh well, I could've done that job" than miss a deadline because you're overextended. Unless you're a hot dog, throwing caution to the winds and taking on whatever comes your way, having decided that you'll pull an all-nighter if that's what it takes. If you've got the stamina for that approach, I can't argue with it, because one thing's for sure: you'll learn your limits in a hurry.

The Big Kahuna Just a note about taking on long-term (three weeks or more), full-time assignments. A company had better be paying me very handsomely to do that, because there will very likely be a significant "opportunity cost" in lost business when I cut myself off from my network—and from taking other work—for an extended period of time. But, big jobs are awfully tempting, especially when they're sporting $5000–10,000+ fees.

Just make sure that you couldn't make a similar amount of money in the same time period with a normal work load, doing a series of jobs (is variety important?) and staying well-connected to your network. Of course, if the job is in an arena you've been trying to break into for awhile, by all means, go for it, as one successful foray into new territory can open up more doors down the line.

Think Before You Say No... There have been times when I've turned down a job because I thought I was too swamped, only to find that I really could've done it by working a little harder for a couple of days.

If it's been very quiet and all of a sudden it gets really busy—very common—one or two projects may *seem* like a lot, when you're simply comparing it to nothing. Needless to say, always be responsible to those who have hired you and never put a promised deadline in jeopardy by overextending yourself.

And as discussed, it's even more of an issue if a call comes from a new client and someone with whom you've been wanting to work. Then it's not just another job. It's a key audition that if it goes well, will lead to lots more work. It's not like he'll never give you another chance if you turn it down. He may even be impressed that you're *that* busy, but the bottom line is, you won't be on his mind after he hangs up.

So, if you can find a way to make it happen, do so. Work a few extra hours, come through for him and he'll think of you that much quicker the next time... instead of calling the writer he used when you couldn't do it.

Ride the Waves Don't think this job is similar in schedule to working for someone else. In the typical working world, you can count on working at least from 9–5, Monday-Friday. In this field, the work ebbs and flows, which is one thing I love about it. Not that you can completely control your schedule at all times, but you've got a lot more freedom than most, minus the daily commute.

When the work comes, and it often does seem to come all at once, ride the wave and work extra hard. When things slow down, take it easy, sleep late, work out in the middle of the day, meet friends for lunch, catch up on "errandy" stuff, go to the beach on a Wednesday—in short, catch your breath and smell the flowers (or the ocean). If you're a freelancer at heart, and I assert most of us are, once you get the rhythm down, you'll never want to go back.

Seasonal Swings This business has seasonal ups and downs that may be very different from other businesses. Again, if you're a crack marketer, you can minimize the highs and lows, but few of us are that consistently disciplined to always be stirring up business.

January can start out slowly, which, as we discussed in the direct mail segment of Chapter Eight, is a great reason to do a mailing that will land on people's desk the week they come back from the holidays. This past January, I hit the ground running with a big job, but that's not always the case. Things pick up steadily into the late winter and if the word is out about you, can continue all the way to the summer.

Summers in this business (mostly July/August) are generally slow, though they don't have to be, especially if you time your mailings to get an extra boost of work in that mid-late summer. People on vacation mean projects get back-burnered and end of fiscal years (June 30) mean new projects may not have started yet. Right after Labor Day, however, there's usually a burst of activity which can go right through the end of the year.

Don't count on a quiet December. Procrastination is alive and well and many clients are scrambling to get it done before the champagne corks pop. You'll be amazed at how packed your holiday dance card can get as you try to juggle a bunch of juicy jobs, parties, doing greeting cards, and the beloved shopping crush. But look on the bright side. You'll have a very merry Christmas.

The Tease I just love this: Someone you've been contacting for a long time with no success, or even better, a referral, calls *you*, anxious to have you come in and show him your work. "We've got a lot of projects coming up and we've heard good things about you." Great, you're thinking. After all, aren't calls like this the goal? Yes… and don't get too excited too fast.

Several years back, I got three or four such calls in a one-month period. Went in, met everyone, they liked my work, seemed very excited about working with me, I went home, followed up on all of them regularly… and nothing happened. Never got even a return call from any of them, much less a job. In fact, I didn't hear a darn thing from any of them for six months.

At the six-month mark, one of them actually called me about a project. I went in, met with her, got a folder with background reading and contact list, and we made up a tentative timetable for the project, which was to kick off after I got back from a trip ten days later.

When I returned, I called her, as requested. No response. I called her again several days later. Still nothing. And you know what? She never called. Never took one minute to call me up to tell me: the project got scrapped, the client went flaky, we found another writer, you've got B.O., nothing.

Very tacky and unprofessional, but it happens (albeit rarely), and there's little you can do about it. Every six months or so, I rattle her cage with a call just to bug her and maybe stir up her guilty conscience. I get voice mail, leave a message, and again hear nothing. Amazing. The moral: Always have so many irons in the fire that you don't end up fixating on any one particular client or job.

The second moral: Never ever turn down real work that's in your hands because of a promise of work from someone else. As the song goes: "It don't mean nothin' till you sign it on the bottom line." Calls are just calls. Meetings are just meetings. Only assigned, "let's get moving" work with (preferably) a deposit check is work. Treat each as such and you won't get as frustrated when the inevitable mirages rise up to alternately entice and frustrate you.

Big Deal … No Deal As I write this section, I'm amusedly shaking my head over a "Big Deal" that was going to make my year last year. Along with a video producer, I first met the client in late January. It was a CD*i* scripting job that was to take eight to ten weeks, and we all figured—client included—that my portion would get started March 1, and finish up in early May. Every few months during the year, I'd get status reports, always the same: It's not a matter of *if*, but *when*. Any day now. Blah, blah, blah.

Finally in November, we got the word. It was dead. But I'd stayed busy enough all year long that it didn't matter. Then, in February, guess what happened? You got it. I got another call, saying it's alive again, and we'll keep you posted. You do that. I pretended it didn't exist. A year or so later, still nada. I'm learning.

Easy Business A few months back, I got a job that took virtually no real writing talent. How so? Well, herein lies one of the realities of the freelance commercial writing business and one that should comfort those who feel they're not overly creative writers, but certainly able to deliver solid "meat-and-potatoes" writing.

You will often pick up jobs that on the surface seem so simple, from a writing standpoint, that you wonder why the clients didn't do it themselves. Well, it happens all the time, for one simple reason: they don't have the time to do it themselves, but they have the budget to have someone else do it. Or sometimes, if it's a very creative project, they may've "hit the wall"—tapped out, no more ideas and they need fresh thoughts and a new set of eyes.

The job I mentioned above was a trade show brochure, a second-round mailing to prospective exhibitors for a show coming up in a few months. It essentially needed to be a rehash of the first round piece that went out several months prior, plus a few new sections. No reinventing the wheel, just a bit of writing and then arranging the different components in a logical structure – not too difficult, since the material lent itself to a certain sensible flow.

On a Monday afternoon, I was given the parameters, the old literature, the gist of the new sections, the main contact person and phone number, and off I went. I got the job done at a leisurely pace in about 10–11 hours over the next two days before turning in my draft on Wednesday morning. A few minimal revisions, and we were done. Flat fee: $1000. As the corporate world gets increasingly overworked and you get more established, count on picking up more and more of these relative no-brainers.

DAY IN THE LIFE Many people have the wrong idea about this job. Plenty will ask, "How can you sit in front of a computer all day long and just type?" Well, in the nearly seven years I've been doing this, there's been precious few days of just sitting and typing all day.

More likely, you'll end up with a mixed bag. Generally, the more creative a project is, the less copy-heavy it will be, and the less time you'll be camped out in front of your screen.

"Concepting" Time Notice I didn't say that it takes less time. The *concepting* process is just as important as the actual writing of the copy. FLCWs—and most clients who know what they're doing—understand that you need to have a certain number of hours factored into most jobs for brainstorming. How you end up approaching that intriguing process is very personal and often, pretty bizarre.

Creativity is Personal For some, it could be as simple as taking a legal pad and pen to a quiet place with a comfortable chair, no interruptions and minimal distractions. Others may need to take a walk in a pretty setting with a microcassette recorder—one of my favorite strategies. For someone else, it might require cranking up Led Zeppelin's "Physical Graffiti," standing on his head in the bathroom wearing only polka-dotted boxers, and munching on pumpkin seeds. Whatever gets the juices flowing.

Speaking of individual tastes, we all have a style, in the clothes we wear, the music we like, foods we're into, sense of humor and … how we work. Do you like to focus on one job at a time and don't like too much going on at once? Or do you love juggling four or five different things simultaneously, savoring the variety and constant freshness of such an approach? Somewhere in between?

Figuring out your "work style" can go a long way toward not only easing the transition to self-employment, but just as importantly, allowing you to see that there's no right way to do it.

I prefer to have a number of pots cooking at once and love jumping back and forth with my big spoon stirring up each one in a cycle. Every day I prove the old adage about often getting the solution to a problem or some inspiration about a project I'm working on while busy doing something else.

Even more reason to carry around a microcassette recorder wherever you go. You might just knock out that killer headline or concept you've been struggling with in about one minute flat. Often, however, a deadline is such that you need to focus completely on one project and get it done.

So now that we've got a sense of how life goes for folks like us on a day-to-day basis, let's take a look at the personalities of the people for whom you'll be doing your fine work. What kinds of clients will you encounter out there? Nice ones, scary ones, stupid ones, unbelievable ones. Let's go meet them….

Chapter Twelve

Clients and Other Fascinating Species

OH, WOULDN'T IT BE NICE ...   Let's fantasize for a moment, take an other-worldly trip to the Land of the Perfect Client. A place where clients live to make our lives easier, where they offer to pay us more than we've asked for, heck, where they do our job for us and still pay us. OK, OK, let's talk about the *Imaginable Perfect Client*—the one you actually might run across at some point. What would be the characteristics of such a wondrous creature? Well, we'd want someone who:

- *Understands the creative process.*
- *Is knowledgeable about the whole arena of copywriting and what it involves.*
- *Is accommodating to a reasonable time frame and budget.*
- *Is helpful in providing, at the first (and only) meeting, everything you need to do your job or the people who can get it for you.*
- *Knows their subject matter and doesn't waste your time going off on unproductive tangents.*
- *Is organized and goes out of her way to facilitate the process.*
- *Doesn't over-manage and actually lets you do the job you were hired to do.*
- *Gives you lots of referrals and hires you again and again.*
- *Pays you in ten days.*

OK, let's return to earth for a moment and discuss how most clients *really* are and the more common types we'll encounter. I say most, because truthfully, I have had several clients that do come awfully close to the above description. However, we won't expect that, and when we do find it, we'll be pleasantly surprised.

CLIENTS LOOKING FOR A "MASSAGE"   Am I suggesting something a little improper here? Not at all. This often happens with clients whose employee has written some copy or who consider themselves writers. The latter are easy to spot: they'll adopt a somewhat modest, pleased-with-themselves tone and say something like, "Well, I dabble a little bit in writing myself," the underlying message being, "I'm pretty good at it, but I'm not really one to toot my horn." Be afraid. Be very afraid.

They'll typically introduce a project (that you've been told you'll write from the beginning) by saying, "I've (We've) pretty much written the copy. I just need you to *massage* it a little." Other red flag terms? *Tweak, polish, spruce, jazz, spice, etc.* Translation? 'I don't want to pay you very much, so I'm making it sound like a minor job.'

If after such an intro, such a client tries to pin you down to a fee, politely tell him your hourly rate and say you'll really need to see what they've done before you can provide a firm quote. That's not always possible if he wants some idea or he's going to check with someone else. Just be careful. Copywriting, if you're good at it, is a whole lot more than just using the right words to convey a client's message. The structure and flow of the piece is as important as the words you choose.

If a client's written their own copy, just "massaging" it may not be enough if the piece isn't structured effectively. Of course, if that's all he wants (ie., he's told you this is simply going to be an editing job), then give it to him, as long as he understands that he may end up with something less than it could be.

CLIENTS WITH LIMITED BUDGETS   When starting out, before penetrating the hallowed halls of the Fortune 500, reality often dictates dealing with clients with little money.

As is true in most businesses, the smallest customers are usually the most demanding. When you have a small budget, your priority will be maximizing that money. While these can often be unpleasant experiences, they certainly don't have to be. By handling certain issues up-front, you'll avoid a lot of problems down the line.

Get Specific Determine exactly what the job is, i.e., the nitty-gritty of what you're offering for what price. For example: "Copy for one marketing brochure including two revisions, one face-to-face meeting, all phone consultations, and so on."

An hour-by-hour itemization of your time is generally unnecessary and as discussed, could bite you if hours set aside for "revisions" aren't used and the client wants them subtracted. I've rarely provided that kind of detail and have never been questioned. Just be prepared for the remote possibility that your client might want to see an itemization of your time.

As we've already discussed, a formal contract is probably not necessary. Simply create a bid letter like we discussed in Chapter Eight with the details clearly outlined and a place for the client to sign at the bottom.

Editing for the Budget-Conscious With budget-sensitive clients, assuming the job is pretty small, you might even suggest that they write it and you edit it. Have them put down what they're trying to say—even if it's terribly written—and in what they feel is the proper sequence for optimal flow.

Being typically human, if it is terribly written, I'm always a little relieved, since it clearly isn't going to take a superhuman effort to make a big difference for them. Editing can also be a very viable option in several other cases besides budget sensitivity:

The "I'm Not So Sure I Need a Writer" Client In cases where the client has yet to fully grasp the awe-inspiring miracles that a professional writer can accomplish, you might suggest editing as a cost-effective insurance policy: "You write the copy, Mr. Prospect, and when you're done, I'll edit it, which will be a fraction of the hours it would take if I'd handled the project from the start." Once you see what you'll be editing, you can give him a firmer estimate of hours. It still probably won't be as good as if you'd written from scratch, but it could be the foot in the door.

The client saves some money, and once he sees what a difference your talents can make, the next time, you might just get the whole job. There are few things more satisfying than converting a skeptic to a believer.

The Technical Writing Client I've had several clients over the years who sell very complex software packages. Rather than pay me for the many hours it would take for me to get up to speed on how the whole thing works, they write the brochure or product spec sheet.

They then give me a quick and dirty technical overview (enough to grasp the overall concepts and how the pieces fit together, without getting bogged down in the minutiae) and I edit the piece, spending four to six hours on each one, depending on size.

By distancing myself from the technical complexity, I avoid getting frustrated, which I absolutely would do if I had to write it from scratch. They get their copy prettied up nicely at a low cost. Win-win all around.

CLIENTS WHO WANT YOU TO TAKE DICTATION   Sometimes you'll feel like little more than a stenographer, as the client essentially spoonfeeds you what he wants you to say. Of course, if he's paying you $75–85 an hour, it tends to cushion the disappointment somewhat. A few years back, I wrote a speech for a major hotel chain's new EVP of Marketing for an upcoming conference. He had a lot of ill will to reverse and hence the speech had to be very strong in some very specific ways. Almost every time I'd put any creativity and zip into it and not just rehash what he'd handed me, it was cut. It was a classic case of feeling like I was simply taking dictation, not really creating or even writing.

Although, from time to time, a juicy and nicely budgeted "yes-sir-no-sir-whatever-you-say-sir-I-have-no-independent-thoughts-sir-except-to-think-up-new-and-better-ways-to-serve-you-sir" project like this can be a welcome gift.

CLIENTS WHO SAY THEY WANT CREATIVITY   I just love these. They've done pretty safe stuff in the past. It's gotten the job done but never been too exciting. Bring me something different, they say. Let's push the envelope a little, take some chances. So you do. You're having fun, trying out some funky stuff, thinking to yourself, finally, a client who's letting me roam wild a little.

Then, when they see what you've done—still light-years from 'outrageous'—they get nervous. Turns out they're not quite so brave after all. Then it starts. Why don't we just say *this* here instead of *that*. Let's *soften* that text a little and *smooth out* the rough spots there.

The More Things Change ...   Pretty soon, lo and behold, you've created something virtually indistinguishable from everything they've done before.

And you want to ask—scream, actually—why did you hire me? When you could've just taken your old brochures and shuffled the copy around a little. You could've just lifted your old copy out verbatim aaAAAAND PUT IT IN A BRAND NEW LAYOUT!! BECAUSE AFTER ALL, YOU SPINELESS, GUTLESS WEENIE, YOU ENDED UP WITH THE SAME BLANKETY-BLANK THING YOU DID LAST TIME, THE TIME BEFORE AND THE TIME BEFORE THAT!

You think it, but of course, you don't say it, because you're a professional. And furthermore, by now, you've learned to laugh it off. Right? Right. (gnash, gnash…)

CLIENTS WHO THINK THEY'RE WRITERS   And lest we forget that certain breed of clients that wouldn't know good copywriting if it came up and smacked them between the eyes with a two-by-four. And as we touched on briefly before, the worst part about this group is that they fancy themselves as writers.

Get used to the fact that, in the eyes of many, copywriting is viewed as something anyone can do. It's amazing how many people out there think they can write, and equally amazing how high a percentage of those who think they can, can't.

Fortunately, many others know their limitations, know the profound difference that a good copywriter can make, and are smart enough to not spend money to massage their own ego, but rather to get the job done right. So take heart.

Knowing One's Limitations   I have one client, a gentleman for whom I ghostwrote a book several years back. He owns a successful mortgage business and is very good at what he does. He does success seminars on the side and wanted to expand that part of his business, so he hired a marketing consultant who told him he should write a book ("Author" after one's name is a proven reputation booster). He replied that he wasn't a writer, they found me, and voila—instant "author"!

Anyway, he's since hired me half a dozen times to work on various marketing pieces, and he's one of those wonderfully evolved human beings who understands on a very fundamental level that, 1) he doesn't have to be good at everything, and 2) writing isn't one of the things he's good at.

He sends me these comically bad pieces for rewriting/editing, but, because I know his business and him, I know precisely what he's trying to say.

When I'm done and he sees my work, you'd think I had a halo and wings. He's just in awe, saying over and over, "You GOT it!!! That's EXACTLY what I wanted to say!! You're amazing!!!" Talk about an ego boost. People like him make it all worthwhile.

Coping Strategies   The dilemma with "writers-in-their-own-mind" is how to be diplomatic when they foist their version of "how they think it should be written," clearly enamored of their own abilities, which often, are at best a notch or two above the average sixth grader. How does one gently suggest massive revisions while not getting their skivvies in a wad?

You could just shut up, suck it up, give 'em what they want, collect your money, and exit stage left. On the other hand, if you really feel strongly about the piece, that it could be a really great project if they'd just get out of the way, there's nothing wrong with shooting straight. And if you do it right, they might just thank you. Something along the lines of:

"I think we need to talk about this. I'm assuming you hired me because you felt I had a particular skill that you did not possess, in much the same way you have talents in a lot of areas in which I'd be lost (stroke, stroke…). But, I'm feeling like I'm not really being given the opportunity to show you what I can do, and the difference that a professional copywriter can make.

"I really want to do a good job and create a solid piece that gets the job done for your business. But I can't do that if you keep changing what I've done into copy that I don't feel, as a professional, is as impactful. If you don't trust that I know what I'm doing, then maybe I don't really need to be here."

Certainly don't be nasty about it, but firmness is often what's needed. And pick your battles. If the client wants to change a word here and there, even if it's not needed, but it doesn't hurt much, let it go. However, if the meaning, comprehension, clarity, or effective flow of the copy is compromised thanks to his meddling, don't be shy about speaking up.

If they're smart and honest—BIG IFs for sure—they'll appreciate your outspokenness. It shows you're more committed to the success of the project than to protecting their ego. Of course, in the end, it's their call. But as long as you've said your piece, you can sleep the sleep of the untroubled. We'll talk more about "taking stands" in the section on speechwriting in Chapter Fifteen.

MULTIPLE DECISION MAKERS   This is a fun one. In this scenario, you've got several people, presumably peers, generating input to a project. Normally, it's just not logical to structure a project in this way, but logic is not always in plentiful supply in corporate America. Or, it could just be an unusual situation. Typically when you have some sort of collaboration between several different entities, they're all going to want to contribute their two cents.

In cases like these, you want to designate, up front, a "point person" through whom all suggestions, revisions, and feedback flow. Even then, you can't guarantee that you won't still have a kitchen full of cooks. DO NOT set yourself up as that point person, or you'll invite a veritable avalanche of input from a small army of wannabe-writers. No fun, believe me.

An Example … I'm just finishing up a project that's been dragging on for 3½ months thanks to a multiple decision-maker scenario. Eight non-profit organizations with similar missions decided to collaborate on a brochure. Well.

At the first meeting, I diplomatically suggested the single-point-of-contact idea. They all agreed, no problem, and named their representative. While they've kept their individual lobbying down to manageable levels, their personal feedback times eight has still made it to my desk. Add to that the sheer time it takes for eight people to get feedback to even one person, and you've got a surefire recipe for a loooooong haul. And seven of the eight are in the same building! I can't even imagine if they were spread far and wide.

Make It Easy On Yourself Instead of having each group dump a stack of literature on me, from which I'd ultimately generate about one paragraph, I created a uniform questionnaire.

They all answered the same brief questions about their organizations and provided fast facts, statistics, and a few sentences about how they envision the brochure, what it should accomplish, who it should speak to, miscellaneous comments, etc. So, eight 2-pagers comprised the sum total of my source material. That's working smarter.

IGNORANT CLIENTS

Type #1 - Out of Their Element This is someone entrusted with a project out of the scope of his normal responsibilities. In cases like these, you end up educating him tactfully as to how it all works: project phases, typical hours, timeframes, edits, fees, etc.

In situations like this, not surprisingly, you've got egos involved, because they perceive they have to prove themselves (to their boss or you), and as such, they may often be more inflexible and controlling than might otherwise be the case. Because you end up spending more "educating" time, if you know this up front, make sure you build some additional hours into your bid.

The good news is that if you can do a good job of educating clients like these and not make them feel stupid in the process, you'll create a friend for life. Think about it. If someone's had something dropped in her lap and feels like she's in over her head, and you work with her, cover for her, and make her look good, you can't help but endear yourself to her.

If she's the one approving hours and budgets, you shouldn't have much problem having your bid approved. In addition, you'll end up with someone who's a lot more confident with the process the next time around.

Type #2 - New to the Game These are folks who've never done any litera-ture for their company and are simply unfamiliar with the process. Up till now, it's been Xeroxes of typed product sheets in store-bought folders with compa-ny-name stickers… you get the picture. Finally, they take the plunge to do their first project and it's your job to get them up to speed on how it all works.

Spell It Out The first step is to quickly determine what kind of piece they envision. Then get it all out up-front—the sequence of the process, how much it's going to cost, exactly what they get for their investment, how many revi-sions, time-frames, etc. As for your fee estimate, you'll either blow them away or if they're even reasonably savvy, they won't flinch.

These are good situations for calling your graphic designer friend with whom you team and putting a turnkey project together (See "Dos, Don'ts, and Don't Forgets" in Chapter Thirteen). Clients like these are particularly receptive to the team approach, because it's minimal hassle for them.

They already feel overwhelmed, and if you can demystify the process and deliver finished product for a reasonable cost, that's a dream come true. And incidentally, doing it this way ends up being a lot less expensive for them than if they took it to an ad agency, marketing company, or graphic design firm.

Hang Tough on Rates If they balk at your rates, which you know are com-petitive, and you also know they're not financially strapped, by all means, encourage them to shop around and find out for themselves that you are indeed, in tune with the market—if not low.

Just suggesting this confidently is often enough to have them drop the issue and move ahead with the project. If so, they were calling your bluff to see if you'd lower your rates. When you don't, they'll stop trying. They don't want to waste time, and if you've come across as competent and knowledgeable, even if they believe they could find it cheaper elsewhere, they'll probably take the deal.

If they insist you drop your rates, don't be afraid to walk away from the deal. Again, the more work you've got and the more irons you have in the fire, the harder ball you can play.

Certainly there are other types that have slipped my mind at the moment, but trust me, you'll find them and then can add your own appendix to this chapter. So, what's next? Well, over the years, I've picked up a lot of little dos and don'ts about this business. Shall we?

Chapter Thirteen

Dos, Don'ts, and Don't Forgets

Over time, I've learned a lot of lessons in this business, things that can make you more successful, keep you less stressed and make the experience of freelance commercial writing that much more enjoyable and rewarding for you … and your clients! Some we've already discussed, but they're worth repeating.

NEVER MISS A DEADLINE Just don't. If you say you'll have it done by a certain time, make sure it happens. It doesn't matter to the client that your car broke down, you had to take your dog to the vet, you had an anxiety attack, etc. Miss one or two and you might just not get hired again.

Granted, once you establish a good relationship with your clients, it's more likely that they'll cut you some slack here and there, but why not develop a reputation for coming through like clockwork? People love to surround themselves with things and people on whom they can depend.

USE EVERY ADVANTAGE YOU HAVE My sales and marketing background proved to be a very strong selling point for a lot of potential clients. At least in the beginning, leverage whatever existing expertise you have. If you come from health care, approach that industry. Your lack of professional writing experience will be more than offset by your knowledge of the industry, the vernacular, etc. If you have a travel and leisure background, go after those clients. Once you're established, then you can diversify but why not make it a little easier for yourself out of the gate?

PICK A SPECIALTY… MAYBE   In this regard, I'm different from a lot of writers, though not necessarily the majority. Many will recommend picking a particular specialty and sticking to it—which makes sense. If you can establish yourself as an expert in say, video scripting, direct mail, or annual reports, the word will get out and people in the market for that skill will seek you out. Once you're at home with a particular field, quickly cranking out a high volume of work at a premium rate becomes relatively easy.

The downside to this approach, at least as far as I'm concerned, is that doing the same type of work day in and day out can, for some people (like me), get old after awhile. Strictly a personal preference.

Being a generalist, I'm not married to any particular type of writing or any particular industry. You name it, I've written it and for a whole spectrum of industries. I may not be known as "The _____ Guy," but I like it this way because things never get boring and every day is a new adventure.

Turning the Tables   Several years back, I interviewed with a company involved with retail catalog work. I'd done some work with a subsidiary of theirs, had pumped them for referrals after the project, and they'd steered me to these folks. Their volume of work was heavy enough that, even with a staff of three full-time writers, they'd occasionally need to farm out some of it to freelancers.

After talking for the first five minutes about the occasional freelance possibilities with their firm, the tables unexpectedly turned. The three writers began asking me, somewhat wistfully, it seemed, about the types of work that I did. It soon became obvious that they were, to put it graciously, pretty weary of doing the same type of work day after day, for years. It was clear that they would have gladly switched places with me. Can't say I felt the same.

I think the ideal situation would be about three ad copy writing jobs a week paying $500–700 each. And that's not all that hard to do, once you're positioned. Which is what we're really talking about here: building sets of relationships and structures where you become the first person that a company or key individual within a company thinks of when they need specific copywriting skills.

In a Perfect World   One client—a small advertising agency—hires me almost exclusively for concepting. This is where the job gets really fun. I come to his office, meet with him and his graphic designer, and we'll brainstorm a concept for one of his clients. Invariably, we have a ball, laugh a lot, he buys me lunch and when I leave, we add up the hours—including lunch—multiply it by my hourly rate and I bill him. It averages about $350-500. Gotta love it.

Is this a typical day in the life of a freelance commercial writer? Not really, but it's sure sweet when it does happen. Nothing says you can't position yourself to get jobs like that with clockwork regularity. After a while, you'll discover what you're really good at and if you happen to love that aspect of the job also, it just makes sense to pursue work in that niche and promote yourself accordingly.

Another Pro-Generalist Reason As time goes on, I find I'm taking on projects that require a variety of skills. For example, I just did an annual hall of fame awards ceremony—sponsored by Junior Achievement and our local business publication—where each year, three prominent Atlanta businesspeople are inducted as laureates.

For starters, it involves writing a bio on each inductee for a special newspaper insert. Secondly, I put together three-minute video scripts for each of the honorees, an undertaking that calls in major research skills in gathering the visual elements and building the story. Finally, I craft the evening's event script, which is a start-to-finish chronology of the evening: all the stage direction, who comes up when, what they say, all the bridge copy between the speakers, the timing of the videos, acceptance speeches, etc.

These are three very distinct components requiring very different skills, and I've done a good enough job that they've hired me to do it six years in a row. And none of this work is particularly difficult.

Year one, my fee was $800. Year six? $2900. They even hired me to do the "Voice of God" voice-over (not a heavily advertised service in my repertoire) during the evening presentation last year, which bumped my fee up an additional $250 for a total of about 5 minutes of talk. A sidebar here: because this is a non-profit organization, I give them a break on my hourly rate and always end up "donating" a lot of extra time to the project. But I don't mind. It always comes back to me many times over.

Since I'm so experienced with this particular event, they wouldn't think of hiring anyone else for it. Point is, being a generalist helped tremendously in taking on this and other multi-faceted jobs.

GET REFERRALS Always ask your clients for referrals, within another division of their company or elsewhere. Assuming they're happy with your work, you've got a ready-made introduction to your next contact. All in all, it's a much better and more promising bet than making cold calls to companies that have no clue who you are.

Take UPS or Coca-Cola, where you have literally dozens of departments that might have a need for your services at some point in time. Make sure that multiple individuals within an organization know how to find you.

SOW THE SEEDS   I'm always amused when I'm discussing with friends the latest high-profile project with some prominent Fortune 500 firm, and they'll ask, "How'd you get that job?" Like it's such a divine mystery how one would penetrate the inner sanctums of such hallowed corporate entities.

It's no mystery. It's about putting in your time, making the contacts, doing your follow-up work, staying on top of things, and so on. By your second year or so, you'll be amazed at how steadily the referrals start coming in.

REMEMBER: NOTHING IS FOREVER   I look back on the companies for which I was doing a lot of work several years ago and, with very few exceptions, it's not the same group of companies that I'm working with today. And through no fault of my own. They may not have had a staff writer and now they do. Their business may have headed in a different direction and now they need less copywriting. Which is just another way of driving home the point that you must always be marketing, always seeking out new business, always making more contacts.

STAY VISIBLE   As discussed, most people don't want to work very hard to find a writer, and this very human tendency favors the "visible." If you happen to be right in front of them when that need arises, you've got an excellent shot at the work. Even more reason to stay in front of people—whether by phone, mail, or in person—as often as possible. But, be respectful of someone's time and professional space. Most people certainly don't mind hearing from you every two to three months, but skip the once-a-month thing unless they've specifically requested that kind of check-in schedule.

Follow Up Regularly   Do follow up when you've agreed to. This is where a good contact management program comes in handy. In fact, the only good reason for not keeping in touch is that you're so busy with work that you simply don't have time. Even that isn't a very good excuse, because invariably it's going to get slow.

Every successful FLCW knows the feeling of being in that amazing "zone," where the work seems to be flowing non-stop forever. Well, the bad news is that it *will* come to an end and get real quiet. If you've got a few free minutes, make some calls.

Knowledge is Power As we've discussed previously, the more you know, the more valuable you are to a client. I've recently done a series of internal newsletters for one division of a big telecommunications firm. In the process, I've learned a huge amount about this group: what they stand for, their goals and aspirations, where they're headed, how they communicate, the tone they want in an internal publication, what you can and can't say and how, etc.

If they had to hire someone else to do a job, there'd be a huge learning curve involved and even then, they probably wouldn't get the quality of work that I could turn out. Yes, I'm a good writer, but I come through largely because I'm so familiar with them. The upshot is I get regular calls from other people in the division for completely unrelated projects like brochures or speeches because I'm "in-the-loop" and can hit the ground running.

TRUST THE LAW OF AVERAGES In God and The Law of Averages We Trust. When making a lot of calls, it is your best friend. Remember that lesson about tying an order book to a dog's tail: eventually, someone's going to buy from him.

I capitalize The Law of Averages because it deserves your respect. As sure as the sun rises in the morning, if you get on the phone and make 50 calls, even if you only talk to two people and leave voice mails for the rest, someone will call you with a job within a few days. Not necessarily one of those 50, but someone will call. It's almost as if your efforts shook the trunk of a big fruit tree and a juicy apple on a distant branch dropped off.

Now, I'm not talking about going home right now and making the first 50 calls you've ever made and expecting the phone to start ringing. It's going to take a lot more than that to get the momentum going. But once you get the machine up and running, it will feed you well.

Momentum is Everything Try turning the steering wheel on a stationary car. Darn near impossible, isn't it? And when you start moving, you have to push on the gas for awhile until you get up to a cruising speed. But get it out on the highway going about 60 miles an hour and now, light pressure on the gas will keep it going. And how hard is it to change direction? You can do it with your pinky.

If the speed dips, all you need to do is tap the gas and you're up to speed again. It's all about momentum. I started my business by making about 700 phone calls in a month. That got the car running. Then it was a matter of keeping my foot on the gas with steady (but less) prospecting. It took a heckuva lot less to keep it going than it did to get it started.

GO OUT AND "PRESS THE FLESH"   Meet your prospects as often and as soon as possible. We've already discussed this. It's worth saying again.

DON'T GO "DIRECT"   If you're working with a big corporation through a MM (middleman) company who's paying you, never, ever approach that big company directly for work unless you've received the blessing of your immediate MM client. Many won't have a problem with it and will encourage you, glad they were able to get you in the door. With others, however, it's a surefire way to bring the wrath of God down upon you.

Why? Because you're "their" copywriter and they can bill you out to the big company at a higher rate than you're charging them, and pocket the difference. Standard operating procedure. It's also egg on their face because Biggie Corp. now gets you for, say, $75 an hour when before, they were paying your client $100 an hour for you.

It doesn't matter if the company approached you first with the offer to work with them directly. If they know you're good *and* they also know that they can save a chunk of money by hiring you directly, it probably *will* happen at some point.

If it does, be ready to say, "I sincerely appreciate the vote of confidence but I really need to stick with XYZ Design. They've taken very good care of me and I need to do the same." If you accept without asking your client, count on not only never working with that client again, but getting a reputation as well. Think hard.

The Right Protocol   Should you get the job through an MM like a design firm, but they let you bill the big company directly, then you shouldn't have anything to worry about in contacting them directly for work, though I would still check with your MM client as a courtesy. It'll demonstrate your sensitivity to a potentially sticky issue.

Moreover, if you're working with Biggie Co. through an MM who's paying you, *never* discuss money or hours with the big firm, but only with them that brung you... and signs your checks.

One last note: No matter how closely you're working with that big company, even at your MM's direction, always route copy through the MM first unless they tell you differently. Nothing irritates an MM faster than a copywriter who gets too chummy with the end client and starts acting a little too independently—not consulting the MM or making decisions about content and design on his/her own. Again, never forget who's the boss.

ROLL WITH THE PUNCHES I had an interesting situation pop up recently, along with a very funny story that underscores the occasional role of serendipity in the whole process. I got a call from an account executive (AE) at a PR firm that I had cold-called a year earlier, though nothing had materialized in 12 months. Evidence, of course, of the power of "sowing the seeds." Just because you don't get immediate work from a major or minor prospecting effort means nothing. There's always a gestation period.

The AE explains that they have a newsletter job for a big local telecommunications client and was wondering if I'd be interested in taking a look at it. Sure. So, I show up at their office for the meeting and here's where it starts getting a little surreal.

Through the Looking Glass The AE greets me, brings me into his office and says, "Well, we're really excited about seeing your design work." Huh? "Um, I'm a writer, not a designer" I reply. "Oh, we know that you write, but you're also a designer too, right?" No, I reply, I don't do any design work. I'm strictly a writer.

AE pauses, perplexed, letting that sink in. I'm thinking about my business card, which he has, that clearly has "WriteInc." as the company name. "Hmmm. Well, since you're already here," he says, "we might as well take a look at your writing."

This last line was clearly delivered in a tone that implied that it was the courteous thing to do under the circumstances—since he'd screwed up—as opposed to anything he really had any interest in doing. All-righty then.

Curiouser and Curiouser So off to the conference room we troop and in walks the president of the company, who's still in the dark, along with another guy. He introduces himself and then turns to the other person and says, "And this is So-and-So, the writer on the project. So, let's take a look at your design work." I turn to the AE and say, "Do you want to break it to him or should I?"

Prez looks a little confused now. I say, "I'm a writer, not a designer, and I'm not sure where the mix-up came in," trying my darndest not to get the AE in too much trouble. The prez gets this look on his face, remarkably similar to the one the AE had just moments ago, picks up my card, examines it and without looking up, ponders out loud, "Now, how do you get designer out of WriteInc.?" A sensible question. AE sinks even lower into his seat.

Being a very polite guy as well, the Prez also suggests they take a look at my work. Well, now I'm starting to get a bit uncomfortable, and say, "Well, I feel a little funny under the circumstances. I don't want to step on any toes," glancing over at my fellow scribe.

Not to worry, let's just take a look, says the prez. As you wish. To make a long story short, I got the job. Having done similar work for that end client, my experience was a perfect match for the project.

And according to the president, when I later mentioned feeling sorry for the other writer, he said it was a tough call to make but that they'd worked a lot with him before and would again in the future, so they'd make it up to him.

Can You Top This? Here's where it gets even more fun. Just as background, this job was a "trial" of sorts. The telecomm firm was trying this PR firm out on the first newsletter, and if it went well, they'd get the contract to produce it every month for the next year.

I do the job, the end client is thrilled with my work but unfortunately for the PR firm, not nearly so enamored with them. Not that they did anything glaringly wrong.

I imagine that she was thinking that by the time she explained to them everything about a project: content, contacts, timetable, and still had to review it every step of the way, she might as well just do it herself and save herself a chunk of money. So, at the project's end, she went to them and basically said, we've decided to go ahead and try to manage the project in-house and… we want your writer.

Do the Right Thing Well, needless to say, the PR firm wasn't overjoyed with this outcome, and I knew what was coming next. They called and proposed that, while they certainly didn't want to stand in the way of a positive working relationship, they felt they were entitled to a small percentage of the fees that I stood to earn for the upcoming work. Very fair sentiment.

We agreed on 10%, which given the relatively healthy budgets assigned to the projects by my new client, was a fairly painless bite. In addition, the agreement was for just one year and only on that one newsletter. Any other work I get referred to within the organization is all mine—and there have already been two other sizable jobs in five months (news of a good copywriter travels fast!).

I could have played hardball and refused and the PR firm could've done little. Except of course, never hire me again and bad-mouth me to anyone they met. As it is, they're happy about the check they get every month for doing nothing and we keep the relationship nice and healthy. More importantly, they deserve it. I wouldn't have that work if it wasn't for them, so I do the right thing—and the smart thing—and happily write the check each month.

SEND THANK-YOU NOTES   In Chapter Six, we talked about the importance of sending out follow-up letters to prospects after first phone calls or meetings with them. In that same vein, get in the habit of sending out thank-you notes to clients after you've done your first job with them, and ideally, after each job.

You can certainly send a nice short letter on your letterhead, but an even better idea is to buy some simple note or thank-you cards, ideally with attractive artistic renderings, watercolor scenes, flower arrangements, and so on. No teddy bears.

Get several different styles, both masculine and feminine. It's a nice personal touch that I promise they'll appreciate. While it certainly shows professionalism, in a subtle way, it establishes a human connection with them that goes much deeper than relatively sterile letterhead would.

On at least three occasions, I've been in a client's office or cubicle a few weeks after I'd sent them a card and have seen the card stuck to their bulletin board or cubicle wall. They were attractive New England-themed watercolors and served as a mini-painting in an otherwise fairly drab setting. As long as it's up there, every time they look at it, they'll think of me. A good thing.

Make Up Reasons   Don't stop with thank-you notes just for work. Make up reasons to send out notes: as an acknowledgment of a job well done, to someone who helped make your life so much easier during a recent project, as a "nice to meet you" after a networking gathering, etc. People feel special when they're remembered and will in turn remember you when it counts. And speaking of notes...

Do Personal Christmas Cards   Every November, I come up with all kinds of compelling rationalizations for not doing my client Christmas cards, then say, "Thanks for sharing" and do them anyway. In addition to the obvious opportunity to thank those who've paid your mortgage and sent you on nice vacations that year, it's a great way to once again get in front of your regular clients as well as promising prospects.

Don't get fancy, embossed cards or the ones with the printed "Thank-You-For-Your-Business" message. Just send a nice regular one, like you'd send to your friends (they're cheaper, for starters), and jot a few notes inside: either a "enjoyed working with you," "thanks for your business," or "look forward to working with you soon." Make them feel less like clients and more like friends.

PROJECT A GOOD ATTITUDE   Regardless of what the snafus might be on a project, you want a client's experience of working with you to be hassle-free, especially for new ones. Even if the screw-ups were all their fault, if you're easy-going about it, they'll walk away thinking pleasant thoughts, and bottom line, people like to do business with those who provide them with pleasant experiences. It's the basic pain-pleasure principle. You do it too.

It's essentially your real-life application of the saying, "The customer is always right." Which, by the way, I absolutely don't believe is always true. Be easy to work with, but don't be a doormat.

GET SAMPLES OF YOUR WORK   This is VERY important. Samples are gold for your business. A portfolio stuffed with gorgeous, beautifully written, four-color masterpieces across a wide spectrum of industries will open just about any door. Ideally, you'll have so many things to potentially show a client that you pick the 5–6 pieces most applicable to their business and/or the proposed project. Getting samples sounds so deceptively simple. What should be so hard about it? Well, let me tell you a story.

In the fall of 1996, I got in the door of a design firm that did a lot of work with that big soft drink company in these parts. Over the next nearly three years, between brochures, proposals, and headlining projects, I did probably 50–60 jobs with these designers for the big company.

After all that, I have exactly two samples of work. Incredible? I'm obviously not trying hard enough, you say? I've asked them no less than 10 times, often as the only point of a particular call. Unusual? Actually, believe it or not, it isn't all that strange.

The Elusive Sample Take a guess at how many jobs end up yielding a sample or "clip" (or "tear sheet" in the case of an ad). 75%? 90%? I've talked with many of my colleagues—both writers and graphic designers—about this and we figure the number's about 20–25%, if you're lucky. How can that be, you ask?

What happens to the other 75–80%? Well, a certain percentage of work never gets printed for a number of reasons. If it's headlining projects for instance, you may get paid for your time, but the client may not end up using your stuff.

Sometimes the client changes directions completely and gets another copywriter.

Another not uncommon tale is that a client micromanages a job to the point where the design and the copy are so dreadful that you wouldn't *want* to put your name to it and show it to anyone.

On the flip side, one colleague noted that her "hit" rate for samples is closer to 90% and that maybe a closer relationship with the client contact might help. By all accounts, 90% is unusually high, but apparently it can happen.

Always ask your client to put 6-10 samples aside for you once they get printed. They probably won't remember it on their own and if it's important to you, take the initiative to remind them. Repeatedly.

A Well-Spent "Sample" Day Given that a good sample (amongst several) can open a lot of doors, it's hugely worth it to invest some time driving around town to pick up three or four good samples from your customers.

Don't wait for them to send them to you, even if they've promised. Go pick them up in person. It not only speeds up the process, it gives you yet another opportunity to get in front of your client. Just as importantly, samples sent through the mail can get beat up pretty badly unless they're well-padded, which most clients, I hate to say, rarely take the time to do. Last thing you need is a half-dozen bent copies of a good piece.

SAVE YOUR JUNK E-MAIL   You know all that unsolicited stuff you get from your friends, neighbors, acquaintances, and total strangers on e-mail? All the pithy quotes, jokes, clever stories, and the pieces that tickle your funny bone or tug on your heartstrings? Start viewing them in a completely different way.

Take a moment to read them and if you can see the possibility of using them in a speech, brochure or some other writing project, hang on to them. Obviously, we're not talking about the off-color stuff, but there will be plenty of possible gems. Keep them in separate computer files, like *Quotes, Jokes, Clever Stories, Heartstrings,* etc. You never know when one might just be perfect.

LISTEN MORE, WORK LESS   Say you're working on some creative piece, like a marketing brochure, ad copy, etc., and you need a good concept and some strong supporting copy. If you let your client just talk away about what she's trying to accomplish with the piece, all the great things about the product, stories about how the company started, why customers like it, what she wants to emphasize, the desired tone, etc., eventually she'll give you everything you need.

And if you're paying attention, you'll recognize a creative concept for the piece. You spend less time guessing and less time writing.

For Example Early on, I did a seminar marketing brochure for a chiropractor who traveled the world to international athletic competitions, including several Olympics, lending his chiropractic services to different teams. He planned to start teaching other chiropractors how to become Olympic doctors and along with a freelance art director, I helped him create this brochure.

I was looking for just the right concept that would get the reader's attention. So I asked him a lot of questions about all his experiences—which were fascinating—and just listened. I knew if I listened long enough, he'd give me what I needed. He didn't disappoint me.

He was sharing with me the story about one of his athletes/patients who'd won a medal at the 1988 Seoul Olympics. After receiving his medal, the athlete came off the stand, came right over to the doctor, took off his medal, put it around the doctor's neck, and said, "Thanks, Doc. I couldn't have done it without you." Now, is that a great concept or what? What more do you need?

We hired an illustrator, who did a stylized re-enactment of that moment, showing just a waist-to-neck perspective of the medal hand-off, with the "Thanks, Doc…" line prominently displayed and we had a winner of a piece that got a great response. Moral of the story: Let your client talk and they'll make your job a lot easier *and* make you look like a genius.

KEEP YOUR WORD Want a simple no-cost way to put yourself ahead of about 95% of the pack? I had a very enlightening experience several months back as I set out for a scheduled appointment. This company had been given my name by a designer friend of mine.

They called me, said they'd heard good things about me, had a lot of copywriting projects coming up and could I come in and show them my portfolio (also incidentally, known as your "book"). We met, they liked my work and a week later, called me for a project. Great. We set an appointment the following Monday to get going.

Monday morning rolls around and an unforeseen little emergency has me running about 15 minutes late, so I call to let them know. I ask for my guy, and I'm told he's not in. I explain we had an appointment scheduled for 10:00 and that I'm running a few minutes late. Long pause. "Um, he was called out suddenly by a client and I don't think he'll be back for a few hours." Sure glad I called before I came in, I said lightly.

Why don't you give him a call in a few hours, the gentleman suggested. I politely countered with, "Please have him call me when he returns." Only fair under the circumstances. OK, not a crime to miss an appointment especially if one of your big clients is screaming. Just clean it up later.

So, when 3:00 came and went with no return call, I called him and left a cordial voicemail: "Hey, John, this is Peter Bowerman, sorry we couldn't hook up this morning. I'm trying to set my week up here, so give me a call and let's figure out a good time to reschedule our meeting." He never called me back. Ever. A few months later, I called back and left another message. Still nothing.

It's a Sloppy World... Some might argue that I clearly needed him more than he needed me, so his little brain cramp didn't really hurt him. Beside the point. It's indicative of a larger trend of overall sloppiness in the professional world: People missing appointments, forgetting deadlines, and not delivering on promised actions. And then coming up with an excuse for why it never happened.

Philosophically speaking, one could view this pattern as symptomatic of human behavior in general. Personally and professionally, so many people seem to have a very casual relationship with their word. Quick to promise, slow to deliver. They shoot for that first impression, and then somehow believe that their lack of follow-through won't be noticed.

Well, unfortunately for them, there is a small collection of intrepid souls who are committed to something more than short-term appearances. It's a matter of pride for them to not only keep their word, but to *be* their word. And guess what? People do notice.

The Standouts We all know them. When they tell us they'll do something, we don't give it a second thought. We know it'll be on time and well done. They return their phone calls. They consistently deliver more than they promised. They don't make excuses; they make it happen. They quietly and humbly reek of competence and integrity. They're a breath of fresh air. What's sad is that they stick out for their relative rarity. But, they've discovered one of the simplest, most powerful, and least practiced success formulas.

Woody Allen once said something to the effect that, "90% of success in life is a matter of just showing up." You don't necessarily have to be the best, brightest, fastest, or sharpest. But "show up": Do what you say you're going to do. Be where you say you're going to be. Make your word count for something. Deliver more than you promise. Do all this, and you'll shoot to the head of the class.

I recently got a call from that president of the PR firm to whom I'm paying the 10% referral fee for the newsletter job. He had just received my fifth or sixth straight check and was calling to *thank* me for sticking to our deal. I called him back and said "you're welcome" but that he didn't need to thank me for simply doing what I had agreed to do. This was, apparently, in his estimation and in this day and age, quite noteworthy.

People Do Notice   I have a client with whom I'll be working on a corporate image package soon. In our first meeting, he said to check back with him the following Wednesday. When I called Wednesday, he commented on how I'd gotten back to him exactly when I said I would. No big deal, I thought, but it made an impression on him. It communicated, "Here's someone who's reliable," and I promise you, he feels good about having me on the project.

If I hadn't called on the exact date, he probably wouldn't have dropped me, but it might have left a slightly unsettled feeling with him. We're talking almost subconscious messages here, which is even more reason to make a good impression when you have the chance, because the subconscious is what drives people's actions and beliefs.

Built-In Padding   Get in the habit of promising drafts to clients one day later than you think it'll be. If you get it done a day earlier than he expects, he's happy, impressed, and can get the next step of the process moving that much quicker. Should a quick-turnaround project come up that you'd like to take on, it'll be that much easier to get them both done if you have an extra day built in.

GIVE BACK   Early in the book, we discussed the role that *pro bono* work can play in helping to create a portfolio from scratch. But at the risk of sounding like I'm delivering a morality lecture, you shouldn't just do charitable work when you want something. Get in the habit of doing at least one *pro bono* job each year. In addition to just making you feel good and really doing something nice for a worthwhile but budget-conscious organization, it can serve another purpose: If you're the type to have any lingering guilt over all those jobs with flat fees that took you way less time to finish than you originally thought, all these unpaid hours will quickly get you right with your Maker again.

EARN YOUR MONEY   One doesn't earn $60-100/hour or more for no reason. I recently picked up a client through a solo graphic designer—a very fruitful avenue. They'd had some unpleasant experiences with freelance copywriters before, which is something that, unfortunately, you get used to hearing. I asked for almost twice what she really wanted to pay for the job, but she agreed. I turned the project around when I said I would, gave her lots of concepts to choose from, and even made a few suggestions for improving their marketing—a true "value-added" service.

When we were done, I asked her if she'd had a good experience. Absolutely, she said—that it was so easy working with me. Meaning? Well, according to her, when she tried to explain to previous copywriters what she did or didn't want, often they couldn't quite grasp what she was asking for (or didn't try very hard), putting the burden on her to figure out very specifically what she was looking for, which meant more time she had to spend at it.

I say that's the writer's job and he/she should be asking enough questions at the outset to tease out exactly what it is the client wants. Clients won't always drop it into your lap in a neat, bite-size nugget. It's your job to figure it out. That's why you're getting the big bucks. They hired you so they don't have to do it themselves, so the more time they have to spend on it, the more it defeats their purpose.

STAY IN TOUCH WITH PEOPLE   Every few months, when making calls to your existing client/prospect list, it's going to occur to you for about the umpteenth time that you're probably wasting your time with 50% of these people—the ones you call, but who never call back. If all we're talking about here is a 15-second investment in a voice-mail message every quarter, keep doing it.

I can think of about a half-dozen instances where I got work from people two years after I initially started calling them, and often the only time I'd spoken to them since the beginning. Or I'll get a call from someone referred to me by the person who never returns my call. You may not think they've noticed your calls, but they'll surprise you and often pleasantly.

If a prospect gets a half-dozen calls from you—even voice mails—over several years, it tells them that you're still in the game, must be enjoying a reasonable amount of success and ergo, you probably aren't a lousy writer. In and of itself, your continued presence in the business is a testimonial of sorts.

PARTNER WITH A DESIGNER   I'm a big fan of this concept because it opens up a lot more opportunities and can put some nice money in your pocket. I've briefly discussed hooking up with a designer twice: early in the book, when discussing your portfolio, as well as in the last chapter. Remember my solo designer client who became one of my biggest customers?

Fairly soon into your career, you'll run across a healthy number of freelance graphic designers through clients, referrals, by networking, etc. Unless they're just absolutely slammed all the time (haven't met many of those and if I do, I ask them their secret), you can bet they'll be very receptive to the idea of collaborating.

Pick Your Partners Carefully These folks will vary greatly in talent (just like writers…). Obviously, if you meet them on a project, you should be able to get some idea of their work. If you meet them through a referral or at a function, definitely take the time to look at their work and figure out if they're good. Just as importantly, do you click with them?

No matter how talented someone actually is, life is simply too short (and there are way too many other good designers out there) to deal with someone who's temperamental, unreliable, or a major *prima donna*. Ask around, find out who the industry thinks are the best, and contact them. If they're way too busy and aren't that interested, ask them to refer you to someone they know is good.

Typical Scenarios OK, so you've found two or three designers who you like personally and whose work and reputations are solid. Chances are, you won't be doing three jobs a month with these new friends of yours. Most of your work will be of the "we've-already-got-a-designer-and-just-need-you-for-the-copy" type, but every few months or so, you'll run across a client or be referred to one who would be a perfect prospect for such an arrangement.

As described in the last chapter, typically, that would be a small company that's growing fast and up till now, hasn't had or made the time to put together a really good marketing piece. Or perhaps it's a small company whose staff has been writing their own ads but is smart enough and now has the budget to bring in some professional talent—and going to a pricey ad agency is too rich for their blood.

True Professional Fulfillment Assuming you're working with good clients— ones who actually plan on taking your advice (what a concept…)—these kinds of jobs can be some of the most professionally fulfilling of any work you may do, and here's why:

For starters, there's something very rewarding about being truly looked up to as the professionals, the people with the answers, as opposed to just a copywriter or designer, one of many a company has dealt with over the years.

While being part of a big project for a Fortune 500 company can put you in some exciting arenas, it's the "little fish in the big pond" scenario. With these smaller clients, however, you're definitely the "big fish in the small pond."

Because this is probably their first serious marketing piece, and they're looking to you for expertise, you'll have a lot more creative autonomy and they're that much more likely to accept your suggestions and direction than might be the case with MegaCorp.

Remember, oftentimes they really don't know what they're doing in this new arena. They need your help. And when you put together a powerful piece that effectively boosts their professional image in the marketplace—and they're delighted with it—you will have really made a difference for them.

Since the reality in this profession is that most of your jobs will be largely directed by your client, you'll savor the opportunity to take more ownership of the production process, especially when it means having your ideas win and your creative vision realized.

An Attractive Proposition To inexperienced clients, hooking up with a designer/writer combo can be a very attractive proposition. Typically, on their first serious marketing piece or professional ad campaign, these folks haven't thought it out very far. They may know they need a writer but past that, how the whole thing is going to come together is still this vague and foggy notion.

Then I come along and ask: "Would you folks be interested in a turnkey situation, where a graphic designer and I team up to create a piece for you, and handle the project from the first meeting to final delivery of printed product?" Much more often than not, with this class of small but growing clients, their eyes light up and they respond with "You bet we would!"

Their life just got infinitely easier, they only have to deal with two people, and best of all, they get it for an excellent price—one of the key selling points to this scenario.

Because we're both freelance, and in all likelihood, work out of our homes, we don't have the huge overhead an ad agency or larger design firm would have, and can pass on these operational efficiencies to the client in the form of lower costs. Typically, the total fee would consist of my time, the designer's time, the printing cost, and an additional amount added in for "project management." I've seen the total be far less than half of an agency's fee.

Don't get me wrong. There absolutely are times when a company needs the full service that an ad agency or graphic design firm can offer in terms of a multi-faceted marketing campaign—TV spots, media placements, etc. However, often, a savvy two-person writer/designer team is more than enough and far easier on the wallet.

Project Management Unless you know all about the printing process, which I would certainly recommend you get up to speed on at some point, you'll need to find a designer who does, which fortunately, is most of them. So, as we've discussed previously, they'll be managing the project, which they're happy to do for a small additional fee: generally about a 20–25% surcharge on the fee for their time (similar to your rates: $60-85+/hr.)

I have managed several projects when the designer didn't have that expertise, and then of course the fee came to me. It was a great experience, and if you get some guidance (and referrals to some good printers) from other designer friends, and pick your printer's brain to help get you up to speed, the process should go very smoothly. As we've mentioned earlier, however, don't underestimate the complexity of this arena.

A Final Huge Plus Some of my most profitable clients came from graphic designers who, because they've worked with me on a variety of projects and are now comfortable with my skills *and* with me, refer me to their big clients. It's basically risk-free for them and their clients. So seek out the solo designers and opportunities to collaborate.

PARTNER WITH ANOTHER WRITER   I've mentioned this before but it bears repeating. A few months into my career, I found another writer and a true prince of a guy. I only knew him over the phone, and he was kind enough to help me with all those questions you always have when you're starting something new.

When I'd rather look dumb to one of my own than to a client, I'd call him up with questions about contracts, estimating fees, how to do different kinds of writing, you name it.

I can't tell you what a difference it made, just knowing I had someone I could call on who knew the ropes. Don't try to do it all yourself. Remember: in most markets, there's plenty of work for everyone, so there's no reason for someone not to help out their colleagues. I'm sure it made him feel good to play that role for me. Which leads me to the next suggestion…

START A WRITERS GROUP   At about the three-year mark of my career, I started a writers group. I'd assembled a short list of 8–10 folks I'd heard about or with whom I'd crossed paths, including my above-described mentor, and approached them.

While several of us were part of a larger freelance creative network of designers, photographers, and writers, FLCWs have their own unique set of issues and challenges and we had no forum in which to discuss them. My idea was very warmly received.

I kicked it off by hosting a brunch at my house and then every 4–6 weeks after that, another member would host for what eventually turned into a Sunday pot luck dinner. At the first meeting, we all brought our portfolios and shared our work with one another. To our delight, we discovered that each of us was an excellent writer, and while there was plenty of skill overlap, there were some very distinct talents in the group as well.

Many, Many Pluses The upshot is that I now know the work of 6–7 writers, people I'm very comfortable referring to clients when I'm too busy, out of town, or if the project is out of my scope of expertise. We have an unwritten rule that if we're referred to an existing client, we do the one job but never try to take the client.

Most of us have referred each other and been referred in return. We've become that much more valuable to our clients because now, we're a resource even when we're not available.

Most importantly, it's a wonderful social venue for us, one that we all very much look forward to. It's been an absolute smashing success, if for no other reason than we all really like each other and so enjoy "talking shop" with our peers. Consider it. You won't be sorry.

KEEP YOUR SPACE CLEAN Have you looked around your office lately? When the phone rings, does it take three rings to locate the pile under which it's hiding? Do you cling tenaciously to the battle cry of insufferable slobs everywhere: "I Know Exactly Where Everything Is!"?

My office certainly wouldn't pass the white glove test every day, but I know the precise moment when I can't stand it anymore. Get ruthless! If you haven't used that piece of paper or magazine article for three months, toss it. I promise you won't miss it, Murphy's Law notwithstanding. It's amazing how much more clearly you can think and operate when your work space is in order.

CLEAN UP YOUR MESSES I'm talking about a different kind of mess here. If you're in business for any length of time, chances are, you'll probably screw up with some clients. You get upset, say the wrong thing at the wrong time, don't deliver what you said you would and then snap at them about it, or any number of other unfortunate transgressions.

Assuming the client is now not talking to you, and will probably never hire you again, there's a temptation to just say, "Well, what's done is done. Better to just move on." Wrong.

The situation may very well be unsalvageable, but you don't *know* that. More importantly, there's something very powerful that's available out of communicating with that person. You may have little control over what that client's ultimately going to hold on to, but you certainly have a say in giving him or her a few options.

In order of preference, do it in person, call them up, or as a last resort, write a letter. Whatever the mode of communication, the tone should be, "I want to sincerely apologize for my behavior. I have no excuse, it was unprofessional, and I'd completely understand if you chose to not work with me again. And whether or not you do, I needed to communicate this." Regardless of the outcome, you'll make an impression. Sincere apologies are about as rare as winning lottery tickets these days.

More importantly, you'll feel a burden lifted. Maybe you'll even realize that there are other people—like friends and family—with whom you've got similar stuff to handle. Take care of those issues, and watch what happens to your business.

GO BACK TO THE BASICS   At the beginning of my second year in business, in the wake of a wonderful first 12 months, and with tons of wonderful credits, a bulging rolodex, oodles of goodwill, and money in the bank, I just knew, that by January 4th or so, I'd be swamped once again. Instead, I got silence. For weeks on end. It freaked me out.

But, instead of sitting around wondering what happened, I returned to what had brought me such a banner year: phone calls, mailings, and follow-up, follow-up, follow-up, follow-up, follow-up. Lo and behold, after only about two weeks of that old familiar drill, the happy sound of ringing phones once again filled the air.

OK, let's talk writing, specifically the types of work you'll get, how to write them, and how they differ from others. Sharpen your pencils ....

Chapter Fourteen

What Will You Be Writing?

YOU KNOW HOW TO WRITE, RIGHT?   Since the answer should be yes, we'll talk instead about common writing projects, with some brief overviews. If you're a good writer and a quick study, then writing, to a certain extent, is writing. You'll catch on as you go.

Obviously ad copy differs from technical documentation, but after awhile, you'll know what clients are looking for from the context, along with what has and hasn't worked for them in the past.

If you take to specializing in a particular type of writing, like brochures, direct mail packages, or press releases, again, experience will teach you much more than I could ever tell you in a book. The thrust of this book continues to be the actual building and running of a freelance commercial writing business.

One Writing Tip   That said, I can't resist offering this one tip on writing that works in virtually any arena and has served me extremely well over the years: *Write like you talk.* Do this one thing and your writing will improve 100%. I can't tell you how many times I've seen very articulate people put a pen to paper and end up with awkward, stilted, wooden copy.

FIRST QUESTION – WHO'S THE AUDIENCE?   When I started out in this business, with my meager portfolio and abundant enthusiasm, the one thing I leveraged to death when I spoke with prospects was my 15 years of sales and marketing experience. It's now more like 20+ years, because, as discussed, this business is, first and foremost, a sales and marketing venture.

I would tell them that, because of my experience, I brought a sales and marketing mindset to the table: I write to sell, not just to communicate.

At the start of every project, the absolute first thing you have to ask is, "Who's the audience?" *(Hint: By making this your first question, it shows clients that you have at least some clue what you're doing.)* Obviously, how you'd write to reach 50+ year-old married women would be very different from a piece targeting teenagers.

It's All Sales Now, my work takes me primarily into the marketing arena, and chances are good that you'll be operating there for the most part as well. That means writing pieces that attempt to sell, persuade, and convince the audience about the merits of a particular product, service, and/or company *and* spur that reader/viewer to take some sort of action.

Arguably, any project—even technical documentation, corporate training modules, or grandiose documentaries—requires you to sell the audience on your approach or point of view and ask the same "Who's the audience?" questions.

So when you've got a new project, whatever it is, and you've determined who the audience is, you start asking questions of your client to discover that audience's hot buttons:

* *What's important to people in this group?*
* *What motivates them?*
* *How do they think?*
* *How do they talk?*
* *What words and language will get through to them?*
* *What's going to turn their heads and get them to pay attention?*
* *Once they pay attention, what will it take to get them to take action?*

"Take action" can mean: buy the product, or more likely, visit the store, take a test drive, make the call, order the bigger brochure, return the reply card, or whatever.

Get Into Their World I'm in the midst of writing a corporate brochure for an importer who specializes in finding, designing and/or manufacturing cosmetic-related products in the Far East—brushes, sponges, applicators, and an array of packaging, like baskets, bags, etc.—for the big cosmetic firms.

Once I'd determined that the primary and secondary audiences for the piece were purchasing agents (PA) and product development managers (PD), respectively, the next step was to figure out how to best speak to those groups.

So I started asking questions of both my client *and* her clients—the PAs and PDs themselves—to discover what their world is like. What pressures do you face? What's a typical day? What sort of demands are placed on you? And most importantly, *How has doing business with my client's company made your life easier?*

It turns out that a PA's life is endless meetings, reports, and deadlines, not to mention constant pressure from marketing to deliver new ideas, new products and the next "winner." They're also used to product vendors who *they* have to track down for answers and status reports.

These people have no time to waste and no patience for problems. Well, through these little chats, I discovered a whole host of ways in which my client simplifies the lives of her customers: reliability, follow-up, intimate knowledge of her clients' needs, and success in consistently bringing them new products or meeting their requests for new designs.

So these become the copy points (See p. 233 in Appendix B), the things that we emphasize in the piece to get the attention of those prospects who face the same challenges and as such, stand to reap the same benefits. The audience needs to see themselves in the copy for it to have any relevance to them.

Speak Their Language Another more fun example is some headline concepting I did for a snack company. They needed a catchy slogan for a display that was going in a college snack bar/cafeteria to promote the sale of some snack products, and obviously geared to the late teen/early 20-something market.

We know the audience, so how do we talk to them? In their language, of course. In addition to a bunch of straightforward ones, I came up with a few "outtakes." Though I had tongue firmly in cheek when I wrote them, note the P.S. to my client afterwards:

Being Hungry Sucks.
Hunger Sucks.

P.S. OK, so I'm kidding here, but if 18–24 year-olds are indeed your market, you'd sure sell a lot of snacks with these…

And I firmly believe that. Of course, corporate America—still an essentially conservative bunch—just can't push the envelope that far, as much as they might like to.

You've got to get them to read it, and they have to walk away having understood the message you were trying to convey. It can't just be cute. It has to sell. It's been said that the advertising business is incestuous, in that the industry decides which ad campaigns deserve the awards and it's not always the ones that were "bottom-line" effective as much as the ones they deemed the most clever.

It's fine to be clever, but anytime you write something, remember who your audience is and ask yourself if this copy communicates effectively to that audience. If it doesn't, start over.

And it doesn't require some extraordinary creative instinct to write good copy. Sure, some writers are more talented than others, but if you undertake the process formulaically as I've described it, you'll end up with copy that communicates powerfully.

OK, let's look at the different types of work we'll be doing.

MARKETING BROCHURES   Just about every company that sells a product or service needs to create a marketing brochure at some point. As the company grows, if the owners are smart, they'll keep improving and upgrading their literature to reflect new directions, products, industry trends, and market demands.

Oftentimes, the brochure that a prospect sees is the first and only impression that individual has of that company and their product line. So, it had better be good.

Brochures can range from a simple black and white tri-fold (8½″ x 11″—folded twice, so why do they call it a tri-fold?) all the way up to a large, multi-page, full-color production with pockets, flaps, die-cuts, slip sheets, and every bell and whistle under the sun. (See next section.)

If you do a good job on a company's first brochure, chances are excellent they'll use you again when it's time to create something a little more ambitious. They know you do good work, and more importantly, you know their business. Refer to Chapter Six for a review of the highlights of a simple marketing brochure. Study brochures you get in the mail. Figure out which ones "get through" to you and why, as well as which ones don't and why not.

CORPORATE IMAGE/IDENTITY PIECES   As a company grows and begins to assume its particular niche in the market, the next logical step often is to create a signature piece that captures the company's identity, what its mission is, its standing in the industry, and a relatively brief (vs. the more-in-depth treatment in product brochures or catalogs) overview of the product line. In a sense, these are marketing brochures, but much more polished versions.

They tend to be slick, glossy, image-driven, light on copy, and are designed to leave the reader with any number of powerful and overriding impressions, depending on the nature of the business: professionalism, stability, creativity, reliability, consistency, international reputation, financial strength, etc.

Often, a multi-page four-color brochure is the cornerstone of a corporate identity package, also including product brochures, spec sheets, and smaller brochures that share common design elements. The whole set of literature works together cohesively to make a singular and powerful statement about the company.

To successfully produce an image package, the writer needs to be able to think "big picture," think more abstractly, and be able to communicate in loftier, more grandiose terms.

Vanity Pieces? The cynics in our midst might say—and not altogether without merit—that the brochure portion of most corporate image packages is just non-substantive fluff. They'll mutter that the real purpose of creating such a package is as a vehicle for ego-gratification and to wow clients.

For better or worse, our business culture today does demand a certain amount of such self-important posturing, and if you can deliver the hard-hitting nuggets that'll bring a lump to the throat of a target audience member, you should stay pretty busy.

Sweet Rewards Please don't get the impression that I'm painting this corporate arena as a sort of well-paying "sellout." In many cases, this can be one of the most challenging, rewarding, and creative arenas you will ever operate in and here's why: when the leaders of a company set out to put down on paper who it is that they really are, it can be one of the most difficult things they have ever done.

If they are committed to getting at the heart of their mission, this forces them to do some serious soul-searching as to what exactly it is that they stand for. And that is vital for them.

In such instances, your role can be as a facilitator, to help gel their thinking, and put a voice to what's floating around in their collective psyches. There's no better feeling than coming up with a few lines that has the company president exclaim, "That's it! I couldn't put my finger on it, but you nailed it!"

BUSINESS LETTERS   A business letter or sales letter is generally the first line of attack in most promotional or informational packages sent to a client or prospect. A well-written one can make the difference between a piece of communication that gets canned quickly and one that gets read and acted on. That translates to real bottom-line impact.

If you're comfortable with the sales/marketing mindset (ie., writing to sell, a features/benefits orientation, what's in it for the reader, etc.) and feel confident in your ability to quickly get a reader's attention and spur him to the desired action, sales letters are one more arrow to add to your quiver of expertise.

Vast Experience Unnecessary   However, an absence of an extensive sales background doesn't preclude you from being an effective scribbler of business correspondence. It depends on the demands of a client. If they're specifically looking for someone who can write strong, persuasive, grab-'em-by-the-throat copy, and that's not comfortable for you, you might take a pass … or not. The only way to learn is to try.

If, however, a client is simply looking for a well-written introductory letter to material that's been requested, and as such, doesn't need to be as aggressive, you shouldn't have any trouble pulling it off. Believe me, I've seen some business letters that are so frighteningly bad that simple coherence, proper grammar and spelling, and a reasonably logical flow would have made a 1000% improvement and thrilled the client to no end.

Double Duty Makes Sense   While small to medium-size companies are probably your best prospects for business letters, your best bet is to get this kind of work as an add-on to bigger projects and often from your regular clients.

For instance, if you've just worked on a client's marketing brochure or corporate image piece, why not suggest that you also write the sales cover letter that will accompany the package in marketing campaigns? It only makes sense to keep the tone and writing style consistent.

In fact, make the suggestion *before* you start that big project and get anywhere from $150–300+ extra dollars out of the deal. It'll show your client that you possess that crucial "big-picture" sales mentality. There are few things more tragic than a beautifully written marketing brochure or corporate identity package fronted by a clunky, bland, client-written cover letter.

It's like an incompetent, inarticulate receptionist at a successful well-managed company. It's the first thing the recipient usually reads, so it has to be good. As the saying goes, "You don't get a second chance to make a first impression."

As mentioned earlier, my standard opening paragraph to a variety of business correspondence (marketing, meeting/phone follow-up, etc.) is this:

As a freelance writer, my goal is to enhance your image, improve your profit picture, and make your life easier. If it carries your name, shouldn't it be the best reflection of you?

Perhaps I should vary it and come up with ten different versions for different scenarios, but I like its simplicity and how, right up front, it addresses those issues nearest and dearest to a client's heart: image/reputation, profit, and simplifying his/her life. I'm speaking to my audience.

Who wouldn't agree that there are few things more important to any businessperson? Did you notice the use of a question to draw in the reader? Can you see how questions involve the reader right from the start and force him or her to consider your proposition? You're still reading, aren't you? Be sure to check out the business letter "before/after" scenario in Appendix B.

ADVERTISING COPY Personally, I find writing ad copy to be some of the most fun work out there. Generally, you get to be creative and persuasive, an often challenging combination. Of course, the level of creativity is going to depend on what kind of ad is being written.

Study advertisements in magazines, newspapers, and billboards. Try viewing them from an academic perspective. Your study could lead to a healthy increase in your income, so learn to enjoy the process. Which ones get your attention? Why are they effective?

And remember, ads in national magazines are often written by the best in the business. Use this piece of information two ways. First, to explain why certain ads are so good (and to realize that you don't have to be nearly that good to write ad copy for smaller clients). Second, when you see a splashy, big budget ad that really isn't effective—and there are plenty—be emboldened that you too can do this. To see the type of ads you're more likely to be working on, check your local newspapers and magazines.

If an ad doesn't get the job done and boost the bottom line, it doesn't matter how many awards it wins. It's not effective. By the same token, if it's just solid, unflashy, meat 'n' potatoes but brings them in the door or gets the phones ringing, then it's a good ad.

If you're not comfortable writing catchy, funny stuff, don't worry. There's a big market for solid ad copywriting that communicates the key sales messages and spurs the reader to action. If you come from a sales/marketing background like I have, you've got a head start in this department.

A Changing Industry Over the past several decades, the advertising industry has changed dramatically. It used to be that advertising, especially for large national corporations, was just something you had to do because the other guy was doing it. Because technology was extremely limited, you generally had little way of gauging the effectiveness of a campaign.

As a result, creativity was king, being easier to measure, at least within the industry. Now, however, the assessment tools exist to determine a campaign's success, literally by the hour. Accountability to results is now the order of the day. Yet, as discussed, that doesn't stop the advertising industry from lavishing its awards on those campaigns deemed most clever and catchy, regardless of how ineffective they may have been in moving profit figures.

Chances are, you won't be working on too many big national ad campaigns, unless you find you love that niche, decide to go to work for an ad agency, and work your way up. More likely assignments for freelancers will be smaller ads for small- to mid-size companies. While more and more of these firms are becoming receptive to lighter, more humorous approaches, first and foremost, they want to convey information and get results.

As discussed, the smaller the company, the greater the chance that your creativity will end up seeing the light of day. With bigger firms, you get into more legal and bureaucratic issues, trying to come up with something that's not trademarked, or hasn't been done before, the old "nothing-new-under-the-sun" thing.

Ideas and More Ideas I've done a lot of headline concepting for the big soft drink company through my client, the design firm. More often than not, I'm coming up with a bunch of ideas for their POS (point-of-sale) store displays, most of which will never see the light of day.

I still get paid, but they're often getting input from a lot of sources. They have deep pockets and can afford to spend a healthy chunk of money to buy lots of ideas. If they get a few workable ones in the process, it was worth it.

With ad copy, again, the first question should always be, "Who's the audience?" Quickly followed by "What's the purpose of the ad?" Image-building? Straight information? Retail sales ad? Special offer? Make sure you always give your client a number of versions from which to choose. Chances are good that you'll agree on how many at the outset, but I always end up giving more.

Here's an interesting phenomenon. I can't tell you how many times I've finished what I consider to be three or four good concepts and I'm about to send them off to the client when one last idea occurs to me—what I'll call a "throwaway" concept. And wouldn't you know it? That's the one they like!

For a more in-depth treatment of the art of ad copy writing, you might take a look at Bob Bly's *The Copywriter's Handbook*. You can't help but improve your skills with this solid book.

HI-LEVEL PROPOSALS   If a major event production company is pitching MCI, for instance, on securing all its trade show business for the next four years (an actual proposal I worked on), it's not a two-page flyer.

Typically, it'll end up being a binder with ten or more different sections covering every single aspect of the process: introduction, rationale, creative ideas, drawings, photos of other relevant work, production details, financial details/breakdown, summary, and more.

If a huge computer firm is pitching a Fortune 100 company on being the vendor of choice for its company-wide technical infrastructure overhaul (another actual example), again, there will be many sections, literally many hundreds of pages of specs, and a gargantuan coordinating effort necessary to bring all the disparate pieces together in one "voice"—a uniform tone and flow to the whole document.

And believe it or not, as complex as this type of project sounds, it's really not all that difficult. It's still just writing. There might be a different tone for the creative brief section than for production details, but it's writing nonetheless.

Different Kind of Writing   A few years ago, I had a very intense week-long proposal writing experience that fell into the "nothing-like-I-expected" category. It was the computer firm example I just used. About 12 departments were contributing sections to a 1000+ page document and I was brought in to write sales-oriented copy for several segments while bringing all the pieces together in one voice.

In the end, however, I wrote virtually nothing new and instead was entrusted with physically setting up the document on the computer, diplomatically staying on top of people (you're never *just* a writer…) to get their contributions done and submitted, and occasionally doing a bit of editing.

Simply put, the client didn't use me for the things I was good at—my writing ability and sales perspective—but rather, I was primarily handling technical issues of formatting and importing documents, areas with which I wasn't nearly as comfortable.

Well-Paid Frustration   I even shared my frustration at mid-week with the project leader, expressing my desire to do what I did best and give them their money's worth, as opposed to being a basically overpaid and not terribly technically experienced (which they knew going in) assistant project manager.

He appreciated my integrity, admitted it hadn't been an ideal situation from the beginning (I was brought in on two days' notice), but added, "It's well-paid frustration, no?" OK, I thought, I've gone on record. And at 65 hours over six days at about $70/hr., though certainly a problematic scenario, I somehow found the strength to go on.

Seriously, any project can unfold completely differently than expected. Some of the most fun and rewarding projects won't necessarily pay well, but don't miss creative opportunities by focusing on the bucks. Meanwhile, the taxing, "can't-wait-for-this-to-be-over" scenarios will put a bundle in your pocket. It all works out.

Added Benefits Nonetheless, many of the proposals I've worked on have been a lot of fun, mainly because it often got me out of the house and into a client's office for a few days. When you're spending too much time by yourself—the most common occupational hazard of this job—a well-paid change of venue is like manna from heaven.

You get plugged into the teamwork dynamic and feel connected to the human race for awhile. Then, just about the time the office politics of that particular situation are starting to wear on you, you get to go home, once again secure in the knowledge that you'd rather be in your shoes than theirs.

EVENT SCRIPTING   Another growing area, which I suspect even many people in the industry aren't aware of, is event scripting. As mentioned earlier, this year, for the sixth year in a row, I scripted the annual awards ceremony of a prominent Atlanta business hall of fame, an event sponsored by the state branch of Junior Achievement.

A few months later, I did another such project for the annual two-day regional conference of a growing fast food company based in Atlanta. I was initially involved with the creative brainstorming of the show's theme and structure, and then generated a two-page description—or "treatment"—of our creative vision. Once the client bought off on the concept, my next task was to actually script every moment of the two-day event.

Much more than just a parade of speakers, it featured an involved talk-show format, with 12 distinct segments and tones. The script included all the 'blocking'—i.e., "*Host walks onstage—a small elevated platform with host desk and three comfortable chairs. Host banters with audience about morning session before intro-*

ducing first guest."—and the bridge copy: intros and exits to and from each guest's presentation or interview.

Each of the speakers/guests provided his or her own copy points and answers to questions. Since most of them weren't writers, it was my job to clean up their masterpieces, work them into the overall flow of the program, and make it all sound conversational, while preserving a uniform tone throughout. It was a chance to get very creative with the directions and details of the event and happily, few of my suggestions were nixed.

The big event production companies (EPCs) we discussed in Chapter Five are a primary source of this kind of work, along with many other types of projects—brochures, speeches, convention literature, etc. Additionally, think of any firm that puts on a very well-orchestrated event each year involving many different kinds of media. Remember: the Junior Achievement event involved three totally distinct writing tasks plus a few others I didn't do.

VIDEO SCRIPTING   While video will certainly be with us for a long time, it will just as certainly decrease in popularity as more versatile CD technology (see below) becomes a more realistic, potent *and* cost-effective medium.

Where video will undoubtedly continue to hold a strong position is when a piece needs to evoke strong emotions or tell a compelling story that builds slowly and powerfully. While CD is superior to video in many ways, it has several inherent drawbacks.

Because CDs are primarily played on computers (CD*i* technology, which we'll discuss shortly, is played on a TV and *is* beginning to change that), the quality of the image just doesn't have that larger-than-life crispness and "bigness" that video can offer.

Secondly, because CD technology is, by definition, a "stop-start-stop" type of programming, it just isn't able to capture moods and tug heartstrings like a nonstop story-crafting medium like video can. Probably most importantly, at the moment, video is significantly cheaper than CD technology, so when budget is an issue (it rarely isn't), video will be the preferred choice for training programs, how-to demonstration tapes, and corporate image/identity pieces.

How Do You Write for Video?   Well, simply put, writing for the eye *and* ear (video) is very different than writing for just the eye (print material). If someone handed you a well-written video script for the average corporate industrial piece, you'd be struck by how elementary it read, as if it was being written for the junior high school level. Short sentences, simple structure, and few if any overly complex words.

The same subject, covered in a written brochure, would be very different. The reason is simple: when someone watches video, his attention is split. He's taking in the sights *and* the sounds. Since your words are competing with the visuals, you need to make it easy for your viewer to hang with it and get the message.

If the sentences are too long or too complex in structure or vocabulary, your audience is going to tune out. How do you structure a video script? Well, I've used two different formats and I'll tell you right now, one is a lot easier than the other.

Video Format #1: For the longest time, I did the standard side-by-side format, like so:

VIDEO	AUDIO
Med CU (close-up) of Graphic Designer sitting at monitor kneading a pile of Play-Doh® and placing the green pieces in his nose.	The story begins in the same place where all your large-format poster production starts: at your graphic designer's PC or Mac. The image is manipulated in the same manner.
Designer puts a fresh pile of Play-Doh in the little grinder that comes with it, snaps the star-shaped attachment in place and cranks out long, starry ropes of dough.	After the image is enhanced through the dynamic Error Reduction Program, it is then processed through Spectragraphix BlasterServe, the state-of-the-art digital imaging software.
Designer takes ball of Play-Doh and presses it onto a piece of newspaper, peels it off, leaving a reverse "printed" image on the Play-Doh.	Once through these steps, the image will move on to your electrostatic printer.

Now, in *Microsoft Word,* you'd use a *table* to create this format, which creates two independent columns (VIDEO/AUDIO), where one isn't affected by the other, as opposed to doing just a page with a two-column format, where whatever you type in the left column will quickly affect the right one.

The only problem with the table approach—and it can be a big one—is that when the page you're working on 'breaks' into the next page as you get to the bottom, the program occasionally ends up hiding your text.

You'll have just painstakingly typed a whole page in, the page breaks, and all of a sudden, the page you just typed is gone. Now you see it, now you don't. Where did it go? I don't know. It's still there, I'm told by my techno-gurus, but I can't find it and don't know how to get it back.

Maybe you've figured this one out, but in my case, I have to go find a digital high priest (my techie friend) to chant some incantation to appease the great god Cyberius so he'll give it back to me. Why bother?

I bring this up only because you might run across clients who insist you give them a script in the 'side-by-side' format, but most will be fine with Option #2.

Video Format #2: I picked up this very simple second way earlier this year from a very experienced video producer. It's apparently been around for eons and I just had no clue. Just type your audio portion and preface it with the video directions in itals:

> *Cut to van pulling up to facility. Shot of driver looking around furtively as he pulls a flask out and takes a long draw. Unsteady but smiling, he gets out and helps patient to reception area.*
>
> Once you arrive, your professional driver will happily escort you to the reception area. When your surgery is finished, he'll be waiting for you! Just a few cups of coffee and he'll be as good as new!
>
> *Staff dressed in Mouse ears engaged in spitball fight, stops suddenly and smilingly greets patient. Picking up phone and speaking (bkgrnd. talk saying "Ms. Jones is here for her procedure.") Cut to split screen with surgical coordinator, dressed as Bozo the Clown.*
>
> Our courteous and professional staff is expecting you, and after signing in, they'll notify the surgical coordinator that you've arrived for your appointment.
>
> *Cut to surgical coordinator (SC) stuffing clown mask in back pocket, then greeting patient. Cut to entering SC's office, shot from inside office.*
>
> The surgical coordinator will greet you and take you back to his office, where he'll be conducting a few tests prior to your operation.

You get the idea. Much easier, which is why I now ask every video client if I can give them a script in this format. No objections so far. You spend your time being creative, instead of wrestling with mysterious and infuriating technical issues.

CD-ROM AND CD*i* SCRIPTING   As technology marches on and the cost drops, CD-ROM and CD*i* technology will become more and more the vehicle of choice for electronic marketing brochures, training programs and myriad applications we as yet can't even imagine. All of them have to be written and the projects range from pretty straightforward vanilla to outrageously creative.

While you're probably familiar with CD-ROM, CD*i* may be new territory. In a nutshell, CD*i* offers a similar interactive experience to CD-ROM, except CD*i* disks need no computer. Instead, thanks to an inexpensive and portable player, you run it on your TV.

The Advantages of CD-ROM or CD*i*

1) CD-ROM or CD*i* are interactive, as opposed to video, which is a passive, linear medium. Viewers physically click their way through the material, and in the case of training modules, take tests and review exercises.

Programs can be designed so students can't move to the next module until they satisfactorily pass the present module's test or review. Because interactive programming is non-linear, viewers can choose where they want to go (though often within the boundaries described above), instead of being limited to the single info path of video, for instance.

2) In contrast to formal classroom training, CD-ROM or CD*i* training can take place at the viewers' own pace, on their own schedule, and, given the universality of TV and to a lesser extent, home computers, in the comfort of their own home. Just the fact that everyone has a TV can give CD*i* technology an edge over CD-ROM. A company merely purchases a number of CD*i* players and instantly expands when and where learning takes place.

3) Again, as opposed to classroom training, with CD-ROM or CD*i*, the delivery of material is uniform: everyone sees and experiences the same thing, which is critical when disseminating information on a nationwide basis.

With an interactive medium, because the viewer does have choices, the emphasis is always on making the material as engaging, compelling, and user-friendly as possible. Ergo, the need for writing creativity is particularly high in this arena, and because it's still such a relatively new medium, writers who can bring that fun, edgy spark to CD projects are in high demand.

CD Writing Style CD copy needs to be simple, short, punchy, to the point. Less is more (good advice in any copywriting scenario). The American attention span gets shorter by the hour. Remember that. The audio portions are obviously similar in simplicity to writing video, in that if it seems almost overly elementary to the eye, it'll be just about right for the ear.

The big difference, however, between writing for linear video and writing for non-linear CD is that, with CD, you never know where the viewer is going next. Consequently, each piece needs to essentially stand on its own, in order for it to effectively mesh with whatever happens to precede *and* follow it. Accommodating and non-committal are good ways of putting it.

SPEECHES Writing speeches can be a very lucrative niche all by itself. In my second year of operation, as I've mentioned, I was contracted by an event production company which had produced the annual global franchisee sales conference for a worldwide hotel chain for six years running. My job: write the speech for their new EVP of marketing.

Involving 10+ rewrites over six weeks, it was a monumental and somewhat delicate undertaking, given the prevailing sensitive political issues within the company. Since no one knew the ultimate scope of the project, I was paid by the hour. The final tally: $9,000. Three months later, primarily on the strength of that job, I picked up a 20-minute speech for the General Manager of a huge international credit card company for their regional conference. Fee: $2,600.

These examples showcase two places you can pick up speech writing: middle and upper management of large corporations. Additionally, small- to medium-size companies can be just as good prospects since they're less likely to have in-house staff to do the writing. The second is the Event Production Companies (EPCs), described in more detail in Chapter Five.

Your Job… When writing speeches, you typically encounter some common scenarios. In all cases, the client should be supplying you with large, meaty chunks of source material. In the case of sales conferences, that will often mean facts, figures and charts as a recap of the past year's (or quarter's) performance. Connecting the sections with fluid bridge copy will generally be the easy part.

What's more challenging (and interesting) is coming up with a powerful way to begin and end the speech. While often there is a predetermined theme to which you need to write, you may be called on in the client meetings to come up with a creative concept for the speech. In these meeting(s), you'll be asking scads of questions, many of them familiar:

1) Who's the audience? Always, always, always…the eternal first question. What are that audience's hot buttons? What are the concerns of its members? What will get their attention? What *don't* they want to hear? With what sense do you want them left? And related to these questions are:

2) What's worked before? (if there was a 'before') What hasn't? As we indirectly covered in Question #1, it's really important to know this: To what has this particular audience responded well in the past? *And* what have they tried that went over like the proverbial lead balloon?

The last thing you need is to spend bunches of time coming up with a great theme only to have them say, "Oh, we forgot to tell you (read: you never asked), we tried that last year and it didn't get a very good response." Back to the drawing board.

3) What's the theme? Your clients may already have a theme for the speech or they may be looking to you to help them create one. If you'll be helping out, make sure you factor some concepting time into your bid. I used the theme of "Relationships" for the speech I wrote for the credit card company.

I defined the word according to the dictionary and outlined the different relationships that existed within the company: client/company, company/vendor, co-worker/co-worker, management/employee.

Throughout the speech, I kept tying things back to that theme and emphasized the growing importance of relationships in a business climate where a company's offerings were often a commodity and something else was needed to set them apart from their competition.

This might be a place to use a good quote from *Bartlett's Quotations* or the *International Thesaurus of Quotations,* the speech aids I mentioned in Chapter Six. It's a small investment that will make you look good. And don't forget those heartwarming, inspirational, clever, and/or instructive e-mail treasures you've saved over the years. I've used numerous e-mail gems in my speeches.

4) What style and tone do they want? Humorous, straightforward, modest, assertive, challenging? It's critically important that you capture the "voice" of the speaker, so he'll feel comfortable speaking the words you write. Remember: this is not a brochure or corporate image piece, where your own professional writing style will work just fine.

This is something your speaker will be delivering to an audience, and if he's familiar to his audience, for it to be optimally effective, it has to sound like words he would say. If the audience gets the idea the speech has been over-scripted, and that words have been put in the speaker's mouth, it'll compromise the credibility.

You'll get a sense of the speaker's style just from interacting with him, gathering as much from observing his mannerisms and bearing as you do from his actual answers to your questions. Make a point of talking with the people who know him well and work closely with them to get their input, as they may realize things about him that you won't hear from the horse's mouth.

All this assumes, of course, that you will be meeting with the speaker before you begin writing. You'd think this would be a given and it usually is, but in large corporations or when your speaker is very busy, they may not even have thought about it.

In these cases, always push for a meeting. If you stress that you'll undoubtedly come up with a better end result by doing so, your professionalism and commitment to doing a good job will come through. If an in-person meeting is not possible, at least try to land a phone conference.

5) Are there any negative audience attitudes or sensitive issues that need to be addressed? (We talked a little about this in Chapter Twelve and these comments would apply to any project, not just speeches.) This is a very important question and it may take some digging. I've always been amazed at people's potential for self-delusion. As a writer, I've been in a number of situations, where in the initial fact-gathering meeting, the client is telling me what points to cover in the piece—whether a speech, brochure, internal communication, etc.

When they think they're done, I dig a little deeper and discover this hugely important political issue of great significance to the audience, that the client never even mentioned. One of those things which, if the speaker doesn't address it (i.e., the downsizing of a corporation, and all the anxiety inherent in such a situation, or a huge customer service issue that's caused a lot of ill will that needs to be reversed), the audience will tune him right out.

Yet they'll sit there, ostrich-like, happy to just deliver some pabulum, the usual dog-and-pony show, not for a second considering that their credibility will be neatly and swiftly annihilated if they go ahead as planned.

They'll Listen or They Won't ... In cases like this, I've had to ask them, almost like you would a five-year-old, that while you'll be happy to give them whatever they want, how do they want their audience to react? In a nice way, you have to ask, "Do you really believe that your audience is going to listen to a word you have to say if you don't acknowledge this pink elephant of an issue looming over the whole discussion?"

Often, it's like you've reminded them of something they're trying to forget. Sometimes they'll listen to you and make what they consider to be the difficult decision to include it, and sometimes they won't. If they don't, then they're probably the types that continue to scratch their heads when employee morale goes into the toilet, they lose market share, or any other consequence of avoiding the necessary conversation.

Separating the Men from the Boys I say it's this kind of extra effort that separates good copywriters from outstanding ones. When you have a commitment to effective communication that truly reaches the target audience, everyone wins. Sure, you can just give clients what they want and not get into the sticky issues, but I assert that *not* taking the easy way out is part of our job. It's one of the reasons we get paid what we do.

More than one client has shared with me that they like working with me precisely because I dig a little deeper and ask a few more questions, which ultimately results in a more effective end product. Of course, we always have to remember the rule we discussed earlier: *The Client Is the Boss.*

Sometimes all you can do is make your professional feelings known and leave it at that. If a situation is just way too surreal, with a client more interested in denial than reality, don't hesitate to walk away if you sense that you're getting into a classic no-win scenario.

GHOSTWRITING Speechwriting is actually a subset of the larger category of ghostwriting, which means nothing more than writing something—a speech, article, book—for someone who will put his name or voice to it as if he wrote it. The fact is, most people in corporate America aren't writers and happily for us, many of them have no problem admitting it.

My first ghostwriting experience came 3½ months into my career (I told you it can happen that fast). As I shared earlier, I got the nod to ghostwrite a book for that local businessman who wanted to add "Author" to his credentials, but wasn't a writer.

Ripe Markets I haven't begun to tap the ghostwriting market, but I'm certain it's huge. For those inclined toward medicine or law, there are undoubtedly zillions of doctors and lawyers who want or need to get articles published on a regular basis. They usually don't have the time or inclination to do it, but they do have the money. Obviously, you need to be able to step in and with a relatively small amount of background and supervision, crank something out.

But just in the corporate arena, many opportunities abound. It's the kind of work that you can scout around for as you're doing other things like brochures, corporate image pieces, video scripts, and of course, speeches. Again, if you can leverage past experience, you'll be that much further ahead of the game.

Ask your contact people if they know how that stuff gets done. Often, in the case of upper management, they may have in-house staff handle things like that, but in this day and age of leaner organizations, don't assume for a moment that that's the norm.

Opportunities Everywhere I had another interesting ghostwriting experience that I mention simply to demonstrate the unusual opportunities that present themselves. I got a call from my writer's agent—who incidentally got me the book job as well—about a unique situation.

The CEO of a local medium-size business was being considered for a prestigious CEO of the Year award in Atlanta. He had to submit five 250–300 word essays addressing five specific questions as part of his application. Not being a writer, he decided he'd hire one to write them for him.

While he ultimately didn't win (the competition was obviously very stiff that year, which of course, is my way of denying that the copywriter had anything to do with the outcome), he was delighted with what I came up with and I was equally delighted with the $1750 fee for one long meeting and about three days' work.

RADIO SPOTS Writing radio spot copy is similar to writing for video, since both are written for the ear. While video has the visual competing with the audio, people listening to radio are puttering around their bedrooms or kitchens in the morning, or in their car to and from work, so you're competing with whatever else they're doing. As such, radio spots need to be simply written and easy to follow by a distracted listener.

The easiest way to figure out which companies may need your help with radio spots is to tune in. It'll be mostly consumer-oriented products: retail, automobiles, leisure travel, financial services, banks, etc.

Writing radio spots can be a lot of fun, especially when the client lets you get creative and funny—and most are open to that. Humor works because an entertained listener is an attentive listener. But remember, funny is only good if the spot is effective in boosting sales, calls, interest, or whatever the desired result.

If you're unsure of your abilities in this arena, just listen to the lame, awful stuff that's circulating on the airwaves these days and you'll get your confidence back in a hurry. It's just not that difficult. As a rule, you'll be writing 30- or 60-second spots, which actually translates to about 27–28 and 57–58 seconds, respectively.

Always build a radio spot around the core information that needs to be communicated: the who, what, where, when, why, how, and how much of a product or service. Think of innovative ways to position those important facts within a compelling (which can mean funny) storyline and remember to keep the copy simple, with few big words or long phrases. See the samples in Appendix B.

"On-Hold" Message Copy Writing An interesting variation on radio copy that's risen in popularity in the past decade or so is "on-hold" messages—what people hear when they call in to a company and are put on hold. Sure, many companies still use Muzak or a radio station, but more and more are taking advantage of the captive audience they have to deliver low-key sales messages, new product announcements, product/customer service enhancements, etc.

Not surprisingly, small- to medium-size companies with a limited and easily definable product line will be the companies best suited for this kind of writing. This is an ideal example of work you can pick up as an add-on to something else you're doing for a company, as opposed to something you'd seek out specifically.

Here's an idea: If you've been contracted to do some work for one of those small- to medium-size firms whose product line lends itself to "on-hold messages" as a marketing tool, but they're not currently doing it, why not suggest it? You'll not only pick up extra work but you'll be viewed much more as a consultant than a writer. See Appendix B for examples of some on-hold message copy.

TRADE ARTICLES The most depressing thing about writing articles for publication in most magazines is the pathetically low fees you earn in relation to the effort expended. However, if you can get into the arena of writing articles for trade publications—those fees can jump dramatically. How much can you make? For trade articles, generally, don't settle for any less than $1 a word and I've got colleagues who've been paid $2 a word. Contrast this with the typical $0.10–0.50/word offered by most periodicals. Here's where someone coming from a particular industry like retail, high-tech, financial services, or healthcare can do very well. (See Appendix B for a sample trade article.)

A Very Sweet Deal Often, a trade publication is a wholly-owned (but deliberately unpublicized) subsidiary of a company who uses the magazine as a venue for promoting their own products and services. It's a pretty sweet little arrangement—and smart too. They get to toot their horn in articles while calling on other industry experts to confirm their ideas and directions.

They might do a piece that highlights the growing trend toward a particular digital screen printing process or an innovative technology for shoring up landfills—trends which, when acknowledged and acted on by their readership, will create a demand for the very products and services they sell.

And since the publication is viewed as an advertising medium of sorts, one that should yield real bottom-line profits, they can afford to pay pretty well. I just finished a trade article of about 800 words that involved briefly interviewing three people by phone and incorporating info from a previous piece. Not a tough piece at all for an $850 fee. Not too shabby for a little over 10 hours of work.

I have a colleague who writes regular articles for a trade publication serving a specific livestock industry. Regardless of the length, she always gets $2000 for each one. This, by the way, is the "I-don't-pick-up-a-pen-for-less-than-$500" woman. Hey, more power to her. So it's out there.

NEWSLETTERS At this writing, the lion's share of my income comes from writing newsletters. Where can you find this business? Everywhere. Every large corporation *is* generating or has the potential to generate any number of newsletters, both internal (employee-directed) and external (customer-directed).

Internal newsletters are designed to keep one's employees informed. They serve many purposes and provide many things: information, inspiration, motivation, recognition, employee input *and* are vehicles for building *esprit de corps*.

This last function is especially important in this day and age, when companies are becoming more employee-oriented and are reaching out to their "most valuable resource." In an employee's market, like we're experiencing at this writing, where good people are hard to find and harder to hold on to, it's just smart business to make employees feel like they're part of a family and that they're valued—whatever it takes to keep them where they are.

Just the Beginning However, an internal newsletter is far more important than just a good employee-retention tool. High performance in today's ultra-competitive business climate requires that companies be nimble, cohesive, and responsive and that means everyone working off the same page. An internal newsletter is certainly a valuable tool for making that happen. In a big company with many divisions, it's not at all uncommon for each division to have its own publication.

I write a monthly internal newsletter for a major division of a local telecommunications giant. This piece is a venue for new product announcements, profiles of newly-hired managers in charge of key profit centers, and success stories to be modeled by the troops in the field. Other articles will showcase new initiatives designed to move the division closer to achieving their short- and long-term goals. Indeed, the piece is touted as the major communications vehicle for this group.

As Intranets (a company's internal Internet) become standard fixtures in large corporations and increasingly common in smaller firms as well, internal newsletters are likely to be web-based. The one I write appears in both print and on-line versions, with the latter providing more detail and expanded content over the print.

Still, far from becoming obsolete, print versions are still prized by companies for the portable "hard-copy-in-hand" factor. Intranet versions, while certainly convenient and low-cost, can get lost in the e-mail crush common in many companies.

Customer Connections External newsletters, in addition of course to being informational, are often designed to create a subtle yet powerful bond with one's customers and make them feel like they're part of a special group. The ultimate goal, of course, is customer retention: keeping those customers coming back and hopefully, spreading the word to others.

As mentioned, I've been doing a quarterly newsletter for the credit card division of a luxury auto manufacturer (drive the car and you're eligible for the card). The goal here is definitely customer bonding/retention.

You might imagine that, in terms of importance, a company would rank internal newsletters below external ones. And in most cases, you'd be wrong. Now, don't misunderstand. External pieces have their place and they can serve a valuable function. But often, they can be somewhat "fluffy" in content and regardless, few companies consider them to be a legitimate substitute for their aggressive, ongoing marketing efforts.

Internal newsletters, by comparison, can be terribly important. With a company's industry ranking, market presence, and financial performance on the line every day, a communications piece that can keep their people all marching together and armed with the information they need to do battle, is critical.

Newsletter Prospects Everywhere Just about any mid- to large-sized company is a prospect for multiple newsletters—both internal and external—if they don't already do them. If they do, they may just need writers. Oftentimes, an employee is writing newsletter content as an additional responsibility but the company may be very receptive to outsourcing the task. This is where it can get fun and profitable over the long haul.

In the case of my internal piece, I've been brought into the inner workings of this organization and feel I'm making an important contribution to their growth path. More importantly, the longer I do it, the more I learn and the more valuable I become to them. Because I know what they stand for, how they operate, what's important to them and what they can and can't say in print, my learning curve on new articles is virtually nil at this point.

Couple that with the fact that I'm doing good work and I'm working with minimal supervision, and the bottom line is I've dramatically simplified their lives. It just doesn't make any sense for them to go elsewhere and start over again.

Of course, at some point and for any number of possible reasons, this particular wonderful opportunity will come to an end and I know that. Nothing is forever. But for now, I'm enjoying the ride. This sort of gig is every FLCW's dream: monthly and well-paying.

What's the Tone? While I don't think it's appropriate, not surprisingly, internal pieces tend to be fairly sober, especially if they've been written by in-house folks for awhile. It's as if because it's an internal piece, companies feel it needs to be serious and businesslike.

Of course, I disagree. As far as I'm concerned, an internal piece should be as engaging and readable as its external counterpart. Employees are very important to a corporation and should be wooed just like any other audience.

Make It Creative Consequently, on internal newsletters, I will push the creative envelope at every opportunity and move the copy towards a chattier, more conversational and engaging tone. Be aggressive on this point because in nine out of ten cases, the more engaging the piece is, the more likely it is to be read, the more positive the employee feedback will be, and the more brilliant you'll look. Sometimes they go for it, sometimes they don't. Ultimately, of course, they're the bosses, so give them what they want.

By definition, external pieces should be lively and engaging, even edgy, if that's appropriate. The company is trying to get its customers' attention. It had better be worth reading.

Make a point to read the newsletters you get in the mail from the different businesses you patronize: your airline's frequent flyer publication, inserts in your electric, gas, or telephone bill, and pieces from your insurance company, financial advisor, real estate agent, health care provider, etc.

In addition to giving you a sense of both newsletter content and style, these pieces offer a perhaps unexpected bonus: a chance to see that not all newsletters are alike in the quality of the writing. And where they're not, you've got an opening for business, especially if it's a local company. Why not call up these folks and find out who does their writing?

Team Up with a Designer Chances are good that if you land a job writing a newsletter, your client will already have a graphic designer to put your verbal gems into a sharp layout. When you're dealing with a small- to medium-size firm however, that may be less likely. Scenarios like these are golden opportunities to team up with a graphic designer compadre.

A writer/designer team that can handle the publication of a newsletter end-to-end—creative concepting, content development, graphic design, layout, research, interviewing, writing, and printing—can be a dream come true for a company. The client will typically provide ideas and contact people for articles, but suggestions for secondary content are always welcome.

The Big Time Here's something to think about. The external piece I'm doing for the credit card division of the car manufacturer is produced by just me and a graphic designer. The company was using a larger marketing company for both the newsletter and their direct mail campaigns and was undoubtedly paying dearly for it. I was brought into the deal by the designer (I say it again: get to know several good solo designers).

We're now doing both projects, giving them better work than they were getting before at certainly a significantly lower cost. We've produced some very slick, sexy stuff. We get to be very creative, are very well-paid, and are collecting some magnificent pieces for our books. These folks have the bucks to hire any ad agency but they chose us and are delighted with the results—and the bottom line. This is where it can go.

Nuts and Bolts Newsletters come in all sizes—two, four, six, eight (or some other multiple of two or four) pages, with most a standard 8½″ x 11″ size. With graphics factored in, figure approximately 500 words per page, ± 50. Like any other job, price it in your head by the hour to come up with a flat rate (unless you're billing by the hour). Be sure to factor in time for meetings, concepting, phone interviews, any research, writing, and editing.

DIRECT MAIL PIECES   The best piece of advice I could offer to give you a sense of direct mail is what I mentioned for newsletters: start reading and analyzing your junk mail instead of just tossing it. In any given week, you'll probably receive four or five examples in several categories.

Talk about accountability… Unlike most other arenas of writing you'll work in, direct mail can be a little daunting. Why? Because it's very easy to measure its effectiveness. When you write a marketing brochure, corporate identity package, newsletter, or even an ad, it's hard to gauge just how effective it is.

Sure, in the case of an ad, you can get a rough idea of its impact by increased sales, incoming calls, appointments, etc. With direct mail, however, you just can't hide from the numbers.

You write a piece and your client sends it out to, say, 100,000 people, and within a few weeks, you know to the third or fourth decimal place what percentage of the recipients responded back.

The Letter   The reality of this is especially pointed when the focus of a direct mailing is a long, multi-paged letter. Then it's all about hard-hitting, attention-grabbing copy, both the catchy teaser on the envelope as well as the letter. Depending on the product or organization involved, it could be a strong sales close or perhaps a powerful emotional hook.

Non-profits are frequent users of letter-based direct mail. Typically, they have a pretty involved story to tell: their good works that justify a healthy donation or conversely, all the horrible things their enemies are up to that justify a healthy donation, all of it in order, of course, to keep the world safe for democracy, from Republicans, the evil real estate developers, the liberal media, you name it.

Maybe, it's an emotional pitch to start supporting a foster child or to buy this money-making program so you can really take good care of your family ("You *do* want the best for them, don't you?")

The Brochure   In other direct mail packages, there may be a letter, but perhaps a four-color brochure takes top billing with a few other inserts such as news clips, information sheets, reply card, etc. The good news here is that the graphic designer is sharing the hotseat with you. If the piece works well, you both get credit. If it flops, you share the blame.

The Self-Mailer/Postcard More and more companies are using self-mailers and postcards (usually oversize—6″ x 9″) to deliver their messages. A self-mailer is a multi-panel brochure with one outside panel serving as the delivery/return address space. The piece can include all the components of a stuffed direct mail envelope—sales letter, brochure, perforated reply card—except in a much more compact form.

The simpler the businesses—especially consumer businesses: print shops, insurance companies, health clubs, restaurants, automobile services—the more they lend themselves to a postcard. And because of their limited working space, businesses will also use postcards as awareness-boosting tools: to remind the world, in a general sense, that they're out there.

Thanks to the Internet... Postcards are even more popular now because of the explosion of the Internet. When a company of any size at all can and usually does have a web site that tells their entire story, why spend an enormous amount of time and money creating fat packages that probably won't get read anyway, when the firm can use a postcard to steer people to their site? Not to mention that once there, these sites provide even easier ways for a customer to respond (and for the company to capture vital information): type and click.

Writing Style Not surprisingly, the ability to write powerful, impactful, heartstring-tugging copy is the name of the game with direct mail. While the tone will vary widely depending on the audience, this is no place for the safe and bland. For postcards, where space is at a premium, it's even more important that headlines be potent and copy be concise and direct.

As always, the first question is "Who's the audience?" What's going to get their attention and more importantly, make them respond to the piece? If you're not comfortable writing strong, persuasive ask-for-the-order copy, you might want to steer clear. And while your mailbox is constantly full of examples of, and prospects for, direct mail writing business, business-to-business direct mail (all the mail you don't get) provides a vastly larger and even more lucrative potential market.

All That Said... Just a final comment in case you're a bit intimidated by this synopsis of direct mail. The high-end direct mail campaigns I'm doing for the luxury automaker's credit card division are focused on the outer envelope. The graphic designer and I are working closely together to create concepts visually and verbally compelling enough to get the person to open the piece up. The copy on the outside ends up being two to four words! For me, the focus is just a small but potent snippet of copy that speaks to the market in the language of prestige, elegance, lifestyle, quality, fun, etc. The inside brochure is just an extension of the envelope and is mainly informational, not requiring major creative or persuasive writing. The point is, it's not that hard, and we're talking about upper corporate circles here.

WEB SITE COPY   Writing for the web, by definition, is a relatively new field and one that requires a very specific talent. Operating on the oft-mentioned assumption that the average American has the attention span of a gnat and getting shorter by the day, web copy needs to be the ultimate in short, punchy, easy-to-read "get-to-the-point-fast-I-get-bored-almost-instantaneously" copy. Short sentences, lots of bullets, lots of space. Big chunks of copy are deadly on the web. Write so that people can get in and out quickly.

More than most other arenas, web writing demands an ability to look at the site through typical "surfers'" eyes. Give them only what they want and need to know to move them along the sales cycle, not what you (and your client) want to tell them.

Since the web's a high-tech medium, web content has typically been written by technical people, but that's changing. Check out a few quotes from some industry people as to what the future holds for this arena of writing:

"In the coming years, the demand for good creative writing – and thinking – is really going to mushroom in all areas, though especially in the arena of web design. Currently, most web page copy is being written by technical people and it shows. As the competition for a 'net viewer's rapidly shrinking attention span grows even more intense, web designers are realizing the crucial importance of crisp, to-the-point copy and that bodes well for free-lancers."

Norm Grey
President, The Creative Circus, Inc.
(A School for Copywriting, Art Direction, Photography, Design/Illustration)
Former Sr. VP/Group Creative Director, J. Walter Thompson

"Good creative writers are in short supply in the multimedia and Internet communities. The talented ones usually have an abundance of work, earning some of the highest rates paid among multimedia and Internet professionals. As the demand increases for better content and more concise communication in new media markets, especially the Internet, companies that want to stay competitive are realizing the importance of good writing. The idea that "whoever is available from the production team can write the copy" is quickly becoming an obsolete mentality for companies that expect to be in business three years from now."

Britt Stephens
President, Multimedia Registry
(On-Line Resource linking creative professionals and employers)
www.newmediaregistry.com

Where do you find web site business? Absolutely everywhere. These days, chances are excellent that any size company—from tiny to global—has a web site. You'll pick up web site work as a logical extension of any other work you do for a company. Anytime you're in front of a client or a prospect, ask about their web site.

If you've done your homework, you've already visited it and know how well or poorly written it is. Find out if they're happy with it and/or open to have it reworked.

THE Place for Web Work Of course, probably the most fruitful avenue for web work, especially if you want to focus on this direction, are the web development companies, which are sprouting up almost as fast as pricey coffee bars. Just look in the Yellow Pages under Internet or Web and you ought to have your hands full till the 22nd century.

However, before contacting the web development folks en masse, it's probably best to cut your teeth with your regular clients and get some experience under your belt. Even though there are few experts out there in this kind of writing, they will still want to see a few online samples of your work.

Of course, if you don't have a lot of web experience, but do have some good clips of other work in the brief, crisp, snappy category, by all means share it—along with your persuasive contention that, essentially, it's the same kind of writing, which it is.

That segues nicely into a little secret: it's just not that hard to write effective web copy. Always be thinking "How can I convey the crucial information in the fewest words possible and in the most engaging manner possible?" and you'll be in good shape.

Get on-line. Visit lots of sites, especially the award-winning ones—designated by that little "Top 5% Site" logo. They're as popular as they are because (amongst other things), they're effectively written. Study them. Model them when you write. And if they're poorly written (which many are), why not contact the company and propose that you rework it? To boost your odds even more, you might even offer up the first page with revisions to give them an idea of what you could do for them.

TECHNICAL WRITING Another enormous arena of writing which I can't even begin to do justice to in a few paragraphs—and hence won't even attempt —is technical writing.

It's not where my interests lie, but my oh my, there's endless work to be done: web sites, technical manuals, documentation, product spec sheets, product brochures, etc. The word is that there's always a shortage of good technical writers. You need a solid grasp of technical issues, whether they be in telecommunications, Internet related products, manufacturing, etc.

And you need to really like this stuff, because you'll be stewing in it. It's not uncommon for projects to be months long in scope, much more so than in the creative arena of commercial writing. The pay scale tends to be lower than creative marketing rates—$35–60/hr. depending on the project and the writer's experience.

Not surprisingly, you should generally approach such companies directly as opposed to going through MM (middlemen) clients. The only exception for middlemen would be brokers and agents. Because these folks very often specialize in matching technical writers with technical projects, precisely because the fees for six-month projects are hefty, check with them if you want to find this kind of work. Besides that, pretty much all the same prospecting rules apply.

Your Own Association If you want to find out more about technical writing than I could possibly share, and more eloquently put to boot, then check out the *Society for Technical Communication.*

Yes, technical writers (and other professionals related to the field) have their own national association, complete with publications, conferences, local chapters, and of course, a web site: http://www.stc-va.org/. This web site covers society information, conference details, employment opportunities, publications, professional development, grants and scholarships, and more.

According to the STC Home Page: "STC is an individual membership organization dedicated to advancing the arts and sciences of technical communication. Its 23,000 members include technical writers, editors, graphic designers, multimedia artists, Web and Intranet page information designers, translators, and others whose work involves making technical information understandable and available to those who need it.

"Membership in STC provides technical communicators with opportunities for ongoing learning and professional networking. STC promotes the public welfare by educating its members and industry about issues concerning technical communication."

Just to Clarify   I want to draw a distinction here. There is a big difference between technical writing and high-tech marketing writing. Straight technical writing is much less persuasive or "sales-y" than high-tech marketing writing, but it still must do more than just convey information. The writer often has to clarify, warn, and subtly motivate. Pick up the technical manual for a software program and you'll know what I mean. By contrast, high-tech marketing writing is like any other creative/marketing writing but for high-tech products.

If you like the high-tech arena, have a good grasp of the technological issues and can write from a "features/benefits" sales perspective, you'll enjoy the $60–100+/hr. rates, not the lower technical writing pay scale. Several of my colleagues are high-tech marketing writers and they bill out as high as $100 an hour. You'll find a ton of work out there in this arena.

For technical writing, the U.S. mean salary in 1999 was $47,560 (not including benefits). According to a Seattle-based STC contact, most technical writing/editing contractors in that area worked through agencies and were paid in the $38–50/hour range (plus full medical and other benefits), and worked a full 2,000 hours yearly.

While I've covered a broad spectrum of the kinds of projects you'll come across as a FLCW, you'll certainly discover new arenas and new kinds of work. And as business changes and evolves, new opportunities will emerge. Guess what? We're just about done. A little pep talk and off you go into the world ….

Chapter Fifteen

The Home Stretch

ARE YOU READY?   So, here we are, standing on the edge of something. Are you excited? Is your head swimming with possibilities? Or are you scared to death?

You're probably in one of two groups. For starters, both groups finished the book, so let's pat ourselves on the back. Thank you for the time you took to read it. You honor me.

The first group is kicking the idea around. It's intriguing to you and sounds very interesting, but there's a lot of mental ground you need to take before you're really ready to jump in.

Perhaps you're entrenched in a job, from which it would be difficult to extricate yourself anytime soon. People are depending on you for income. You like the lifestyle it affords you and though it's not ideal by any stretch, you're not quite ready to give it all up, strip naked, and jump into this huge scary icy ocean called self-employment. You'll find a way to make it or you won't. You'll know if it feels right. And remember, you can start part-time.

A Way Out?   The other group is much further along. You're looking at this opportunity as a real "way out" of wherever you are. I'm guessing that you're not very light and breezy at this moment. More likely, your head is a'swirl with millions of thoughts—"What if… maybe I could… it might just work… it sounds too good to be true… I think I could do this…"

If you're in that place of head-bursting possibility, running over scenario after scenario, getting giddy, creating alternating mental visions of wonderful success and profound destitution, I feel privileged to have made such an impact.

I've done my best to ensure the accuracy and completeness of this material, so it provides the most thorough depiction of the realities of building this business. Several professional colleagues, a few with 15+ years of experience, have reviewed the book and made suggestions, most all of which I've incorporated.

We've had a lot of fun and hopefully laughed a lot. But make no mistake: this is a very serious profession that can afford you a healthy income, plenty of creative fulfillment, along with highly enviable lifestyle benefits. And no, it's not one long funfest, and you wouldn't (and shouldn't!) believe me if I said it was.

Cloudy Days in Paradise It's like that bumper sticker: "A Bad Day at the Beach is Better than a Good Day at the Office." I have plenty of days when I'm not excited about what I'm doing or for whom I'm doing it, but they're just bad days at the beach.

We're talking about a much more satisfying strain of discontent here. Kind of like being with someone you love who occasionally does stuff to irritate you, as opposed to being with someone you can't stand who's constantly doing things to irritate you.

When you're doing something that you fundamentally love, that's essentially a match for who you are, you simply won't find as many reasons to be discontented. You naturally become a "glass-is-half-full" type. It won't take much effort. It doesn't feel like work.

You won't have to pump yourself up with little PMA pep talks and "What-I-can-conceive-and-believe-I-can-achieve" lectures. All that stuff is true but what they usually leave out is that it sure helps to be doing something that turns you on in the first place.

Where Do You Want to Be? Reminds me of a line from a cassette tape by Marianne Williamson—the new-age author of *"Return to Love"* and *"The Healing of America."* If you feel unmotivated, lazy, and discontented in what you're doing, she says, chances are good that you're not fundamentally an unmotivated, lazy, and discontented person. Rather, "you just don't want to *be* there."

Nevertheless, we keep jamming our round-peg selves into square-hole careers, pump ourselves up with the latest pop platitudes and then wonder why the good positive feelings last about as long as the happy gas after you leave the dentist's office. Try doing something you really enjoy and watch those positive feelings and general upbeat attitude about life put down roots.

So if you're in that place, I appreciate where you are. I've been there—thinking the same things, having the same wonderful visions and the same scary doubts and fears. Yet, at some point, I put my apprehension aside, figured out what I truly wanted, believed I could have it (very key), and trusted in myself, which is the ultimate place you want to get to.

Unexpected Allies Just about all you *can* control is the actions you take and that, incidentally, is more than enough to be successful. This book is simply a guide, a roadmap, a game plan, one way to skin this cat, but it's you and you alone who can pull it off. Just know that when you decide to go for it, you unleash strange and wonderful allies, who will deliver things to you, unpredictably and unexpectedly, to help you along. I'm reminded of a poem written by W.N. Murray of the Scottish Himalayan Mountain Expedition:

> *Until one is committed*
> *there is hesitancy,*
> *the chance to draw back, always ineffectiveness*
> *Concerning all acts of initiative and creation*
> *there is one elementary truth,*
> *the ignorance of which kills countless ideas*
> *and splendid plans:*
> *that the moment one commits oneself,*
> *then Providence moves too.*
>
> *All sorts of things occur to help one*
> *that would otherwise have never occurred.*
> *A whole stream of events issues from the decision,*
> *of unforeseen incidents and meetings,*
> *and material assistance*
> *which no man could have dreamt would have come his way*
> *I have a deep respect for one of Goethe's couplets:*
>
> "*Whatever you can do, or dream you can—begin it.*
> *Boldness has genius, power and magic in it.*"

It's true. It really works that way. Commit yourself and things start happening. Make it happen and let me know about it.

Text of Follow-up Letters customized to specific situations

1) You've met with a prospect, introduced yourself and your work, but no work is immediately pending.

September 16, 2001

Mr. Tom Jones
President
Jones Creative
1234 Lenox Rd. NE
Atlanta, GA 30324

Dear Tom,

As a freelance writer, my goal is to enhance your image, improve your profit picture, and make your life easier. If it carries your name, shouldn't it be the best reflection of you?

Just a quick note of sincere appreciation for your time and courtesy in our meeting this past Tuesday. I truly enjoyed meeting you and discussing possible freelance copywriting opportunities with Jones Creative.

More than 16 years of sales and marketing experience coupled with an engaging, readable writing style translates to copywriting that communicates powerfully to your target audience. Need a light, humorous, creative touch to your projects? That's my specialty!

I welcome the opportunity to make an ongoing or occasional contribution to your efforts and feel confident in my ability to deliver a quality product.

Thanks again, and I look forward to speaking and working with you soon.

Sincerely,

Peter Bowerman

---

2) *You've met with a new client and are about to start work on a job.*

January 15, 2001

Mr. Joe Jackson
Media Services, Inc.
100 Highway 47
Marietta, GA 30067

Dear Mr. Jackson,

As a freelance writer, my goal is to enhance your image, improve your profit picture, and make your life easier. If it carries your name, shouldn't it be the best reflection of you?

Just a quick note of sincere appreciation for your time and courtesy this past Wednesday. I truly enjoyed meeting you and discussing my prospective participation in the upcoming United manufacturers corporate identity program.

I welcome the chance to work with you on this exciting and ambitious undertaking, and feel confident I can make an eloquent and valuable contribution to overall effort.

Take care, and I look forward to talking with you on Sunday and meeting on Monday, January 20.

Sincerely,

Peter Bowerman

2a) An expanded version of the above letter where you feel it's important to elaborate on a couple of key points about your skills that are of particular importance to the client.

January 15, 2001

Mr. Joe Jackson
Media Services, Inc.
100 Highway 47
Marietta, GA 30067

Dear Mr. Jackson,

As a freelance writer, my goal is to enhance your image, improve your profit picture, and make your life easier. If it carries your name, shouldn't it be the best reflection of you?

Just a quick note of sincere appreciation for your time and courtesy this past Wednesday. I truly enjoyed meeting you and discussing my prospective participation in the upcoming United manufacturers corporate identity program.

I welcome the chance to work with you on this exciting and ambitious undertaking, and feel confident I can make an eloquent and valuable contribution to overall effort. As discussed, I feel I can bring much to the table:

1) Quick Study - I pride myself in swiftly grasping the key points of any subject matter and devising a logical structure and flow for the written presentation.

2) Independent - My ability to turn around high quality work with little supervision will free up your time while ensuring that the job's getting done right the first time.

3) Copywriter Plus - With my broad-based experience in sales, marketing, and copywriting, I relish taking an active role – where desirable and appropriate – in the whole process of conception, creation, and ongoing project development.

Take care, and I look forward to our meeting on Monday, January 20.

Sincerely,

Peter Bowerman

3) *You've talked to a prospect, who will probably be a long shot for work in the future, but you're sending out a thank you letter, résumé, and business cards.*

August 11, 2002

Mr. Steve Smith
Smith Multimedia
20 Maple Dr., Suite B
Atlanta, GA 30305

Dear Steve,

As a freelance writer, my goal is to enhance your image, improve your profit picture, and make your life easier. If it carries your name, shouldn't it be the best reflection of you?

It was a pleasure speaking with you on the phone this past week and discussing possible freelance writing opportunities with your firm. While I understand your needs for my type of writing may be limited, I've enclosed a résumé on my interactive/video copywriting experience. Should you have requests for my kind of expertise, I would be very grateful if you'd think of me.

I welcome the opportunity to make an ongoing or occasional contribution to your efforts and feel confident in my ability to deliver a quality product.

Thanks again, and I look forward to speaking with you soon.

Sincerely,

Peter Bowerman

4) *You've talked on the phone with a new prospect, and need a cover letter for a package of samples, résumé, client list, etc.*

May 7, 2001

Ms. Denise Williams
Williams and Partners, Inc.
500 Miller Drive NW, Suite 110
Atlanta, GA 30318

Dear Denise,

As a freelance writer, my goal is to enhance your image, improve your profit picture, and make your life easier. If it carries your name, shouldn't it be the best reflection of you?

It was a pleasure speaking with you on the phone today and discussing possible freelance writing opportunities with Williams and Partners, Inc. Thanks for your time and courtesy, and as suggested, I've attached a résumé listing a very selected sampling of my credits and experience, along with a client list and service offerings.

More than 16 years of sales and marketing experience coupled with an engaging, readable writing style translates to copy that communicates powerfully to your target audience. Need a light, humorous, creative touch to your projects? That's my specialty!

I welcome the opportunity to make an ongoing or occasional contribution to your efforts and feel confident in my ability to deliver a quality product. I'll be in touch shortly to set up a mutually agreeable time to meet, share my portfolio, and explore how I may best be utilized to meet your needs.

Thanks again, and I look forward to talking with you soon.

Sincerely,

Peter Bowerman

5) *You've received a call from an assistant to a creative director or communications manager with the request to send their boss a package, and this letter accompanies that package.*

May 7, 2002

Ms. Denise Williams
Williams and Partners, Inc.
500 Miller Drive NW Suite 110
Atlanta, GA 30318

Dear Denise,

As a freelance writer, my goal is to enhance your image, improve your profit picture, and make your life easier. If it carries your name, shouldn't it be the best reflection of you?

It was a pleasure speaking with Angie on the phone this past week and discussing possible freelance writing opportunities with your firm. In our conversation, she suggested I forward a résumé to you on my freelance copywriting experience.

More than 16 years of sales and marketing experience coupled with an engaging, readable writing style translates to copy that communicates powerfully to your target audience. Need a light, humorous, creative touch to your projects? That's my specialty!

I welcome the opportunity to make an ongoing or occasional contribution to your efforts and feel confident in my ability to deliver a quality product. I'll be in touch shortly to explore how I may best be utilized to meet your needs.

Thanks again, and I look forward to speaking with you soon.

Sincerely,

Peter Bowerman

---

6) *Slightly different versions of the above letters for video/CD prospects vs. print/collateral prospects, where references to "copywriting" change to "scriptwriting."*

August 30, 2002

Mr. Bill Booker
Booker Video Production
3400 Falling Water Lane
Atlanta, GA 30087

Dear Mr. Booker,

As a freelance scriptwriter, my goal is to enhance your image, improve your profit picture, and make your life easier. If it carries your name, shouldn't it be the best reflection of you?

It was a pleasure speaking with you on the phone this past week and discussing possible freelance writing opportunities with your firm. As promised, I've enclosed a résumé on my interactive/video scriptwriting experience.

More than 16 years of sales and marketing experience coupled with an engaging, "listenable" writing style translates to scripting that communicates powerfully to your target audience. Need a light, humorous, creative touch to your projects? That's my specialty!

I welcome the opportunity to make an ongoing or occasional contribution to your efforts and feel confident in my ability to deliver a quality product. I'll be in touch shortly to explore how I may best be utilized to meet your needs.

Thanks again, and I look forward to speaking with you soon.

Sincerely,

Peter Bowerman

Sample Contract

The following contract is one used by one of my writing colleagues. As with the bid letter that appeared in Chapter Nine, the same disclaimer applies:

THE FOLLOWING IS NOT A LEGALLY APPROVED DOCUMENT. USE IT FOR GUIDELINE PURPOSES ONLY. I AM NOT AN ATTORNEY AND WILL NOT BE HELD RESPONSIBLE FOR ANY PROBLEMS, HASSLES, OR OTHER MESSES THAT YOU GET YOURSELF INTO OR THAT MAY ARISE FROM USING THIS DOCUMENT. CONSULT YOUR OWN ATTORNEY AND COVER YOUR OWN BUTT. I'M VERY SERIOUS. GOT IT? GOOD.

Terms (Your Company Name) provides quality public relations and marketing communications materials. My goal is to meet or exceed my clients' expectations with every job.

Billing Procedures: In most cases, I can provide a flat rate estimate when beginning a project so that you can plan your budget accordingly. If the parameters of a project change, or if it involves much more time than originally estimated, I will inform you and we can renegotiate the rate. I submit the final invoice for a project upon receiving client approval. If I have not received any comments or revisions within a week of submitting a completed draft, I send the invoice. For a job with a flat rate of $700 or more, I bill for half of the total estimated cost when I begin the project and the rest upon completion.

I require a purchase order number or an initialed agreement before I begin work on a project. Unless otherwise specified, the flat rate for a written piece includes one telephone interview, if necessary, and one round of revision. Any additional interviews, meetings, research trips, phone calls, and revisions are billed on an hourly basis ($75/hr.). Incidental expenses such as long distance phone calls, postage, courier service, etc. are billed at cost. Mileage to special events or interviews is billed at the rate currently accepted by the IRS. When a piece involves writing, graphic design, and printing, I provide separate estimates for each item, and may bill for them separately as well. I bill 20% extra for rush jobs. I require half of the total estimated cost up front before beginning a rush job for a first-time client.

Parties & Assignment: This agreement is between Bill Shakespeare (You), hereafter referred to as "Writer" and the commissioning party and its agents, hereafter referred to as "Client."

Acceptance: Signature by "Client" constitutes acceptance of these terms.

Expiration of Estimate: Estimated costs are good for 90 days from the date of this estimate.

Estimate: The specified price is an estimated cost based on the initial specifications of this job order only. Any additional costs incurred in the completion of this project will be added to this estimate. Estimated costs are good for 90 days from the date of this estimate.

Client Approval: Client is responsible for written approval of work ordered (i.e., copy, design, photography, typesetting, and other services) required for the completion of this project. This approval can be in the form of initials or facsimile. Upon acceptance of the work, client accepts responsibility for any further processes in which this work is used (i.e., film output, printing, etc.) Writer is not responsible for errors occurring in this work or projects related to this work after acceptance of this work.

Changes: Any verbal or written changes made by Client to the scope of this project following its initiation by Writer are subject to additional charges. Should such changes negate any part of the project already completed at the time of the changes, Client accepts responsibility for payment of the completed work and all services related to it, in addition to charges for the change itself.

Cancellation: Upon written or verbal cancellation, Client is responsible for payment for all expenses incurred and any work done toward the completion of the project based on the percentage of project completed. Should Client cancel the project following its completion, Client is responsible for full payment as per the above estimate plus all other expenses incurred.

Payment and Collection: Payment for this project is due net 15 days from the invoice date. Unless otherwise specified in writing, invoices not paid within 30 days of the invoice date will accrue interest at 1.5% per month. Client agrees to pay for each check returned for insufficient funds or any other reason $25 per occurrence or 5% of the value of each returned item, whichever is greater. Client agrees to pay all reasonable attorney's fees (at least 15% of all amounts due, including interest) if any account is placed with an attorney for collection. Client agrees that the purchase of the services described herein constitutes "doing business" in the State of _____ and submits itself to the jurisdiction of the State of _____ with respect to any suit brought by (Your Company Name) to collect any sums hereunder. The parties agree that the only venue for any suit brought by either of them with respect to the services sold hereunder shall be in the State Court of _____County.

Sample
Brochure

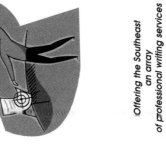

WriteInc.

Offering the Southeast
an array
of professional writing services
in the sales and marketing arena

Joe Johnson
Writer

A powerful partner
for your next
sales and marketing campaign

WriteInc.
1250 Miller Lane
Atlanta, GA 30002
404/987-6543
404/234-5678 (Fax)
jjohnson@cyborg.com

COMMITMENT

Solid Writing

While some projects warrant the unconventional, many others demand the straight-forward. When clear, simple communication is your goal, I'll provide it.

Creativity

When creativity's the goal, count on my 15 years of marketing, sales, and writing experience. I know how people think and make decisions, and how to effectively reach them through writing.

Value

Get good work at a price far lower than large ad or PR agency rates. I don't do everything they do, but you'll get just what you need.

My Best Stuff

Count on it. Good writing doesn't just happen. It takes extra effort and a commitment to find the special angle that will lift it above the ordinary.

And that's what'll keep you coming back.

EXPERIENCE

Tap into nearly 20 years of successful sales and marketing experience, spanning the spectrum from direct sales to business-to-business marketing. Call on me for your:

- Marketing Brochures
- Corporate Image Packages
- Direct Mail Campaigns
- Advertising Copy
- Newsletters
- Video/CD-ROM Scripting
- Speeches

Writing credits include marketing brochures, training manuals, fundraising proposals, video scripting, and press releases for such firms as ABC Telecomm, Biggie Snack Company, American Ear Association, and others.

I am a successfully published local humorist, and my work appears regularly in several area publications. Harness that same creativity and bring new vitality to your project as well.

"We were very pleased with Joe's work on our corporate marketing brochure. He covered all the necessary bases while **keeping the text flowing, concise, and engaging.**"

John Smith, President
Marketing & Training Video Productions

ADVANTAGES

A freelance writer can:

- Improve your bottom line
- Enhance your image
- Increase your efficiency
- Make your life easier

You don't have the time
to be good at everything.
You know what you do best. Do it.
Outsource your writing to me.
Keep up your momentum.

A professional writer really **does** make a difference. Why do it yourself? Doesn't your product or service deserve eloquent presentation? **Hand it off and stay focused.**

The Freelance Advantage

- Reduce costs with the "task-specific" help you need - only when you need it.
- No salaries, benefits, vacation, or sick leave.
- Corporate "downsizing" creates short-term staffing crunches. Fill in with a free-lancer.
- A fresh perspective. New enthusiasm.
- THE solution for sporadic writing needs.
- Allows small firms to compete effectively.

"Joe did a marvelous job both writing our corporate fundraising proposal as well as scripting our fundraising video. His direct and compelling style effectively draws in the reader or viewer."

Laura Williams, Past President
HelpFirst, Inc. Homeless Outreach

PROFESSIONALISM

Consultation/Agreement

After an initial no-obligation, no-charge, Q & A session, I'll share my ideas on the project. We'll discuss finances. Once okayed, we'll sign a simple agreement, outlining responsibilities, time frames, and investment.

Terms

As all jobs are different, quotes will be made at consultation. Short-term assignments (2 weeks or less) can be quoted on a Flat Rate basis. Longer projects may warrant hourly rates. One-third of the contracted amount will be due up front, with the balance paid at negotiable checkpoints.

Revisions

Two rounds of revisions are included in any contracted price. Additional revisions will be billed on an hourly rate. Prices quoted are for copy only. Additional services may be billed separately.

"Joe's work on our services agreement booklet reflected an **impressive dedication to maximum comprehension.** He reduced an enormous amount of material to the salient points."

Jack Wilson, President
Acme Production Services, Inc.

Direct Mail Piece

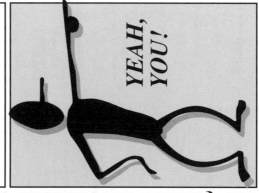

Write Inc. – Joe Johnson
Quality Copywriting

WHAT I DO

Marketing
Brochures
Corporate Image
Ad Copy
Sales Promotions
Video/MM Scripts
Speeches
Radio Spots
Trade Articles
Ghost Writing
Direct Mail Pieces
Business Letters
Press Releases
ASK ABOUT
CONCEPTING
SERVICES

MY CLIENTS

UPS
Holiday Inn
MCI
American Express
Coca-Cola
Harland
Georgia-Pacific
Cartoon Network
NationsBank
Junior
Achievement
Caribiner
Communications
Franklin's Printing
American Heart
Association

CALL FOR

✧ **Free Consultation**
✧ **Samples**
✧ **References**
✧ **Reasonable Rates**

WOW!

Joe Johnson
404/**GET-JJ-00** (Ph)
(404/555-6543)
404-555-5678 (Fx)
jjohnson@cyborg.com

Appendix B

THE SAMPLE COLLECTION

A few notes about the following samples:

1) Remember in Chapter Eight when I spoke about faxing text samples (as opposed to copies of actual pieces)? These samples are in the exact format that I'll use to send to a client by fax.

2) Where a sample says "Excerpt," it's a one- or two-page encapsulation of the original copy—generally enough to give a client (and you) an idea of the tone of a piece.

3) As you look at some of these pieces (i.e., the ads and some of the brochures), note the structure of the copy, as this is usually how you'd deliver it to a client for review. For example:

> *Cover Headline:*
> *Body Copy:*
> *Inside Panel Body Copy:*
> *Back Panel Copy:*

4) On the video script (Spectrographix), CD-ROM script (Korea), on-hold message copy (Spectrographix), speech (Youth Accomplishment), and radio spot samples (The Shoe House/Security), given that they're all written "for the ear," note the simplicity of the copy. Remember: few big words or complex phrases, because you're competing with visuals in the case of video and CD-ROM, or with other things the person is doing in the case of the radio spots and even speeches.

5) In all cases, I've changed company and product names.

BEFORE YOU READ THESE, READ THIS...

After viewing these samples, you'll probably be hit with one of two emotions. Smugness or depression. Smugness if you think that you could write at least as well as I did, if not better, in which case I say, good for you! That's great news and means that you'll have no trouble being nicely competitive in this field.

The other emotion, depression, will obviously hit if you feel that your writing ability just isn't as good as what you see here. To which I'd say, go back and re-read the first few paragraphs of Chapter Three—"So, What Does it Take to Be Successful?"—where I talk about "Writing Ability."

You just don't have to be a phenomenal writer in order to find plenty of work in plenty of fields. Remember, in many industries, they're not looking for flashy, creative copy—just solid communication that conveys the important information.

Let's take a look...

Sample:
Business Letter Before/After Scenario. — "BEFORE"

Dear Mr._____:

   Just over two years ago we founded and started Real Equity Financing Corp., Inc. and secured a license as a Mortgage Broker. During the past 28 months we have seen tremendous growth within the organization. Retail loan closings now exceed $10,000,000 per month with multiple sales locations in metro Atlanta and Charlotte, NC. If you have had any experience with mortgage retail, then you are probably aware of the significance of that pattern of growth and the ongoing potential with that level of volume.

   The purpose of my letter is not to toot our horn, but rather, to possibly spark your interest in a potentially mutually beneficial partnering. I realize that as impressive as the growth has been in our first two years, the next five could be even greater with the right partner. I am pursuing a Community Bank that would have an interest in participating in the growth and profitability of the mortgage industry.

   Our unique concept will continue to attract experienced mortgage professionals and I believe it is safe to expect a doubling of the retail volume in the next 18 months. That's where a Community Bank partner comes into play. As an equity partner the possibilities toward additional profit centers for both organizations is significantly increased. With the strength and quality of our retail volume, we have developed a client base for ongoing products and services that offers tremendous potential.

   If your Bank has considered or perhaps is currently pursuing opportunities in the mortgage industry and would like to know more about our organization and our plan for a partnering please give me a call at _____. If I am unavailable, please speak with my Assistant, _____, to arrange a mutually convenient time for your review of our corporate presentation materials. I hope we will have the opportunity to meet at some future date. Until then, I wish you much success throughout the remainder of this year!

Sincerely,

John Brown - President
Ace Mortgage

"AFTER"

Dear Mr.___:

A 2-year old mortgage brokerage firm with monthly retail closings in excess of $10,000,000? And looking for a partner?

The past 28 months since we founded and launched Real Equity Financing Corp., Inc. have seen growth nothing short of phenomenal. Yes, $10,000,000+ in monthly retail loan closings from sales offices in metro Atlanta and Charlotte, NC. If you're familiar with mortgage retail, then you certainly recognize the significance of such numbers and the growth potential with this level of volume.

I'm not here to brag, but rather, to spark your interest in the possibility of a partnership. As impressive as our growth has been in the first two years, the next five could be even greater with the right partner. With that in mind, I am seeking one Community Bank interested in participating in the growth and profitability of our dynamic company.

Our unique concept continues to attract experienced mortgage professionals and we confidently predict a doubling of retail volume in the next 18 months. And that's where you come in. As an equity partner, the potential to create additional profit centers for both our organizations is significantly increased. The strength and quality of our retail volume is clear evidence of a mature client base - a solid market for ongoing products and services that offers tremendous growth potential.

If you've considered or are currently pursuing opportunities in the mortgage industry, we urge you to learn more about our proven organization and our partnering plan. Please give me a call at _____, or please speak with my assistant, _____, to secure a copy of our corporate presentation materials. Become part of our bright and profitable future! We appreciate your consideration, and until we speak, I wish you much success!

Sincerely,

John Brown - President
Ace Mortgage

Sample Excerpt:
Corporate Image Brochure for import/export firm.

Cover Headline: We Know Your World...
Now Come Discover Ours.

An Intimate Understanding

When it comes to selecting a product vendor, you have high expectations. At ABC International, we know that. But no more than is expected of you every day - and from many different directions. Endless meetings, reports, and deadlines, not to mention the constant pressure from marketing to deliver new ideas, new products, and the next "winner" – and all of it on-time, on-target, and on-budget.

Uncommon Reliability

What you don't have a lot of is time to waste, patience for problems, or margin for error. Because we understand your day-to-day realities, we know that you look for a company that will do whatever it takes to earn and keep your business.

We've built our business and our reputation through competitive prices, rock-solid reliability, and a "can-do" attitude. Not to mention a commitment to constant communication throughout the order process and prompt problem resolution. The long-term trust and loyalty of our customers speak eloquently of our performance.

Contacts and Control in Asia

China. Hong Kong. India. Indonesia. Korea. The richest and most fertile source for the products and manufacturing processes you need to compete successfully in your industry. Through our many, varied, and exclusive supply contacts, we're your passport to the kind of ambitious results you expect and require.

Unparalleled Responsiveness

While our roots and expertise lie in cosmetic accessory items - brushes, sponges, applicators, and an array of packaging that includes baskets, boxes, and bags - our product scope ranges comfortably beyond these parameters. Tell us what you want and we'll find it. Or with the help of our dedicated factories, we'll create it. And with our intimate knowledge of your needs, both immediate and long-term, count on us to continually bring you the latest treasures that'll have you meeting targets, deadlines, and expectations.

Relationships Mean Security

Time-tested relationships with factory owners across Asia - who work exclusively for AI - generate security and benefits for all. For **ABC,** it's knowing that we have reliable producers who will deliver on commitments with precision and excellence. Our **factory owners**, assured of steady work from ABC, now feel comfortable investing in research to source and design new and unique products for us and you.

Finally, it is our **customers** who have the most to gain from these close and well-cultivated connections. In addition to our ability to offer attractive terms to our clients, it means the "order-it-and-forget-it" reliability for which ABC is renowned. And with both ABC and our suppliers sourcing new products, you'll have many eyes searching on your behalf.

Unsurpassed reliability. Exceptional and exclusive Asian connections. An ongoing commitment to understanding and meeting your unique product needs. Come to the source.

ABC International. A New World of Excellence.

Sample Excerpt:

Brochure for FDE (Foundation for Disease Eradication) highlighting new *Worldwide Health Journey Museum* – targeted to school teachers as a field trip site.

The Global Health Odyssey
The Extraordinary Story of the FDE

Finally, a Look Inside...

For years, a curious public has wanted to know more. What is the history of public health? What exactly does FDE do? Where have we been and where are we going? How does what we do impact you? Using a dynamic combination of colorful original posters, historical artifacts, and fun informative interactive displays and video presentations, *Worldwide Health Journey* (WHJ) answers these questions and more.

You'll walk away with a real sense of what's been going on in public health for decades now – an intimate look into the organization that sees itself as the "guardians of the nation's health."

Something for Everyone

Through an informative five-minute video presentation, host Bill Cosby and a collection of FDE professionals offer a warm welcome. Moving through the exhibit, you'll visit a simulated laboratory, a field investigation tent, hazardous waste site and other life-size settings that'll give you a feel for the many arenas in which FDE operates.

Bright catchy visuals – photographs, posters, and artifacts – chronicle the spectacular and historic disease eradication campaigns waged by the FDE around the world. For more in-depth treatments, visitors can turn to the inter-active dimension of the exhibit, the Life Style screens, the FDE TimeLine and the FDE Internet Home Page to explore the rich depths of the FDE story – past, present, and future.

Humble Beginnings

In 1947, new FDE employees, working out of cramped quarters on Peachtree Street, demonstrated some of the legendary teamwork and camaraderie for which the new agency would become renowned. Penny by penny, FDE employees collected the token $10.00 fee for the15-acre plot near the Taylor University grounds earmarked for their new home. And thus began the next chapter in the incredible story of the organization that would change the course of world health. A story that we now share with you for the first time through *Worldwide Health Journey.*

FDE's Milestones...

As you stroll through history, you'll relive the defining moments in public health and FDE. The public health initiative against malaria in the early 1900s. The ultimately successful campaign to eradicate smallpox in 20 countries in Africa, waged from 1966 to 1977. The dramatic reduction in heart disease and stroke achieved through FDE's efforts. The serious present-day viral threats: Hanta, Ebola, and – closer to home - AIDS, and the headway we're making.

The next disease in FDE's sights? Polio. The estimated global eradication date? The end of the century. Find out what they're doing to make this a reality. Just as importantly, you'll get in touch with FDE's ambitious campaigns to promote safe and healthy lifestyles right here at home.

Time Travel, Anyone?

Want to take a trip back in time? Visit the highlight of the exhibit, the interactive FDE TimeLine. Using rare archival video footage, the TimeLine offers truly fascinating glimpses into the role that the Public Health Service and then FDE played – in the U.S. and around the globe – in positively impacting the course of history for millions. You'll travel back and get a "you-were-there" sense of what it was like to be around during those challenging and troubled times.

Sample Excerpts:

Text segments from Educational CD-ROM
Audience: Students - age 10+

Geysers in the Deep

Scientists used to think that all life existed using the energy of the sun and only the sun. Through "photosynthesis," the complex process of using sunlight to create food, life on land and in the sea thrived. Could life have begun in another way? In 1965, a British geologist, John W. Elder, thought so. Using the theory of plate tectonics, not widely accepted at the time, Elder had an idea.

He saw hot mineral springs and geysers such as Old Faithful, which erupts like clockwork every 75-90 minutes in Yellowstone National Park in Wyoming. What causes this phenomenon? Ground water seeps down and hits red hot magma, which had pooled close to the surface. Quickly boiling, the water shoots back out like a huge steaming tea kettle, but this time, full of minerals picked up from below. If this could happen on land, Elder asked, why not on the ocean floor?

If the shifting of the Earth's plates could cause cracks, exposing molten lava, what would happen when ice-cold seawater hits these gateways to the inner Earth? If this was the case, what would it mean? If new ocean floor could form at the mid-ocean ridges, as a result of shifting plates, might it be a good place for life to begin as well? Very possible, thought Elder. Why? Because of the heat, turbulence, and the expected high mineral content of the geysers, this might just make a perfect "stew of creation."

Another point supported Elder's theory. In the Earth's early days, the sun's burning ultraviolet rays beat down, making it impossible for any life to survive. Because there was no protective layer of ozone high above the atmosphere like there is today, shielding us from the sun's harmful rays, life may have started somewhere else, hidden from the sun. What better place than miles below the surface, on the ocean floor? But how could he prove it? His answer came in stages over the next 20 years.

Two years later, in a joint French-American mission, scientists, using submersibles, discovered vast collections of "pillow lava" along the Mid-Ocean Ridge. It was obvious that lava had pumped out of cracks in the ocean floor and had hardened almost instantly into strange, billowing shapes. In much the same way as we see all kinds of shapes in white, puffy clouds on a sunny day, the scientists saw lava in the shape of hot dogs, basketballs, and even a baked potato with a spoonful of sour cream on top! But as yet, no evidence of geysers.

It was in the next expedition in 1977, aboard the ship KNORR, that scientists "struck gold," along the so-called East Pacific Rise, near the Galapagos Islands, off the coast of the South American country of Ecuador. After descending for 90 minutes in the research "submersible" ALVIN, they suddenly saw a patch of water, shimmering with heat and serving as the centerpiece for an incredibly rich array of life at a depth where early scientists were certain that nothing could survive, because of the extreme cold and the crushing pressure.

But here were blood-red tube worms, huge beds of Frisbee-size clams, white crabs, and huge colonies of shrimp, mussels and sea anemones. A teeming oasis of life in the deep. They called these deep-sea vents "black smokers," because the mineral-rich geysers often appeared as black plumes rising from the ocean floor.

One key to confirming the theory was in the smell of the water. Water samples from the "black smoker" areas smelled like rotten eggs, which meant that hydrogen sulfide was present. Seawater contains sulfate, which when superheated and put under pressure, becomes hydrogen sulfide. Using this substance as a food of sorts, a special bacteria actually thrived, right next to water as hot as 750 degrees Fahrenheit. This abundant bacteria becomes a food source for larger animals and forms the beginning of a food web. Life flourishes - where the sun never shines!

Sample Excerpt:

Event Scripting for franchised business regional conference

VOG (Voice of God): Ladies and Gentlemen, Welcome to the 1997 CBA Regional Leadership Conference - "CBA Today, Leading the Way!" and right now, we're proud to present "CBA Coffee Chat"!

Mara enters from back, strolls through audience with microphone.

Mara: Good morning, everyone, and welcome to *your* conference! Well, we're finally here. It's amazing how much time and preparation goes into these conferences and just like that, they're here and then they're over.

It's really wonderful for all of us at CBA corporate to meet face-to-face with everyone we've been talking, struggling, and sweating with all year. We're going to have a lot of fun today, share a lot of good information, while always remembering that today is all about you and all for you. I look around me and see a lot of old familiar faces and some new ones - which I always love to see. The CBA family continues to grow and that's always exciting.

Well, we've got a really great program planned for you today, and we're going to kick it off with a real bang, as we - drumroll, please - unveil the new advertising creative. We thought about waiting until the end of the day, but we want you to have plenty of time to realize what an impact this campaign is going to have on growing your sales, and believe me, it's going to be big! So let's bring up a couple of great ladies who are going to tell you all about it. Please welcome your Vice-President of Marketing, Ms. Diane Martin, and the head of the Marketing, Mr. John Wilson.

- **Marketing Presentation - New Ad Campaign - Diane Martin and John Wilson**
   Diane Martin and John Wilson come up, take seats on the stage, and banter with Mara.

Mara: Hi, Diane, so you've got something pretty fantastic for us this morning, don't you?

Diane: I sure do. I've been antsy all week, couldn't wait for the conference to get here so we could share this great new campaign with the CBA Partners.

John: It's definitely been the hot topic of conversation this week!

Mara: So, John, what do you think of the new spots?

John: They're wonderful and I'm really excited about what they're going to do for everyone's business.

Mara: So, Diane, give us a little background on how we arrived at this campaign — what went into the spots, the creative thought process, anything you think we should know before we take a peek.

Diane: For starters, I'd like to take a few minutes to talk about where we've come from:

Discuss:
• Sales
• Creative Process
• Focus Group Video

Diane: So that's about it. What do you say we show them?

Mara: Sounds great. *(To audience)* Everyone ready? Let's roll 'em!

Show New TV Spots

Sample:

Full Page Ad for
Graphic User Interface (GUI) Technology

Visual Concept: Chameleon

Split Screen featuring chameleon with left side in old un-enhanced green screen, while right side is GUIForm-enhanced - colorful, vibrant, and compelling.

Headline:

This Beauty Is More Than Skin Deep ...

And smart too, when it comes to migrating your legacy applications. Unlike typical "screen-scrapers," GUIForm is beautiful and intelligent, not only learning how you've designed your host screens, but how you want the GUI representation to look.

And while others have to start over from scratch with each and every minor modification, our unique KnowledgeBase grows more brilliant with every use, making application maintenance a breeze. How? By generating your new client application in fully functional Visual Basic. This means that new features and functionality can be added and integrated like never before, at the desktop level.

So you get a migration partner you could be happy with for years, while safeguarding your investment in legacy applications. And all without altering your host application. Why settle for a "screen scraper" when you can have the beauty and brains of GUIForm?

GUIForm. Pretty. Smart. Idea.

Sample Excerpt:

"On-Hold" Message Scripts for Software Products

Short informative and sales-oriented scripts designed for customers on hold. Setting: industry trade show.

#1 - Jack and Bob

Bob: Hey, Jack. Glad you stopped by.

Jack: Hello, Bob. Thought I'd slip behind enemy lines to the Spectrographix booth. What's this I hear about a new Windows platform?

Bob: That's right, Jack. RasterServe for Windows. It's our latest. We're really excited about it. Lot of shops running on PCs these days.

Jack: (hopefully) So this is just some entry level system, huh?

Bob: Afraid not, Jack. We've got a complete upgrade path from Windows. It's easy to get started and our clients can eventually move up to a full-blown system. At their own pace and within their budget.

Jack: (in a low, soft voice) You guys hiring here?

#2 - Straight Voice-Over Script

Spectrographix, the leader in digital imaging technology, is on the move—around the world and on the pages of the trade magazines you read most. Make sure to catch us this month in:

        Modern Reprographics

        Corel Magazine

        Sign Business Magazine, and

        Screen Graphics Magazine

Keep up with the latest in profit-boosting developments from Spectrographix

- the One-Stop source for all your digital imaging needs.

Sample Excerpt:
Eye Surgery "Relaxer" Video
Designed for Prospective Eye Surgery Patients

(Video commands in italics, Audio in regular type)

Med shot of van pulling up to retirement home. Cut to smiling driver helping person into van. (bkgrnd. sound of driver greeting patient) Cut to Van pulling away. Interior shot of driver chatting with patient. (bkgrnd. sound of chatting)

The big day begins at your retirement home or managed care facility, where you'll be treated to our "door-to-door" shuttle service. Our friendly and specially trained drivers will meet you in one of our roomy and comfortable vans for the short drive to our modern Atlanta area center.

INSERT TESTIMONIAL: Comment about how nice the driver was, "how I was a little nervous, but he did a great job of relaxing me."

Cut to van pulling up and driver walking patient into reception area.

Once you arrive, our driver will escort you to the reception area. When your surgery is finished, he'll be waiting to take you right home!

Smiling staff greets patient (bkgrnd. greeting talk), possibly checking name off list. Picking up phone and talking (bkgrnd. talk saying "Ms. Jones is here for her procedure")

Our courteous staff is expecting you, and after signing in, they'll notify the surgical coordinator that you've arrived for your appointment.

Cut to surgical coordinator (SC) greeting patient (bkgrnd. greeting - maybe, "Did you have a nice trip?") Cut to entering SC's office, shot from inside office.

The surgical coordinator will greet you and take you back to her office, where she'll be conducting a few tests prior to your operation.

Cut to Med CU of patient sitting in front of machine having test done, comfortably chatting with SC. (possibly bkgrnd. of patient asking question)

These tests are simple, quick, and painless, and they'll give us the right prescription measurements for your new lens implants. It's actually quite similar to the test you'd have when being fitted for glasses. Feel free to ask any questions. Our staff is happy to explain every step of the process.

Sample Speech Excerpt:

Youth Accomplishment Atlanta Business Hall of Fame Awards Ceremony and Dinner

We are in the midst of exciting and turbulent times. Discussions of the national priorities that will affect the future of this nation are on the table. It is more imperative than ever before that we strive as an organization to bring the message of economic freedom and opportunity home to our youth. To say that our futures lie in their hands is far more than just a common cliché. It's reality. Ensuring the strength of that future is a tremendous responsibility and one that Youth Accomplishment has never taken lightly.

Youth Accomplishment serves more than 21,000 local area youth, kindergarten to the 12th grade, bringing them together with a small army of volunteer businesspeople. Through programs that explore business- and economics-related issues, these young people are guided and prepared for their future in the workplace and society at large. And by providing comprehensive material, training, and support, Youth Accomplishment ensures that even the most nervous volunteer is a success. Volunteers discover that they don't have to be economics experts in order to make a difference. Just honest and committed.

As many of you this evening are past Youth Accomplishment volunteers, who generously shared your successes and setbacks with young people, isn't it gratifying to know that some member of your Youth Accomplishment class remembered a specific story you told, and applied it successfully to their lives? Through your efforts, as well as that of Youth Accomplishment and the individuals honored by the Atlanta Business Hall of Fame, both tonight and in nights past, the free enterprise torch is kept burning brightly.

Tonight we come together to pay special tribute to three outstanding individuals who, during the course of long and distinguished careers - far from complete - have made incalculable contributions not only to the city of Atlanta, but to the fundamental ideals of Youth Accomplishment as well. Each of these men are, in their own way, larger-than-life heroes to the city of Atlanta, and their contributions go far beyond their actual accomplishments. Contributions that were no doubt made possible, in part, by their common roots in Youth Accomplishment.

Through their commitments to their respective causes, these men created a legacy that does great honor to the enduring ideals of Youth Accomplishment: economic freedom, initiative, self-discipline and motivation. And that motivation comes naturally when you're truly inspired by a worthwhile purpose. Something that's true for each of these gentlemen.

And while we're speaking of inspiration, I'm reminded of the story of the unfortunate fellow who was taking his usual shortcut home from work through the local graveyard. It was quite dark and he didn't notice the freshly dug grave awaiting a burial the next day. And in he fell. It was quite a deep hole and try as he might for the next hour to both climb out and call for help, he still remained stuck with no rescuers on the way. Totally exhausted, he sat down in the corner and promptly fell asleep.

Along came another hapless stroller, who made the same wrong step, and into the hole he went as well. With no moon out that night, he didn't notice his fellow grave-mate snoozing in the corner. Struggling mightily for several minutes to no avail, his rather loud efforts awoke the first gentleman, who watched the new arrival making the same futile efforts to escape that he had. From the dark corner of the grave, the second gentleman heard a low, calm voice say, "You can't get out of here." But guess what. He did!

He had some real inspiration. And I must say, I'm inspired, just being in the same room as these guys, so without further ado, let's move on to the awards. Ladies and gentlemen, the Atlanta Business Hall of Fame inductees for 2002 are:

Mr. John Brown, Dr. William Jones, and Mr. David Smith.

Sample Excerpt:

Brochure/Newspaper Insert Showcasing Hospital's "Good Works"

Good Works.

Indeed it does, and in more ways than one. In fact, these two words are at the heart of what Missionary Hospital has stood for since its inception in 1952. Under the stewardship of the Sisters of Charity from the beginning, this full-line not-for-profit medical institution has made caring, compassion, and excellence their very cornerstones.

Missionary Hospital knows that good works for everyone - patients, employees, and the community at large. You already know the Missionary Hospital renowned for its top-quality health care - with some of the finest cardiac and oncology programs in the Southeast. We'd like to introduce you to another face - the good works we do every day to deliver on our fundamental commitments.

We've all heard that "Charity begins at home." And never truer than at Missionary, where employees are special. From higher than normal starting wages to child care and home buying assistance programs, Missionary takes good care of its own. Indeed, their Child Care Center, while a relatively new fixture in most corporate settings, has been continuously operating at Missionary since 1980, recently undergoing a renovation that fully doubled its size and ability to serve employee needs.

And people like Joey and Linda Tass, maintenance and medical transport workers with Missionary, are homeowners thanks to an innovative partnership program between Missionary and the Neighborhood Enterprise Initiative (NEI). With NEI guiding and advising prospective homeowners through the process and Missionary providing assistance with down payments and securing second mortgages, the dream of home ownership has become a reality for many Missionary employees like Joey and Linda.

And this is only the beginning of the good works beyond the doors of Missionary.

Sample Excerpt:

Missionary Hospital "Good Works" Brochure - Stella Jackson Profile

> "I may stop by a widower's house, and a neighboring widow asks how he is. If he was sad, I may say, 'Well, it's raining today,' and she'll understand and may say, 'Well, I'll call him,' or 'I'll make sure he has something to eat.' I love to see community come together."

Stella Jackson feels especially fortunate to do what she does. As a social worker with Missionary Hospital, she works in the nearby Glenwood community. It's a neighborhood with which Missionary has always enjoyed a special relationship, and where they suspected there were many unaddressed needs amongst the largely elderly population.

Stella's mission? To befriend the people, assess their needs, and as an advocate with a keen grasp of available resources amongst residents, the community, or Missionary Hospital itself, steer the person to the solution. Or, in her words, "look after people who might otherwise fall through the cracks."

But far from handouts, which she is quick to point out that the proud people of Glenwood simply won't accept, her mission is to empower the community and its residents to help each other. She explains, "Sometimes, when I go into a neighborhood, I'll recruit one or two of the residents to help out with a particular situation, and that way the community is taking care of its own. By spending time with these people, whom I dearly love, they don't see me as a social worker, but as a friend. And when a crisis hits, people will accept help from a friend."

Stella Jackson walks the world of the forgotten. Elderly people who are often alone and grieving. They grieve for the loss of a lifelong spouse, a loss of independence, and most of all, the loss of their self-worth as a vital member in the day-to-day happenings of their community, which has moved on without them. It's not glamorous work, and there are few "success stories" in a conventional sense.

Yet, Stella Jackson knows the difference she's making. Whether it's a smile coaxed from a timeworn face or a thank-you from a friend who needs so little but needs that little so much, her rewards come in small sweet packages.

Sample Excerpt:
Missionary Hospital Recruitment Brochure

Introduction

Making a difference. As human beings, it's something we all strive to do. For our families, our professions, our communities. At Missionary Hospital, we've been making a difference for people in the quality of healthcare since 1952. We're good at what we do because of our commitment to quality and excellence. And that commitment starts with our people.

Every day, the medical professionals in the Missionary family see the difference they're making in the quality of life around them. And for those with families of their own, that difference takes on a whole new meaning and richness.

Chances are, you're viewing Missionary either as a place to align your professional future or as your provider of choice for quality healthcare. Regardless of your interest, you'll find Missionary to be a sound decision for many reasons. In the pages ahead, you'll begin to see why so many high caliber medical professionals as well as area residents have chosen Missionary for the future of their healthcare.

Conclusion

Quality of life. A common phrase in today's world perhaps, but one that takes on many dimensions in relation to Missionary Hospital. First and foremost, it embodies one of the fundamental goals of our caring and healing institution.

Just as importantly, it speaks to things fundamental - universal longings in all of us: a close, loving, healthy family and the resources to care for that family. Strong faith to provide a solid foundation for our lives. The chance to do a good day's work with an organization that is guided by enlightened and time-honored principles that support and empower our commitments. To have our work make a difference. And when the day is done, to have time with our loved ones to savor the beauty and magic of life.

Quality of life. This is what Missionary offers. And whether you're choosing a career or simply a hospital, we invite you to come be a part of it. Missionary Hospital. The future of your healthcare.

Sample Excerpt:

Product Brochure for Speed One Electronic Printing Software

Introduction: Electronic Printing

Johann Gutenberg would be pleasantly surprised to discover how many so-called "modern" printing methods are very similar to his 500-year-old process. How is it that, up till so very recently, forms printing technology has managed to elude the same automation trend that's exploded efficiency and productivity levels in so many other business arenas? Sorry, Johann, but it's time to move on … and electronic printing is the future.

The Advantages of Electronic Printing?

Obvious and overwhelming. Electronically create, store, and print checks, forms, and labels, by merging data files with forms at print time. Which means you'll save hugely on the up-front costs of printing, shipping, and storing mountains of pre-printed forms. And what happens when, two months into your six-month forms supply, a new regulation forces a forms change? You fill your dumpster and empty your pockets … again.

Do you simply write off such waste to "the cost of doing business"? With electronic printing, it's a non-issue. Need to make a change to an existing form or check layout? With electronic printing, an end user can revise any form on the desktop level without ever altering the application program. And it gets better. Forms get printed to plain laser paper, while checks and labels are output to blank check or label stock. Multi-part forms can be electronically burst and distributed to any printer on your network.

Now that we've determined that staying with a traditional forms printing approach would be like going back to typewriters and carbon paper, what would the ideal electronic printing software look like? How about a product that's incredibly easy to use, very comprehensive - it handles all your jobs: checks, forms, and labels - and specifically designed to interface with the #1 selling computer platform in the world - the AS/400?

Sample:

Trade Article for Digital Imaging Industry Publication

"SHORT RUN" DEMAND FUELING DIGITAL BOOM

Setting: *The Past.* The screen printing marketing rep sighs at his retail client's unrealistic expectations. They want an actual proof of the in-store display signs before printing begins. Then, customized print runs for 15 different stores, each reflecting items of regional interest and local appeal. And all at a price barely above the cost of one straight, uniform run. This guy must be new, the rep thinks. Sure, we can do everything he wants, but we're talking some major bucks. Someday, maybe …

Setting: *Someday.* As in, today. The marketing rep nods and jots some notes as her client hesitantly ticks off his particular needs. An apparel manufacturer marketing in college towns, the company wants its in-store displays to feature starbursts boosting each individual school's football team. Short, custom runs all around. And proofs of all 25 versions of the poster.

The buyer gulps nervously as he presents his budget, afraid their requirements may be too ambitious for the money allotted. After all, he asks, doesn't each of these runs require its own screen? The rep smiles, thankful for her company's recent entrance into the digital arena, tailor-made for situations just like this.

Scenarios like this, once wistful longings on the part of clients and screen printers, are now daily fare in the graphics world. Digital imaging, with its technological breakthroughs coming at dizzying speed, is offering the market an unparalleled level of flexibility and customization, while providing screen printers with yet another arrow for their marketing quiver.

According to Mary Wilson, Director of Government Issues for the Washington, D.C. based trade association SGIA (Screenprinting and Graphic Imaging Association, International), while digital is perceived as pricey technology that still lags behind screen printing when cranking out high-volume output, the technology offers some clear advantages to the screen printer.

"In addition to its contribution to short run and 'proof' scenarios, we're seeing the strong impact of digital in the pre-press area. It's frankly a lot easier and faster to create the initial image digitally. What used to take people three days to do is now taking one. Just as importantly, it's giving the screen printer another viable option to offer their customer base."

Those in the digital industry, however, clearly see their technology as much more than just an adjunct to the screen printer's current modus operandi, but rather, where the entire graphics field is inevitably headed.

Bill Brian, Executive Vice-President of Spectrographix Technologies in Atlanta, a fast-growing digital graphics development company, sees a screen printer's decision to go digital as bottom-line based: they're losing business to digital providers, who can do proofs and custom short-runs in a much more cost effective - and environmentally safe - manner than is possible through labor-intensive screen printing methods.

Furthermore, Brian adds, "We're seeing that the growing awareness of the capabilities of digital technology is driving a whole new set of client expectations. For instance, a client may envision a "dream" marketing campaign, consisting of an overall theme, which is then customized in a virtually infinite number of ways, to achieve true target marketing impact. Now that they're realizing the technology exists to quickly, easily and cheaply implement such a program, they're demanding it."

And yet, because of those same bottom-line realities, the actual acquisition of digital imaging technology is a step being taken by primarily the medium- to large-scale screen printers.

However, thanks to the ubiquitous service bureau and reprographic house, the smaller screen printer has convenient access to the technology on an "as-needed" contract basis, allowing them to remain competitive.

Growing environmental concerns also appear to be steering the industry inexorably toward the digital arena, which prides itself on offering the "greener" technologies: products and processes that are environment-friendly.

At the same time, existing OSHA guidelines along with the new EPA "Title 5 Permit" regulations are pushing medium- and large-volume screen printers to take a hard look at the solvent-based screen washes and inks that have been production mainstays for years.

A not-so-subtle affirmation of digital's secure future is the decision last year by the former SPAI (Screen Printers Association, International) to change their name to the current designation SGIA (Screenprinting and Graphic Imaging Association, International), a move which met with virtually no resistance.

Comments Wilson, "Everyone understands that digital is becoming a part of the screen industry, and that we need to take a look at it and embrace it. It's progress. We're not going to fight it."

At this juncture, a screen printer's main trump card when going head-to-head with digital is the speed of output. Even Brian concurs. "Give me and a screen printer a 100 poster run, from start to finish, and we'll beat them hands down. Give us both a 5000 piece run, and they're going to win. But, watch out, because the speed's coming. And when it does..." His voice trails off, as he smiles. Setting: *The Future.*

Sample:

RADIO SPOTS

Setting: Fairy tale with loose dialogue; sometimes medieval, sometimes contemporary. Tinkly fairy tale music, with story teller-type narrator.

Narrator: The Shoe House presents "The Perfect Pair." Once upon a time, there lived a princess with really ugly feet.

Mixed Voices: Eeeeewwwww....Yuck....Cover 'em up, will ya?

Narrator: Princes came seeking her hand, but rarely made it past her feet.

Prince: Ooo ... I just remembereth....I've got a....um...crusade to fight! Gotta goeth! (voice loud and trailing) I'll write...

Princess: (moaning) I'll never find a prince with hooves like these!

Narrator: One day, she discovered The Shoe House: 30-60% off retail on brand-name, in-season shoes, purses, belts and accessories. Magically, her clodhoppers became charming, delicate footsies. And another prince came to call...

Prince: What lovely feet you have, m'lady. Must be The Shoe House.

Princess: (delighted) How didst thou know?

Prince: I shop there as well.

Princess: (disgusted) Great! A cross-dresser! Just my luck...

Prince: No! The Shoe House carries shoes for princes as well. (Then sadly) Especially princes with feet like royal barges.

Princess: (relieved and delighted) Thou, too? At last, I have found my love!

Prince: (matter-of-factly) On one condition. Our shoes stay on.

Princess: Deal.

(Then trailing off..)

Prince: I've heard about your boats…

Princess: Oh yeah, Mr. "Prince of Clubs"?

Narrator: The Shoe House. Uptown, on Stockholm Avenue, and coming soon to Maryville. Open Friday and Saturday 10-7, Sunday 1-6. Call 555-6543 for directions. The Shoe House - for the perfect pair. And that's no fairy tale.

Security Home Equity Lines of Credit - Radio Spot

Setting: Bob and Jack, two normal guys, just chatting

Jack: So, Bob, did you ever get that home equity line of credit you were talking about?

Bob: Not yet. Sue and I definitely want to build that sunroom, but jeez, those up-front fees are pretty steep. So, we may have to wait.

Jack. Have you heard about Security's *SecurAdvantage* program?

Bob: (chuckling) What's their gimmick? A blender, maybe? Oh, I know: a tune-up and an oil change…

Jack: (laughing) No, they do better than that. No closing costs. And no origination fees on the first $50,000.

Bob: Lemme guess. Prime rate plus 4 or 5%, right?

Jack: Nope. They're competitive. Prime + 1 1/2%, I think.

Bob: (interested) No kidding…

Jack: Oh, and if you make application in the next two weeks, they'll waive the application fee and part of the appraisal.

Bob: (more interested) Really? I might've just run out of excuses. So, how come you know so much about home equity lines?

Jack: (innocently) Oh, I don't know. I just keep my ears open. Didn't you say you were thinking of putting a pool table in the sunroom?

Bob: That's the plan. Why?

Jack: Oh, just curious…

Bob: (skeptically amused) Riiight … Just keeping your ears open, huh?

Jack: Hey, gotta look out for your friends.

SecurAdvantage home equity lines from Security. It just got easier to say yes.

Sample:
Tourist Center Rack Brochure for Hardison Gardens

Headlines - Cover/Inside Combo

Where Nature's the Stage and Every Day's a New Grand Opening …
Featuring a Cast of Thousands

Inside Panel Body Copy:

Quietly tucked away in the North ___ mountains, sits a rare and special
treasure. A botanical paradise fairly bursting with dogwoods, tulip magnolias,
native azaleas, lady slippers, trilliums … and rhododendrons. Oh my, the
rhododendrons. Over 400 varieties - 2,000 plants in all - bloom from spring
through early fall.

Welcome to Hardison Gardens, a truly enchanted spot, boasting the largest
collection of rhododendrons in the state of Georgia. Stroll tranquil pine bark
trails as they wind through lush foliage. Drink in stunning views of Lake
Chattson and the breathtaking countryside, including the majestic rise of
Billsworth Peak, our highest peak. Feel your cares drift away on the gentle
breezes. And remember what peace and quiet is all about. The magic awaits …
at Hardison Gardens.

Back Panel Copy:

The legacy of Jack and Agnes Hardison, the Gardens were graciously
donated to the North Mountain Fair in 1982, and more than 1,000 plants were
eventually relocated to their present site. In 1990, the first Rhododendron
Festival was held in Halderon, and two years later, the Festival earned the distinction of being one of the Top 20 Events of the Southeast Tourism Society.

While every day is a special event at Hardison Gardens, check with us for
peak viewing times. Open year round, free of charge.

For Women Only

At-home Moms/Writers Speak Up!

As a single male, my experience of this business is, by definition, limited. And I assert that freelance commercial writing, with its inherent freedom and flexibility, is perfect for "at-home" mothers looking to carve out a working life while still being there for their kids. So I tapped my network of colleagues and clients and put together the following three interviews with mothers/writers. While each has her own unique story, they share a common reality: juggling marriage, motherhood, and the writing life. I am sincerely grateful for the time they shared with me. If you are a woman considering this path, may their words speak to you in ways that I could never hope to.

And FYI, there is a wealth of information and support on the Internet for home-based working moms. Check out these sites for starters:

Mom Writers
— www.momwriters.com

Mothers' Home Business Network
— www.homeworkingmom.com

WAHM.com — The Online Magazine for Work At Home Moms
— www.wahm.com

Home-Based Working Moms
— www.hbwm.com

Mom's Network — Connecting At Home
— www.momsnetwork.com

National Association of At-Home Mothers
— www.athomemothers.com

National Association of Work at Home Moms — Mom's Home Work
— www.momshomework.com

Bizy Moms
— www.bizymoms.com

Mrs. Marshall

Emily Marshall* is a 26-year old "at-home" mom who left her position as marketing communications manager at BellSouth Corporation in February 1999, following the birth of her daughter. Emily now works with her old company as a freelance writer on a contract basis, juggling work and motherhood. Her husband is pursuing an MBA full-time, and while they've taken out a loan to live on till he's working, her freelance writing income has turned out to be a big help in many ways…

How receptive was your old company to your working with them on a contract basis?

Very. And it was all based on past relationships. Why reinvent the wheel, especially when you're starting out? I just went back to familiar territory and leveraged existing relationships and contacts.

What's the story in corporate America today?

There's so much business out there, especially in telecommunications. My old company just doesn't have the funding to hire full-time people in the communications department. They keep just a minimum number of managers. And that's the reality in many industries these days.

Why are freelancers in demand?

Things are going very well in corporate America today; they're making lots of money and they want to keep it that way, but with the current levels of permanent staffing. Consequently, it makes much more sense for them to hire outside contractors. They don't have to pay full-time salaries or offer benefits, retirement plans, vacations, etc. And I'm speaking from experience here. I hired out so much of my workload when I was there. I know how big the workload is and hence, how high the demand is for good freelancers. If you're a decent writer, it just isn't that hard to get established in this business and get plenty of work.

For a corporation, isn't the contractor relationship different than with an employee?

Absolutely. It's another good reason why companies are going in this direction. As a contractor, I'm going to be much more customer-oriented than I would be as an employee. They're my customer, not my employer and because of that, they're going to get higher quality work out of me. Most employees are

* Name has been changed

working so many hours and have so much going on that the quality of their work starts to decline. When I take on a project, it's because I have the time and the inclination, so I'm going to do a better job. So, there are a lot of good reasons why a company will hire you. You just have to decide why you're doing it.

And why are you doing it?

Well, I'm *not* doing it for financial security. I'm not trying to do it full-time. I don't believe you can be a full-time Mom *and* a full-time writer. I work to have an outlet for myself. This is what I can do to keep my brain sharp. Being a Mom is my double-full-time career and being a writer is my "squeeze-in-during-nap-time-career." Most of the jobs I accept are ones I can do primarily at night, during off-business hours, and there's plenty of work out there that meets that criteria. Just like in college, you don't do all your studying during the day. And sometimes it's hard. You need to have realistic expectations and decide what you're going to sacrifice because you will sacrifice something. My priority is being a parent. And this work direction lends itself wonderfully to doing that. I don't have to drop my child off at childcare, and in that sense, it's very flexible.

Logistically, how easy is it to get started in this business?

It's a very easy-entry business. You need a computer, fax, and e-mail access, which most people have anyway, and that's about it. There's almost no overhead. And with a business out of your home, you can write off part of your house, your computer, fax, Internet access, and anything else related to the business. *(Author note: Please consult your tax professional for specific advice regarding legitimate deductible expenses for a home office.)*

What was the biggest obstacle to getting started?

Given how much work there is, the market is certainly no obstacle. Honestly, it's about having the confidence in your own abilities. I asked myself the question: How do I know that I'm a decent writer? And when I first asked it, the answer I came up with was: "All I've done is change diapers and talk baby talk for the better part of a year. What makes me think that anyone would hire me?" I call it the "mush-brain" affliction (MBA). My husband is getting his MBA and I'm getting mine! The upshot is, I'd lost my confidence.

So how do you deal with that?

You just have to build it back one inch at a time. In the beginning, you'll think they're doing you a favor by hiring you. But remember what's going on in corporations today. In most cases, they're operating short-handed. They need the help. And as your confidence grows, you'll realize you're really doing *them* a favor. Go take a writing class if you need to, take on small jobs, seek familiar territory. My husband and I have a quote on our refrigerator: "It's the journey, not the destination." It's about what you're learning along the way.

Is the confidence issue different for women?

I think so. As a young at-home Mom, I've struggled with this. When I worked with my old company, I was part of the team—a bigger entity—and I could separate me from the job. If someone made a comment about what was going on, it was more about the business. But it's more of a challenge to feel business-like when you work for yourself and *you* are the product. If someone is critical of your work, it's harder to separate, you're much more vulnerable. But it comes in time.

Unlike men, women tend to not believe in their skills. We have a tendency to forget all our past job accomplishments or at least to downplay them. But I finally got to a point where I could see what I'd achieved, realized that it was good and solid and more than enough to leverage it into this new direction. So what I'd tell women is that if you want to start something new and you doubt your skills, look back at what you've already accomplished and know that you're capable. Freelancing is definitely uncharted territory for many of us, but you can do it. Again, start small and work up to the bigger stuff.

Your husband is currently a full-time MBA student and while you've taken out a loan to live on, does your income from writing make a meaningful contribution to the family purse?

Any money makes a difference. The loan we have barely covers our mortgage payment and utilities, so I use the money from writing to send my daughter to preschool twice a week, for groceries, gas, trips to the burrito place down the street, unexpected costs like new tires and brakes for the car, mice in the laundry room, and the three ear infections my child had this winter. And believe it or not, my husband and I have enjoyed a trip to a B&B this past Christmas with my extra money.

It's a great feeling to know the extra money is there, but, we try not to depend on it since we can't really forecast how much business I'll get in a given month. When considering jobs, I can only commit to about 10 hours per week and that's after 8 p.m. each night, unless my husband can arrange to be at home. I could do more if I hired a babysitter, but we haven't gotten to that point yet. As my daughter gets older, I'll probably consider devoting more time to my freelance career. For now, though, 10 hours per week is just right because I also enjoy volunteering, getting involved in my child's preschool and our church, and doing little things like gardening with my neighbor. I like to keep a good balance.

I can count on anywhere from an extra $600 to $1500 coming in per month. That's pure gold for starving students like us! Come to think of it, I think that's more than what I made in my first job with BellSouth!

What's a typical day for you?

Wake up, play with my child, feed her, put her down for a nap, take a shower, eat, fix my hair, and start working. I usually get about 45 minutes in at that point until she wakes up. Throughout the day, I'll work when I can, fit it in here and there. If I have to make appointments for later or chase down clients, I can use a cordless phone and follow my child around. Then, during her afternoon nap and later on at night, I can squeeze more in.

Do you use babysitters to free you up more?

Because I pretty much take jobs that don't require me to be in meetings during the day, I haven't had to rely on baby-sitters. I was using them at one point, but clients kept changing meeting times at the last minute, which got very frustrating. If you can get a baby-sitter or family member to help out from time to time, that will obviously expand the scope of work you can take on.

As a wife and a mother, what do you like most about this business?

I love the flexibility, the ability to work it in when I've got the time. Also, I can do something that takes brainpower and still be a full-time Mom. It makes me feel like a human again. And that's really good for my family too. I can keep my brain together to have an intellectual conversation with my husband and be a happier Mom for my daughter. Your family is a good reason to do it all by itself.

I've done a lot of reading about why women decide to stay at home. Psychologically, if a woman who decides to stay at home is miserable and depressed about her decision, she's doing her child more harm than good. But if a Mom can choose to stay at home and has some work that will give her a sense of self and make her happier, she'll be doing her and her child a favor. And this business is one of the easiest avenues in which to pull that off.

Sounds like this business can give you a more well-rounded experience of life…

Definitely. There's been a lot of press recently about how the home can be a lot less welcoming than it once was—a lot more hassles, discord, turmoil, etc. And thanks to this business, I don't have to contribute to that trend. A lot of mothers talk about passing off the baby like a football to the husband the moment he walks in the door from *his* full and tiring day. Having this business for myself allows me to be more balanced. So now I'm not counting the minutes till he gets home so I can hand him the baby. I'm doing things, talking to people, staying busy. I have a life.

What are the biggest challenges?

Being able to do the business and all the other things I want to do. But you have to make a choice. Anyone who decides to be with her child and work is going to have to make some choices. I laugh when pregnant women talk about how, once they have their child, their company is going to let them keep their jobs and work full-time from home. As if their child is going to sleep quietly in their bassinet and let Mommy work all day. That's just not realistic.

With this business, the biggest challenge is fitting it in where you can, and delivering the level of quality that I'm committed to bringing to my work. I'll only take on a project if I know I can do it well. Sometimes it's a challenge to say no. And the ebb and flow of work can be tough. When you don't have much going on, it can make you a little crazy.

Is isolation a big issue?

Being at home can be very isolating and that's tough to deal with sometimes. You have to make yourself get out and meet other people, especially other at-home Moms. Check around in your area for groups of part-time working Moms who meet and talk, preferably, of course, about more than just baby stuff! I found some on the Internet: "National Association of At-Home Mothers" *(www.athomemothers.com)* and "F.E.M.A.L.E."—Formerly Employed Mothers At the Leading Edge *(www.femalehome.org)* are ones I'm looking into now. I don't know much about them right now except that one has a magazine with great articles and good stuff on home businesses. Anything you can do to build your circle is a good thing. And besides talking with my husband, I'm committed to having at least one adult conversation every day!

Do you sometimes long for the steady paycheck and security of a 9-5 job?

No way. Especially given the flexibility of this business and the fact that I can make $60-70 an hour. Where else could I do that without going back to work full-time? I've made a choice to be a mother and I'm proud of that choice, despite the fact that so many people in society don't value it. My biggest pet peeve is people who think that a mother who stays at home with their child doesn't work. In fact, I don't like the term "stay-at-home Mom" because it implies that I'm standing still, not moving forward. I have definitely moved forward. I have grown so much spiritually in the past year and have a much better perspective on things. I prefer to call myself an "at-home mother." And the truth is, I'm staying very busy and my writing business is an important part of the mix.

Mrs. Singer

Natalie Singer*, a 41-year-old wife and mother of two children, 12 and 10, makes a full-time income as a freelance commercial writer. She spent four years in the early 1980s in Atlanta in TV production with Headline News (CNN) and as an assignment desk staffer with CNN. She followed that with freelance production work and a three-year tenure as an on-staff marketing/communications writer with Digital Equipment Corporation in Boston. With her husband working out of the home as well, they enjoy being a steady presence in their children's lives. The inherent flexibility and variety of corporate freelancing has been a perfect fit for Natalie, creatively, financially, professionally, and spiritually. And her family would agree.

How did you get started in this business?

I began in TV news, aspiring to be the next Barbara Walters, but after a few years working in local TV and for CNN as a producer/writer, I decided I wanted something a little more flexible in terms of lifestyle, and not quite as grueling with overnight hours, etc. So in 1984, I started freelancing by cold-calling production companies. I didn't even really know what corporate communications was, but I figured if I could produce for TV, I could do it for video production companies. I got my feet wet producing multi-image shows, mounting slides, and not actually doing much writing at the beginning. I transitioned into writing later after realizing that producing was more hands-on than I really wanted. I was looking for a more flexible lifestyle.

How did you find your work?

I just sold myself, my existing skills and the credibility of CNN. As I advanced along the independent freelance path, I had several opportunities including a three-year stint as a staff writer with Digital in Boston in the marketing communications group, where I got a lot of hi-tech and corporate experience. With Digital, I was probably one of the first telecommuters, having had my first child in 1987. I loved the freedom and realized that writing was the way to go and that's the path I've stayed on ever since.

How has it worked out?

It's worked out fabulously well. I've made a lot of money and had a lot of flexibility and most importantly, I've been around for my two children. Of course,

* Name has been changed

it's not without its challenges but they're far outweighed by the advantages. Almost all of my business at this point comes from word-of-mouth; I do very little marketing. It's all about repeat business, getting to know companies, becoming a resource for them. And also being a resource for middleman clients like production companies and graphic design firms, marketing companies, and others. That's a great situation: they always need writing services to execute their projects, so they essentially do the marketing for you and contact you when they have work.

As a wife and a mother of two, what do you like most about this business?

There are a lot of very positive things. Certainly the flexibility and being able to be home. You can set your own hours to a certain extent. If someone asks you to be available for a meeting, you can decline. And they don't have to know whether you're busy in another meeting or doing laundry.

I always felt I wanted to work, never thought I could just stay home without working at all, whether it was for economic reasons or just for my own self-satisfaction. If you're happy with yourself, you're going to be a better mother. I don't think it would have been the best thing for my kids to be home every minute of every day. When they were young, I did use day care, putting them in a loving home environment with other kids to play with and it was fun for them. This business is an excellent option for women who have children.

Other pluses of the business?

It's an incredibly satisfying business. Sometimes I'm in a meeting with a major corporation and I'm hearing their strategic messages for the entire year. And I'm totally responsible for getting the word out for a new product or service that can mean millions of dollars in new business. It's so exciting to be able to say, here I am and it's all on my shoulders to come up with a powerful way to communicate all this information. It's really fun. And because you get to come in at the end when they've gotten their creative strategy together, you don't have to sit through all the BS and the corporate politics.

How do you like playing the consultant role?

In almost every industry, the consultant, the outsider, is more valued than the staffer. There's this perception that because they're bringing you, the writer, in from outside, you must be important. It gives you a certain elevated status, which is a nice feeling. And also, when you're working by the hour, you're going to be more motivated on a project than if you were an employee making the same salary, regardless of the hours you put in.

What are the biggest challenges of this profession?

Because you don't always get paid on time, it can be tough to plan on a steady income, because you may not know when the next paycheck or the next project is coming in. You might get three in one week and then nothing for three weeks. Which is also why you need to make time for marketing yourself, making phone calls, following up with people—making sure you're continuing to prime the pump. But it's a solid income.

Speaking of that, does your income from writing make a significant contribution to the family bottom line?

Yes, it does. You can definitely make good money in this business. Hourly rates are anywhere from $50–80 or more, if you're good, reliable, and people like you. On a part-time basis, that can easily translate to $25,000 a year and on a full-time basis, $75–100,000 is very doable. My goal is to make $100,000 a year, which translates to one good-sized project or two every week.

What does it take to hit a mark like that?

You have to be willing to recognize your own value and not sell yourself short. In the earlier days, I undercharged because I didn't feel I was experienced enough. If you know you can do the job and your clients are paying the going rate for writing or passing on a charge to their clients that those clients expect to pay, then don't be shy about asking for a healthy rate. You can always come down in price. It's a lot harder to go up.

What's the reality of marriage, motherhood, and freelance writing?

Could you hold on a moment while I talk to my daughter?

(One minute later...)

Now, there's part of your answer right there. I'm walking around with my cell phone. I'm on my way to middle school to pick up my son for a lesson. My daughter is home and can't find a friend to play with. This is the biggest challenge: you think you're flexible, because after all, I work at home. And people think you're so lucky that you can be home with the kids. But that flexibility comes with a lot of pressure and sometimes you feel, hey, what's the point of being home with your kids if you're always on the phone and ignoring them?

So do you get most of your work done while they're in school?

That's the goal and usually I can. Though because I'm a very early riser, I can often get a lot of my non-phone writing work done in the early morning for a few hours before anyone's even up. That's when I think most clearly and it's nice and peaceful and quiet. Which points to a very big advantage of this business. Once you get the work you can pretty much do it on your own time.

Do you consider this a full-time or part-time career?

I don't actually think of it in those terms. I certainly don't look at it as a part-time career and yet it doesn't seem full-time, like a 9–5 job would, because it is so flexible. But it can certainly be a full-time income. I can say pretty confidently that I will never go back to a full-time job because I'll never be able to get the flexibility and diversity in one single organization. Or the hourly rate, which *really* makes it no comparison. And once you get established and get a steady client base, theoretically, your checks should be coming in regularly. You do have to be disciplined in paying your taxes quarterly and all that.

Are there unique challenges for women in this business?

For a woman, at every stage, whether you're a new mother or a mother of adolescents or facing a hormone surge that week, there are unique challenges. The biggest is over-committing, which is very common among women of our generation—trying to do too much for too many people. I think about the times I've had the most stress, professionally and personally, and it's been when I'm trying to be a 100% full-time mother and 100% full-time writer. The cliché is "you can't do it all," but it's really true. The temptation in this business is to say, "Well, I'm home, so I can do it." But then something has to give. You end up not being able to do the kind of job you need to do on a project and you irritate a client. Or your kids or husband end up getting upset at you. It's not worth it.

What would you suggest to someone starting out to build their confidence?

Start writing some pieces for publication in perhaps some local papers. There are also a lot of opportunities in newsletters or even on the Internet. They are often anonymous, have longer deadlines, and you can get feedback from an editor. Seeing your work in print can be a big confidence booster. And that's how you need to do it—one project at a time. I've been reading the Freelance Writer's Newsletter on *about.com* and they have a lot of opportunities posted. And when I was first starting out, I contacted local publications and with a one-page letter, I pitched them on writing short articles on topics that interested me. All this helps in building a portfolio, which your prospective clients will really want to see.

If you're not totally confident in your abilities, get your feet wet with one type of work, whether it's writing articles or scripts, and once you get a few credits under your belt, you'll develop the confidence to go after more work. It would also help to mentor with someone or even assist an established writer. If someone approached me and asked to help me out in exchange for some tips, I think I'd welcome the opportunity to share the ins and outs of the business.

In a reasonably good-sized metropolitan area, how easy would it be for some-one to leverage their past business experience into a freelance commercial writing career?

It's never "easy," but I will say this: If you believe something about yourself and are able to communicate it, people will generally accept it. If you tell them that you're the greatest thing in the world because of your experience in even a totally unrelated field, if you can justify it, people are going to give you a shot. I really feel it's the strength of your personality and the way they feel about you more than your résumé or where you got your degree.

If someone is a decent writer and reasonably aggressive about letting people know they're out there, how hard is it to find steady work?

It's not that difficult getting the work, but it takes a certain type of person to be able to do the work. Deadlines are frequently tight, and often you're thrown into a new situation with little information and you need to be able to get up to speed quickly. You have to have the kind of mind and ability to be able to rapidly assimilate information, and communicate it back. And it really helps to not get intimidated easily by people with attitudes.

Do you feel that this work is really that hard?

It's not that the work is so hard. For me, as I mentioned, what sometimes makes it tough is my own inability to say no. I often end up with multiple projects without a comfortable amount of time to get them all done. Each individual project is not that difficult. I think anyone who's a reasonably good writer can be a successful freelance corporate writer. The reality of the market is that very few companies staff full-time writers. Yet, every single business in the world needs writing. There's a lot of opportunity out there.

Can you elaborate?

Everyone from the widget-maker to the computer maker to restaurants, healthcare organizations, banks, all need external and internal communications. In that sense, it's almost a no-brainer. And because so few companies keep writers on staff and don't want to pay high ad agency rates for copywriting, there are a lot of good reasons for a company to hire freelancers. It's like having a staff writer but only when they need them and without the salary, benefits and vacation. And that's a great way to position yourself to these companies: like an in-house resource but without the overhead. You get to know their business, become like one of their staff and over time, your value to them really grows.

What are the different ways to approach this business?

You can be a generalist—sort of an "all-things-to-all-people" type—which has been my path, though mostly by default. Or you can specialize. It might be a particular industry, like healthcare, high-tech, retail, fast food. Or maybe a particular kind of work—like video scripts, speeches, PR work, what have you. I guess I've become a generalist because I can get up to speed quickly in a project for just about any industry, feel out the personalities and corporate culture, and quickly sense what they want. And that brings up an important point that I've learned, which is to leave your ego outside the door. If they want something that you don't agree with, by all means express your opinion, but be prepared to give the client what they want. They're the boss.

Any final advice for women considering a career in this business?

If you have the ability, the talent, personality and self-discipline, go for it. The rewards of being independent and flexible are great and you'll know quickly whether it's something that's a good fit for you. It's really been perfect for me. With this field, I feel I've really found my niche. I feel great about it because it's something I can excel at, something that will never go out of style, there's an endless supply of potential clients for my service and I can make a very healthy income. And, of course, be around for my kids. Ultimately, I want to do more creative writing for myself. But once you do this kind of writing, I think you'll find it hard to do the personal writing because of the immediate gratification—and good pay—you get in writing for others.

Mrs. Parra

Gabrielle Parra* is married and a mother of four children—11, 9, 3, and 7 months. She has been freelancing since 1994, after stints as a staff writer for soft-ware and telecommunications companies and a small PR firm. She has essential-ly been the primary breadwinner for her family of six for seven years, while her husband pursues his Ph.D. in nuclear engineering. During that time, she has earned a "very livable" income through freelance commercial writing, an income that has increased every year.

How did you get started in this business?

After graduating from college with an English degree, I fell into technical writing—specifically software manuals—for about 3½ years. I then moved to a telecommunications company, where I started doing their marketing litera-ture: newsletters, brochures etc., something I discovered I really enjoyed.

When did you decide to go freelance?

After moving to Atlanta in 1993, I went to work for a small PR firm for 1½ years and got a lot of PR/marketing experience under my belt. One day, I real-ized my time was being billed out at about four times what I was earning per hour. So I decided to go on my own. I wanted more flexibility and, because writing can be done from anywhere, commuting to a job just didn't make any sense.

What sort of preparations did you make for self-employment?

I went cold turkey with very little in the way of a financial safety net. I had two kids at that point and my husband was starting his Ph.D. program so there was a lot of risk involved. I just had to shut my eyes and jump, which brings up a piece of advice: If you're waiting for the planets to line up before you do it, it'll never happen. The first year was pretty lean and scary and I pretty much took anything that came along, including some documentation work. I was also inexperienced as far as what to charge and ended up losing money on some jobs. But once I got a taste of self-employment, it was hard to turn back.

Have you always worked?

Yes, through the birth of all my children. I never had a paid maternity leave. I've always put my family first but working was a necessity. And given that, I

---

* *Name has been changed*

wanted to make sure I was doing something I enjoyed. But because family came first, I had to pass up promotion opportunities at my former companies because I wasn't willing to work more hours. Which essentially made those jobs dead ends, because the ceiling was set. That was another reason I started freelancing.

Can you elaborate?

With freelancing, there is no dead end, no one telling you what you're worth or what you can't do. Freelancing was a way I could continue to grow and expand my career while putting my family first. Freelancing is not without stress but it has given me the flexibility to do a lot of things with my family that I wouldn't have been able to otherwise. But, make no mistake: I'm not doing this for pocket change. This is my job and I take it very seriously. I do use childcare and I keep regular hours, generally 8:30–3:00—which is when my older kids are at school—and sometimes after hours as well.

What's a typical day?

Well, recently, because of his schedule, my husband has been able to do more of the child care in the morning, getting the little ones ready to go to the babysitter and the older ones to school before going on to school himself. After working till 3, I pick up the kids from school and day care, and from 3–5, it's usually pretty crazy. I'm helping the kids get settled with snacks and homework and still fielding phone calls from clients. I feel it's important for them to have me be there when they come home. But I think it's beneficial to see their mother working—to learn that work is important. When they see me working, they learn that it's something to be respected and not to interrupt me unless it's very important. And my older kids are at the age now where they can help with the younger ones when I need to take a call.

With all the societal debate about day care, have you wrestled with this?

I've definitely wrestled with it. But, I've always had to work and had four babies while I was working. I've always kept day care to no more than six hours a day and, since my husband's schedule often permits, usually less. Day care is never ideal but working has been a necessity and writing takes concentration. It's not something that can be done in the midst of chaos. And compared to kids who spend 10–11 hours a day in day care, 4–6 hours is a level I can live with and feel good about. Children are very adaptable and do well as long as they're loved and cared for. And frankly, I think it's a good thing for them because it allows them to meet and socialize with other kids. I don't think they're suffering as a result of it.

I also think that the time that a mother spends with her older kids can be even more important than when they're babies. Bonding is very important with little ones, but it's almost more important for older kids to have their parents around when they came home from school, to supervise them, tell them to clean their rooms and tell them which words are and aren't appropriate in the home and so many other things that you can't do if you're not there.

As a wife and a mother of four, what do you like most about this business?

I like the flexibility and that I can be involved in the kids' school and visit it quite often. I like the fact that I can avoid traffic and can generally set appointments outside of rush hour. I can take time off as I need it and not have to ask permission. And this type of job is such wonderful mental exercise every day. I love learning about different people and industries, and there just aren't many jobs that can give you that. In the high-tech marketing writing arena in which I work, I earn more than in any other kind of writing. Where else can you make $70–80/hr. or more? Bottom line, I'm able to bring home a very livable income in less than 40 hours a week. Not that it's all billable time and there's certainly some night and weekend time involved, but it's a solid living.

What are the challenges in this business?

In the past few years, the amount of work has increased, which has increased the hours and the stress level. When I started, the challenge was just to find work, but now there can be too much work. And it's tough to turn down a job because you remember the lean times. That's the seduction of this work: you can end up taking on more than you can really handle. Every job represents money and it's hard to push money away. It's all about striking a healthy balance and that comes with time. My husband has been very supportive and helps out a lot, especially on weekends. It would be a much harder job for a single Mom. Which brings up another downside of any self-employment: by definition, there's no safety net, no time off, no paid vacation, no disability.

Another challenge is knowing what to charge. Charge too much and you'll turn people off, too little and you don't make enough. I did make the mistake in the beginning of not charging enough or getting talked into giving a special rate, and once you do, it's harder to raise those rates with your regular customers.

Besides experience, what would you suggest to learn about fees?

I would recommend joining a writer's group or other groups of freelancers. I'm a member of several groups *(including one started by the author)* that have been very helpful to me in answering so many writing-related questions, especially pricing. Don't be shy about talking about money with as many of your writing peers as possible. You really need to find out what people who are doing what you're doing are charging. The more that people compare notes about rates, the better we're able to get paid what we're really worth. My resources are much better now than when I first started out.

Is it challenging to work at home?

In a traditional 9–5 job, it's easier to leave the job at the office, though with beepers and cell phones, that's becoming harder as well. When you work at home, it can be tougher to leave the work at the office because it's always there. Your work becomes very integrated with everything else you're doing. On Monday, I got up at 4 a.m. so I could finish a project by noon and take my kids to the MLK holiday parade. I didn't like having to get up that early but I'm glad I have the freedom to set my own schedule. Another downside, at least in my experience in the marketing writing arena, is that the deadlines are always tight. People always want it fast.

Working while being a Mom is very stressful, but I don't think I could work in a better situation than the one I have. If I'm going to have stress, these are the circumstances in which to have it.

Are you sometimes tempted by the security of a 9-5 job?

I regularly get offered jobs from my regular clients, which is tempting, especially when it comes to benefits. But even as an employee, I don't think that the deadlines and stress would be any less. And I wouldn't have the flexibility. Yes, I've considered it, but with that security comes a lot of bondage.

What advice would you give other women in a similar position who are thinking about a career in this business?

As far as finding work: I've heard people talk about getting all their work through networking, and how cold-calling isn't that effective. But when I started out, cold-calling was how I got my first good clients. Never turn up your nose at cold-calling. Plan on investing some serious time in the process. Fortunately, because of word of mouth, I haven't had to do any cold-calling for several years, which is nice, but it was really important in the beginning.

Is networking effective?

As far as networking goes, your best bet is to network with your peers, other writers, creative people, not just business people in general. And make sure you ask your steady clients for more work in their organization and for referrals to other prospects.

If someone's a decent writer in a good-sized metropolitan area, and are reasonably aggressive about getting their name out, how easy would it be to get steady work?

It took me two to three years to build up my clientele to the point where I stay busy all the time. With the present economy as strong as it is, it would probably take less than that now. Of course, even the most experienced writers can have a turn in luck. That's why it's important not to depend too much on any single company for your business. It's also wise to constantly network and send out mailings even when you have plenty of work. I don't do that as well as I should because when I'm busy, marketing myself goes by the wayside. I've paid for that in the past, when a client decided to hire an in-house writer, and I was left with a big gap in my income that I had to make up. No relationship with a client is permanent, no matter how good it is. So much depends on the individuals you're working with. If someone leaves a company, the person who replaces them usually changes the status quo.

How good a writer do you have to be in this field?

If you're considering a career in this field, you do have to be a good writer. I recommend getting a second opinion on whether you're good from people who know. If people are going to pay good money for writing, they expect it to be above average. That said, I do think that you can get better with experience.

It's important to realize you don't have to be an expert in the field you're writing about. You just have to know how to ask the right questions and keep asking them—without embarrassment—until you understand the answers. High tech is an important niche for me, but I am not and have never been a "techie" person. That makes me good at translating the stuffy jargon into interesting, conversational prose. I often stop and ask myself, 'What am I REALLY trying to say here?' Then I just say it, without any mumbo jumbo. To be a writer, you have to like the challenge of writing and for me, writing has always been very hard work. But I enjoy the craft. I enjoy finishing a project I can be proud of.

Any final comments?

Don't ever belittle what you do. Especially if you're a mother working part-time. Being a mother doesn't make you less sharp, and you need to take yourself as seriously as if you were in a traditional job. And just like there's no perfect time to have a baby, don't wait till the perfect moment to start this business because it probably won't ever come. Enlist the support of your family. You take what you're doing seriously and expect them to do the same.

Index

Give the Gift of a New, Exciting, and Lucrative Writing Career!

Order extra copies of
The Well-Fed Writer: Financial Self-Sufficiency as a Freelance Writer in Six Months or Less.

☐ YES, I want _____ copies of **The Well-Fed Writer** at $19.95 each plus $4.00 shipping and handling per book (Georgia residents please add 6% sales tax - $1.20)
Allow 15 days for delivery.

My check or money order for $_____.___ is enclosed.

Please charge my credit card:
MasterCard ☐   VISA ☐   American Express ☐   Discover ☐

Card # _____ *Exp. Date* _____

Signature _____

Name _____

Address _____

City/State/Zip _____

Phone _____ *E-mail* _____

Please make your check payable to and return to:

> **BookMasters, Inc.**
> **PO Box 388**
> **Ashland, OH 44805**

Or order by:
Phone: Toll-Free – 800-247-6553
Fax: 419 - 281 - 6883
E-mail: order@bookmaster.com

Michael Höhne
had an enjoyable time designing and typesetting this book
using Adobe types: Minion, Officina Serif, Times,
and miscellaneous others
on Apple Macintosh equipment.
heyyou@heyneon.com

Give the Gift of a New, Exciting, and Lucrative Writing Career!

☐ YES, I want _____ copies of **The Well-Fed Writer** at $19.95 each plus $4.00 shipping and handling per book (Georgia residents please add 6% sales tax - $1.20)
Allow 15 days for delivery.

My check or money order for $_____.___ is enclosed.

Please charge my credit card:
MasterCard ☐   VISA ☐   American Express ☐   Discover ☐

Card # _____ Exp. Date _____

Signature _____

Name _____

Address _____

City/State/Zip _____

Phone _____ E-mail _____

Please make your check payable to and return to:

> **BookMasters, Inc.**
> **PO Box 388**
> **Ashland, OH 44805**

Or order by:

Phone: Toll-Free – 800-247-6553

Fax: 419 - 281 - 6883

E-mail: order@bookmaster.com

Michael Höhne
had an enjoyable time designing and typesetting this book
using Adobe types: Minion, Officina Serif, Times,
and miscellaneous others
on Apple Macintosh equipment.
heyyou@heyneon.com